# THE BUNCH QUITTER

## A MEMOIR

BY

# PHILIP J. BURGESS

Printed in the United States of America.

Print ISBN: 979-8-9885167-1-2
E-book ISBN: 979-8-9885167-2-9

Cover and interior design by Kyle Bateman with Self-Publishing Services, LLC
Edited by Self-Publishing Services, LLC (selfpublishingservices.com)

First edition

*DEDICATED TO MY FATHER, WHO LIVED A LIFE OF TRUE STEWARDSHIP.*

# TABLE OF CONTENTS

*BUNCH QUITTER:*

A colloquial expression generally used to describe an animal, usually a cow or steer, that resists being herded or controlled. This resistance can sometimes take the form of violent and even self-destructive behavior.

# PROLOGUE

This is a brooding place, looking down from the divide across the valley. Rolling grassland breaking down into buttes and ravines as it moves down towards the Missouri River. Badland bluffs form the far side of the valley, a jagged knife blade held to the throat of the sky. The Indians were gone long before my time, and most of the whites who came to show the red men how to live have given it up as a bad job and pulled stakes. The families that I grew up around are almost all gone or slumbering in neat rows behind local cemetery fences.

I know that in spite of the gray in my beard, I've got a few good miles left in me, but whenever I return here, I feel a little like a Rip Van Winkle waking to find himself a lone survivor among the fading artifacts of his civilization. Wheat fields being reclaimed by weeds and native grasses. Unstocked pastureland. Nothing left of the little crossroads settlement that was once nestled where the railroad tracks came to the river from the south.

Standing up here over a grave above that valley, I can see for miles. There are a few ranch and farm buildings off in the distance, and the old, black-towered Snowden Bridge still stands where it has carried trains, cars, and horses across the Missouri since 1912. Here and there, an oil field worker's trailer taking shelter in an abandoned windbreak next to the crumbling, empty foundation, what's left of some homesteader's dream.

A few oil wells are scattered across the landscape, their pump jacks like giant black insects dipping their suckers deep into the earth's flesh. Rusting fragments of barbed wire cling to an occasional fencepost. Across the valley and to the east is the restored trading post, Fort Union, and just downriver from that are the remnants of the old military post, Fort Buford, with its cemetery half-full of suicides and poisonings. In those days, everything the white man used came and went on the river, so the trading post and the fort were both placed here, near the confluence of the Missouri and the Yellowstone Rivers.

Here and there among the artifacts of the rapidly receding wave of homesteads and ranches are scattered clues to what went on here before them. An occasional arrowhead, an old buffalo bone, ancient tepee rings, and campfire sites in unlikely, exposed places on the tops of ridges and hills where young Indian men kept vigil for their visions and old Indian men waited for their deaths. Echoes of sudden death skirmishes between Blackfeet, Sioux, Cheyenne, and Crow hunting parties who happened to stumble into one another.

The white man came and wiped out most of the red man and most of the game, and even the spirits began taking refuge in the roughest and most remote recesses of the badlands. The great Sitting Bull had his day of bloody glory but four years later came trailing in to surrender at Fort Buford at the head of a ragtag column of hungry horses carrying a remnant of his people, hooves treading his pride into the ground along with the buffalo grass.

Across the river from Fort Buford, thirty-one years after Sitting Bull's surrender, my father was born in the tiny little village of Java. A few miles farther west along the Missouri, sitting on a bluff high above the valley, are the ranch buildings where my family lived. The three-room shack that was my childhood home has stood empty for over forty years, but the roofline that my father built, though humble enough, is still as straight and true as my memories of the man himself.

Now some of the game is returning. Elk are beginning to drift back into the country, bald eagles are fairly common, and there are even some buffalo being raised on local ranches. Spirits drift with the tumbleweeds along collapsed fence lines in broad daylight. From where I stand in the graveyard above the ranch, the valley probably looks much the same as it did when my great-grandfather, George Burgess, first rode in here with his wife and children in the spring of 1899, all of them a little worse for wear.

# CHAPTER 1

*GREAT-GRANDFATHER AND THE NORTHERN CHEYENNE*

There is a Burgess family legend, one eroded like some ancient gravestone of such details as first names and dates, that somewhere around the year 1800, a man named Shannon set out from Ireland on a sailing ship with his wife and their small son, bound for America. While en route, Wife Shannon was stricken by some unnamed malady and died on shipboard, and perhaps her death burned the dreams of the New World out of the heart of Husband Shannon. Anyway, for reasons and purposes that remain mysterious to his descendants, upon landing in America, Shannon gave his child over to the care of strangers and took passage back to Ireland, never to be heard from again on this side of the water.

His son eventually exchanged the Shannon name for the name of the family who raised him to his maturity, that name being Burgess. And so, my family came to America in the person of a wandering orphan Irish child who found refuge in a stranger's house and a stranger's name in a strange land. Anyway, that is the story that is told, and I choose to believe it a true one.

*** * ***

My Great-grandfather Burgess's family trail-herded three hundred miles down from the New Ulm area in southeastern Minnesota to Nebraska in the spring of 1871, their back trail haunted by the Santee Sioux Uprising and thirty-seven Santee Sioux warriors dancing among rising dust motes, their death songs choked short by the creaking hemp nooses reluctantly assigned them by Abraham Lincoln. Death songs that sank deep into certain hearts, to be carried like some strange, indecipherable message down through the generations.

Great-grandfather George was sixteen years old when he left Minnesota with his parents and his six sisters, Emily, Mary, Eva, Augusta, Snow Belle, and Hannah. The entire family seemed to have an affection for the view of open country from the back of a good horse. Long-haired riders in long, sun-bleached skirts strung out in the dust of the cattle and horse herd with wreaths of wildflowers bobbing around the crowns of battered straw hats, following their big brother south.

When the Burgess clan arrived in eastern Nebraska, they joined up with the Bruce Colony, a group of settlers who formally organized to found the town of Creighton in a raw and depopulated (of Ponca and Omaha Indians) frontier area where the relatively hospitable weather and terrain of the Midwest begins to give way to the less forgiving environment of the Western prairies. The Burgess family set up a horse and cattle operation outside of Creighton.

In 1874, Custer's Black Hills Expedition opened up southwestern South Dakota to a gold rush, and wagon trains began moving through Creighton on their way to join in the bonanza, triggering restless dreams of open spaces in Great-grandfather George that were complicated by his marriage to a widow lady named Evelyn Lightner in 1879.

Colonel Custer's violent termination by the Cheyenne and the Sioux in 1876 put white America and its humiliated military establishment in a fairly humorless and vengeful mood that did not bode well for the victors, and after surrendering in 1877, the Northern Cheyenne were removed from their home territory in southeastern Montana and exiled to hunger and disease on an Oklahoma reservation. In 1878, a group of around three-hundred Cheyenne followed their chiefs, Dull Knife and Little Wolf, out of their confinement and began the thousand-mile trek back to the Powder River country of southeastern Montana in a quest to reclaim a bit of the freedom that George Burgess was dreaming of.

The Cheyenne men, women, and children were hunted like rabbits by vigilantes and US Cavalry—but the rabbits had guns and fought a series of successful running battles across the open winter hills. There were atrocities committed on both sides, but the Cheyenne were trying to avoid trouble, while the whites were seeking it. A cowboy sprawled amidst dust and cow manure, a homesteader shot off his wagon seat, an Indian woman's naked thighs in the snow with her dress thrown up over her face. Many Indians, men and women, died fighting, and there are stories of Cheyenne women who cut their children's throats rather than see them captured, a story of one woman who held her child up to take a bullet rather than see it captured. Many were shot down just for running away. The white civilians in particular were not kind when successful in cornering their prey. The bodies of the helpless ones—old women, children, even babies—were scattered along the trail, staring at the moon with frozen eyes.

Little Wolf and his hundred or so surviving Cheyenne followers managed to survive a hard winter spent ducking the US Cavalry in the Sand Hills of western Nebraska and made it back to Montana Territory in the spring, where they convinced the American military that hungry, ragged, and almost horseless as they were, they would die fighting before they would be removed from their home again. Today, ribbons flutter over the neighboring graves of Dull Knife and Little Wolf in the Lame Deer tribal cemetery. The ribbons are always there, some faded and tattered, some vibrant and bright.

Around the time of the Cheyenne ordeal, my great-grandfather and the other Creighton area settlers struggled through hellacious winters, drought, and bizarre locust infestations. The Rocky Mountain locust infestation of 1874 stripped crops, pastures, and trees bare, and even bedsheets, horse harnesses, clothing and shoes were reportedly eaten by the little beasties. People starved to death. Most of the original Bruce colonists went looking for greener pastures. However, the Burgesses and some of the Bruce family managed to hang on, and things slowly improved.

In 1885, George Burgess, his sister Mary, and a few cowhands left Creighton, Nebraska, pushing a cattle herd bound for the Tongue River Cheyenne Indian Reservation in the Montana Territory. They arrived in an area that was sparsely settled, with a great many of its people spending a lot of time and energy either threatening or actually committing mayhem and violence upon one another—plus, it could be a perfect bitch for weather. So, Great-grandfather decided that this would be a wonderful place to raise a family.

During the Cheyenne's exile, local ranchers had been using their land for free grazing and now wanted them evicted, utilizing local politicians and newspapers in an intense campaign to convince the federal government that the Cheyenne were a danger to the white community and should be removed.

The Northern Cheyenne found themselves suffering from many of the same hardships they had experienced under the tender care of Uncle Sam in Oklahoma. Half-starving with no buffalo and short rations from the government, pushed to give up their religion and their native language, they had in effect exchanged an unfamiliar prison for a familiar prison, surrounded by a lot of armed and resentful whites.

It was a volatile mix that sometimes led to homicidal violence. Many Northern Cheyenne lived through that time believing that the whites were going to come in and kill them all, and some of them stayed hidden in the hills against just such an eventuality.

After delivering their herd to the government agent in Lame Deer, George Burgess spent the rest of the summer going back and forth between Lame Deer and Creighton, Nebraska, creating a home for his pregnant wife. George Burgess turned thirty years old in 1885, and horsebacked 2400 miles between spring thaw and winter freeze-up. The new baby was my grandfather, Bruce.

My great-grandfather ran his stock on the open range that surrounded the Tongue River Reservation, put together a sawmill enterprise in Lame Deer, and occasionally drove the local stagecoach. Eventually, he was hired by the government to be what was referred to as the "Boss Farmer" on the reservation, teaching the Cheyenne cattle-raising and farming skills.

My great-grandmother, Evelyn Burgess, was no more than thirty years old when she traveled up the trail to Montana in a covered wagon with George and her baby, but she had already seen a lot of country seated on wooden wagon seats, watching distant hills slowly grow over swaying horse rumps. She had left one world behind in New England, and still another behind in Nebraska (where she'd also left two sons by her deceased first husband in the care of her mother). Now she found herself in Lame Deer, Montana, riding herd on another growing family and trying to teach a crew of hungry and loss-crazed Indian children who never brought an apple for teacher and whose parents were not enthusiastic PTA members.

Many of her students were traumatized veterans of their tribe's long journey home and struggled with their English lessons, but Evelyn found that most of them could draw like angels, so she had them spend a lot of time drawing and working at describing their drawings in English. They drew pictures of buffalo, of gunfights between the Cheyenne and soldiers, of their own people wearing transitional clothing: a mixture of buckskins, colorful blankets, and white man's hats. A hundred years later, while closing out our old ranch house, I found a handmade book containing some of those drawings.

It took a little while for Evelyn to wrap her mind around the reality that her students were half-starved and that no one in charge was doing anything about it. She began using her family's own beef to cook up a daily pot of stew with which to fill the children's bellies enough to enable them to concentrate on their lessons. After a few days of this, the children took to wearing leather pouches hidden beneath their clothes to carry stew home to their families.

So, the Cheyenne went hungry on a reservation surrounded by open range stocked with nice fat white man's cattle. The result was fairly predictable, and the occasional steer met its premature demise at the hands of a Cheyenne. It was also fairly predictable that occasionally an Indian would be caught at his rustling and receive rough treatment, followed by imprisonment or even death, as a punishment for his transgression—and once in a while a Cheyenne rustler was overwhelmed by the unfairness of it all and rose up to inflict some fatal injury on his white would-be captor.

And so, Grandfather Bruce came up the trail as a brand-new baby from Nebraska to spend his childhood and early adolescence, from 1886 to 1899, playing and going to school with the traumatized and hungry children of angry, frightened Cheyenne parents; he and his two younger siblings were marked as aliens among those Cheyenne playmates by their pale Celtic hides and their well-fed bellies.

My grandfather spoke of two Cheyenne warriors singing their death songs before charging down a hill into US Cavalry guns, of families hiding in the hills from an expected massacre by the whites. He spoke of almost being killed by a Cheyenne warrior, and it was he who told me of Great-grandmother bringing soup to class every day to feed chronically hungry children.

During the Burgess family's time on the Cheyenne reservation, the place was a simmering pot of fear and anger that was kept simmering by minor incidents of violence and unpleasantness between the whites and the Cheyenne. Periodically, a major incident, usually involving a violent death, would cause the pot to boil over. Cowboys threatening, insulting, and taking an occasional potshot at an Indian without fear of legal consequences. White posses, vigilantes, and US Cavalry stampeding around the reservation. The local newspapers and politicians, controlled by the big ranchers, would "spin" these incidents, both minor and major, to support their case to the US government that the Cheyenne Nation was a danger to the community and should be removed.

By the fall of 1898, things seemed to be on the verge of finally falling apart for the Tongue River Cheyenne, and they did fall apart for the George Burgess family. It was never made clear to me just exactly what happened. It was said in our family that they fled "under the cover of darkness" to get away from an "Indian uprising." My sense is that there was a lot of turbulence and violence on the reservation during this time that never made the history books. All that I know for certain is that my grandfather's family feared for their lives and ran, taking only what they could get together in a hurry. Their nerve, strained by years of turmoil, violence, and stress on the reservation, finally broke.

The little Burgess cavalcade pulled out in a northwesterly direction, driving what they had managed to salvage of their cattle and riding stock, avoiding the few settlements that existed along their route. They turned at the Musselshell River to follow it north to its confluence with the Missouri River, where they found themselves in a huge chunk of nowhere with winter at their heels, a winter for which they were poorly prepared. There were no settlements in that country, and very few people, just a few widely scattered ranch headquarters. I believe that my great-grandfather, an experienced frontiersman, knew exactly what he was getting into and was deliberately seeking refuge from both whites and Indians in the isolation and desolation of the Missouri Breaks. The Burgess family jerry-rigged a shelter out of wagon canvas and logs near the river bottom and settled in for a long winter fighting to keep themselves and their stock alive on short rations.

My grandfather told of finding what looked like human bones in the burned remains of two log cabins. Between the remains of the two cabins lay a log with remnants of rotten rope still attached to it. Thirteen years earlier, Granville Stuart (aka Mr. Montana) and his vigilante group, known as "Stuart's Stranglers," had ridden in there and proceeded to shoot, hang, or burn alive all of the local male residents—thirteen or so, mostly cowboys—whom they accused of being rustlers. Some of them probably were. Some of them probably weren't. So it goes.

Grandfather Bruce spent his fifteenth winter listening to the wolves howl, the ice cracking out on the river, and the dying grunts and whispers of cowboys wishing they'd been kinder to their mommas. Cabin fever and an early thaw pushed the Burgesses out onto the trail in early April, the family apparently preferring the risk of a late snowstorm to the risk of being flooded out. They headed east, downriver. It was in the spring of 1899, and the big cattle outfits still held sway over the open range along the southern side of the Missouri, holding the land with nothing but their guns and political power. The Burgess family put another 250 miles behind them before selecting a good, uncontested spot on the edge of the Missouri River Valley about twenty miles short of that river's meeting with the Yellowstone River. Our family holds ground there to this day.

It was a cowman's dream, with the river bottom for wood and hay, good water, and open rolling hills off to the south for grazing, and George did all right for a number of years with his small open-range cattle and horse operation. However, by 1914, the homesteaders had crowded the Burgesses out of the cow business, reducing them to a 640-acre homestead good only for farming, so Great-grandfather George proposed that he and Evelyn head west to find some ground where a horseman could ride for a while without running into a settler's shack. Evelyn, however, had had her fill of Western adventure, so George rode out alone at the age of sixty-four on one of his big black geldings, with his guns, his bedroll, and his saddlebags, leaving the ranch to his wife and my grandfather Bruce, who by this time was married with two children—one of them being my father, William.

I have a couple letters George wrote to my father during his years in self-imposed exile, letters written with lead pencil on lined paper by a semiliterate man. He spent those years doing light cowboy work such as fence-riding and moving cattle, cowboy work and trapping in the winter—almost always alone. There was no self-pity, regret, or complaint in any of those letters. Just a matter-of-fact accounting of his day-to-day life and inquiries about the family.

In 1928, a rancher was out riding fence line south of Dotson, Montana, when he came across an old man up on a big black, riding bareheaded, with long white hair and beard swirling in the breeze. He sat that gelding like the ghost of Robert E. Lee, but it was obvious to the rancher that something was wrong. There was a deep, blood-crusted gash on the side of Great-grandfather George's head, and he didn't really seem to know who he was or where he was going, even though the rancher reported that when he had first spotted him, the wounded man had been trotting along like he was headed for hot biscuits and gravy.

The rancher managed to talk the confused old man into going home with him and eventually was able to get word to the Burgess family to tell them they'd better come and get their wayward patriarch. They'd just purchased their first car, a Ford Model A, and my father chauffeured Grandfather Burgess across two hundred miles of mostly dirt road along the Great Northern Railway tracks up the Missouri River to Dotson to fetch my Great-grandfather George. Grandfather Bruce was not possessed of a particularly generous spirit, and he grumbled all the way, grumbling even more when they got to Dotson and the object of their rescue mission took one look at the Ford and said, "I've never ridden in one of those things before, and I ain't about to start now."

It was a long slow trip home. They retraced the two hundred miles downriver with my father at the wheel of the Model A and Grandfather Bruce riding shotgun, cursing under his breath every time they had to stop to wait for the old man on the big black gelding. Towards the end, they had to cross the Missouri River on the Snowden Bridge, a recently completed, gigantic iron structure a quarter of a mile long with towers a hundred feet high. Great-grandfather George and his horse had never seen anything like it in their lives, and my father was afraid the high-strung big black would blow up in the middle of the bridge and take itself and the old man over the railing into eternity. However, as Father and Grandfather watched from the south end of the bridge, the old centaur kicked the gelding up and came thundering across at a dead run, sitting straight up in his hand-tooled Miles City saddle with his white hair and beard floating like wreaths of smoke about his head.

That was Great-grandfather George's last ride. He lived for nine more years of deepening dementia, apparently content to rest during the time he had left, settling gently into his final senility as though it were a warm bed on a cold winter's night.

The old man died in deep winter in 1937 at the age of eighty-seven. They put his body in the icehouse, and two days later some neighbor men came in early morning and helped my father build a big bonfire in the graveyard on the hill above the home place. While they waited for the ground to thaw enough to dig, they passed around a bottle of good sipping whiskey, told kind jokes about old man Burgess, and soaked up the view of ten miles of Missouri River Valley spread out before them. When the fire had burned itself out and the whiskey was gone, they dug the hole and laid the old horseman in the ground next to Great-grandmother Evelyn, who had not waited around long enough to see her husband come trotting home on his last black gelding.

The coffin came to rest on top of an empty whiskey bottle that lay partially covered with loose dirt in the bottom of the grave.

# CHAPTER 2

---

*THE GOBLIN, THE HOBO, AND THE KITTEN KILLER*

I missed meeting Great-grandfather George by about seven years, waiting to be born until November 30, 1944, about the time that Nazi Germany was gearing up for the Battle of the Bulge. One of my earliest memories is of waking up as a four-year-old in a hospital room after having my tonsils removed and looking disapprovingly across the room at my mother sleeping in a chair, thinking that she should be home taking care of my siblings.

Our ranch buildings were perched on a high shelf looking out over miles of Missouri River bottom, and on sweet summer mornings I'd walk across our yard on my way to do chores, my eyes filled with the panorama of the badlands and the sprawled-out river valley, the tall grass soaking my boots and pants cuffs with dew as a gauntlet of meadowlarks serenaded me, their piercing cries sliding down my heart like raindrops sliding down a windowpane.

My two brothers, my sister, and I lived with our parents in a three-room stucco house without plumbing or telephone in a community that lacked electricity until the 1950s. Warm summer evenings were spent with a kerosene lamp burning in the middle of the old oak kitchen table, Mother and Father sitting quiet and tired, children playing a game of cards or studying, with no sound loud enough to drown out the singing of the crickets out in the great dark space surrounding the home or the coyotes out running the valley below, wailing their disconsolate glee to one another as they loped along in the shadows of a tree line, waiting for either their nose or the moon to give them something to chew on.

The Great Northern Railway line ran along the foot of bluffs facing across the Missouri River Valley to the high hill our ranch buildings were perched on. The old steam engines were still running when I was a child, and the sound of their whistle echoing across that valley in the night made my young heart ache for things I didn't understand.

Father's parents lived next door in a larger, more comfortable, three-bedroom house. My uncle and his family lived in a third house, and all three homes shared the same large oval driveway that came down the hill from where the main road wound its rutted and graveled way east along the Missouri River towards its joining with the Yellowstone.

Up until I was about eleven years old, my childhood was almost idyllic. My parents were kind and protective and were quite effective at shielding us from some of the harsh realities of their lives. We had a thousand acres with woods and a river for a playground, and all kinds of animals to tend to and play with. I've always had the belief that if the six of us had just been left alone, if there had not been an extended family involved, life could have been pretty sweet for us. Not perfect, but still.

So, I was still a pretty carefree ten-year-old sitting at my school desk daydreaming on an early fall day that was still holding onto the heat of high August. The schoolhouse stood near the spot where a branch line of the Great Northern Railway crossed the Missouri River, and I was idly meditating on the black lines of the old railroad bridge silhouetted against the blue sky. As I was watching, a freight train crossed the bridge, headed south from the main line. It was a common occurrence, so I wasn't paying much attention until the train had passed and a man appeared in its wake, carrying a backpack and walking down the road towards the school.

Now, in our community, you never saw a man walking down the road unless something was wrong—and this was the first time I ever saw a backpack—so I was paying attention. He was dressed in nondescript but respectable working man's clothes and there was nothing dangerous or threatening about him as he turned into the school's parking lot, but our teachers went on red alert and locked all of us in the schoolhouse. After all, those two young women were on their own out in the middle of nowhere, with no telephone to call for help. There were some negotiations through a closed door, but eventually a glass of water was passed through to the stranger, and he went back the way he came.

I watched him carefully as he walked his soldier's walk back up the road and onto the bridge to stand in the shadows of its black iron superstructure. I had no comprehension of the relationship between the man and train, and when another train approached, this time from the south, I feared for the man's life. Sure enough, when the train had passed, the man had disappeared, convincing me for a moment that his squashed body must be on its way south, borne by muddy Missouri water—until finally I realized that he had simply stepped up onto the train.

Like St. Paul on the road to Damascus, I suddenly saw the light. I had just seen a free man. I had just seen that if one could rid oneself of possessions, families, and fear, one could be free. I was going to be free. I was going to be a hobo, a wanderer. This dream, or compulsion, would help carry me through the difficult times that were coming for my family and me, and a war.

*** * ***

Around the age of eleven or twelve, I began to be aware of the simmering resentments on the part of both my grandfather and uncle towards our family, resentments that the two of them didn't bother concealing from us children. These mysterious resentments were never discussed by our parents in our presence, and I was never clear as to their cause or origin. They had a great impact on life on that isolated farm and on our family. Decades after Grandfather had died, I asked my father about it, and all he would say, in the same bleak tone of voice he always used in response to any question concerning his experience in the Great Depression, was that his father had been an ignorant man. An ignorant man passing on some of the wounds inflicted on him and the Northern Cheyenne.

It was about this time, around 1955 or 1956, that the wheels began to fall off the wagon for our family. My mother's mother and brother lived on a little hardscrabble farm just down the road from us, and the brother, a troubled WWII veteran, lost the farm. He moved in with us for too long before leaving with a little encouragement from my father and disappearing for twenty-five years. His replacement in our little three-room cottage was my grandmother, who lived with us for ten years or so, determined to be a burden to my mother.

It was during this same time frame that my father's parents began to die off, first my grandmother after a long illness, then my grandfather, in 1958, also after a long illness. The burden of caring for all these demanding dying relatives along with her own four children eventually broke my mother's health—and our family.

I knew Grandfather as a gruff, heavyset, short-coupled man with a thick brush of salt-and-pepper hair, a large mustache, and deep-set brown eyes beneath thick brows. Beautiful eyes, some might say, but with a broken look about them. I remember seeing those terrible sad eyes twinkle with humor and even affection on occasion, mostly when he was petting his dog or talking to guests in his house, but never when focused on me. Endowed with a deep resonant voice, he used it to punish his own blood for his mysterious miseries like a man firing off a scatter-gun in a crowded room without concern for collateral damage. Most of the time he limited himself to sarcastic comments, but occasionally he gave full vent, and you only had to hear that bull roar once to know that you didn't want to hear it again, much less be its target. It was like being around a volcano that only erupted once in a while. Just the sight of a little smoke rising was enough to get *my* attention, especially when I was alone with him. I learned to walk on eggs around my grandfather—and my uncle, who was a kind of a frustrated wannabe patriarch and, though he lacked my grandfather's authoritative presence, seemed to have inherited his need to punish others for his own miseries. It was through my uncle and grandfather that I learned the downside of living in the bosom of an extended family, one that often made me feel as though my immediate family was under a strange kind of siege. There always seemed to be someone doing or saying something hurtful or making unreasonable demands of my parents.

On those isolated farms and ranches, in that time and place, the matriarch or patriarch was king of the hill, and my damaged grandfather with his damaged psyche and with no one to answer to or question his behavior, was king of the hill on our ranch. Grandfather was one of those people who can never trust loyalty unless that loyalty is coerced. It was his way or the highway, and there was really no highway option for my father during the Great Depression.

My father's parents deliberately worked at breaking his spirit, at convincing him to accept the role of sort of a cheap hired hand. Pulled out of school in the sixth grade to become the workhorse on the family ranch, he sweated his youth and early manhood away, mostly as a solitary figure clearing brush down in the river bottom, trailing flocks of seagulls across the hills behind his plow, bringing the stock into fall pasture beneath incoming flights of refuge-seeking geese, and trying not to dream. By the time the Great Depression was over, my father was thirty years old, without an education or any work experience outside of the ranch.

Despite the way his parents treated him, he was unwaveringly loyal to them. He knew that the survival of the family ranch depended upon him, and he knew that if he left, he would be going out without training or education into a strange world where there were no jobs and people were starving. He was caught in a trap that was not uncommon for those of his generation. The necessities of survival can create uncomfortable bedfellows—and family units.

My grandfather mistook my father's loyalty and tolerance for surrender, and he must have been shocked and angered by his son's marriage in 1942 to a strong-willed, hard-working woman, and his obvious allegiance to her and the four children that followed. Suddenly, Grandfather realized that not only was he losing control of the situation, but that he had never really been in control. That, and he was getting old. My father and mother would look after Grandfather and Grandmother Burgess to the end, out of kindness and responsibility, and Grandfather hated it. He would never forgive our family for our disruption of his rigidly ordered little kingdom. Not to his dying day.

My other grandfather died just after I was born, so for me, Grandfather Bruce was the only game in town. However, he pretty much ignored me, except for the occasional harsh comment or criticism. His treatment of others was what made me genuinely afraid of him. Once, when I was three or four years old and being baby-sat by Grandmother Selma, my grandfather noticed that some of our neighbor's cattle had gotten into our alfalfa fields in the valley below our ranch buildings. He got into his green Kaiser and went down to correct the situation, choosing for some reason to take my grandmother and me along. Looking back on it, it occurs to me that my grandmother, knowing my grandfather's temper, might have insisted upon going along to fill her usual role as the ineffectual peacekeeper.

The neighbor's fifteen-year-old son was already there on horseback, moving the cattle back across the downed section of fence. Grandfather Bruce drove up to him and began bellowing abuse at him through the open car window. I was too young to understand much of what was being said to the boy, but I did understand that my grandfather was saying terrible things about the boy's family, and that the boy was sitting up there in the saddle weeping while my grandfather continued his diatribe and my grandmother tugged at his shirt sleeve, begging him to stop—and I sat petrified in the back seat.

Grandfather Bruce liked cats to the extent that he refused to get rid of any of them and, as a result, there always seemed to be two or three litters of kittens around the barn. This was fine during the warmer seasons when there were a lot of field mice for them to eat and enough cow's milk to afford the cats a share. But in the winter, there was nothing for them to hunt and very little, if any, extra cow's milk, so some of them always froze and/or starved to death, to the frustrated outrage of my mother. When I was eight years old, I found a kitten frozen to Grandfather's kitchen window where it had died trying to absorb some warmth from the smooth, hard glass. The old man's affection for cats was a bit seasonal and didn't extend to inviting any of them in to share the warmth of his fire during the wintertime.

I woke to my last memory of my grandfather late one night on a cot in the unfinished bathroom of Grandfather Bruce's house. I was sleeping there while Mother nursed the slowly dying old man, just as she had nursed Grandmother through her last illness. I'm not sure why I was there, but it may have been to act as a runner to fetch my father if my mother needed him. On this particular night, I was awakened by the sound of Mother's sobbing and Grandfather's bull roar of a voice. I peeked out from my tiny room and saw Grandfather Bruce somehow up and out of his deathbed, standing in his nightshirt in the middle of the living room ranting on at the top of his still formidable lungs about what a lazy, worthless son-of-a-bitch my father was, while Mother stood weeping into her hands. That night, my fear of the old man changed to hate.

When the old man died, immediately after getting home from the funeral, Father had me change into my work clothes, and the two of us made our way down the hill with the mild afternoon sun filtering its golden light through the changing leaves, to where two litters of kittens played around inside the barn. One calico kitten played with dust motes in the light cast through a south-facing window. Father picked it up by the scruff of its neck and went outside into the corral where he grabbed the kitten's hind legs with his other hand, then snapped its head against the roping post, throwing the body on the ground between us where it lay bleeding from its eyes and mouth. "Clean out both litters and bury them on the north side of the barn." He turned away and headed back up the hill to the house. Someone always has to do the dirty work.

Browbeaten Grandmother Selma had slipped away at home late one night in the fall of 1957, still trying to go unnoticed, although the night she died our dog, Rex, howled inconsolably and my youngest brother, Steven, remembers her coming over to our house to say goodbye to him. Grandfather Bruce followed a year or so later, raising considerably more of a commotion as he made *his* exit. Even death offended him. I was fourteen years old that fall when they put what was left of the old man in the ground, and I was glad that he was dead. For that matter, neither of my grandmothers' deaths registered much with me because I didn't seem to be much more than a stage prop to either one of them. They weren't so much unkind as they were preoccupied: one by the demands of her malevolent husband, and the other by her own neediness.

*** * ***

Our ranch was a textbook example of just how crowded and claustrophobic a couple of thousand acres in the middle of nowhere can be made by the presence of an unpleasant personality or two. The situation was made even more difficult by my mother's condition. The stress of raising four children and dealing with a demanding and somewhat demented extended family created some health issues that should have been manageable, but incompetent doctors put her well on her way to becoming a semi-invalid by the time she was in her forties.

A small working ranch like ours required two strong partners to make things work, and my mother went from being a human dynamo to being a semi-invalid for reasons that no one understood. Life became more difficult for everyone.

In 1925, her father's drinking and gambling spree had cost their family a promising little cattle ranch in the hills twenty miles south of our place, reducing them to a hardscrabble struggle for survival on a sorry little farm in the valley. Life had been hard on the ranch out in those hills, but now it became harder and rather hopeless, especially with the Great Depression beginning to really sink its claws in. The cattle ranch became in my mother's mind a kind of lost paradise, a time when her family still had a future, and her father was still her hero on horseback. I suspect that she saw the dark side of her father in me and was determined to weed it out with the occasional cruel comment, for my own good. As I said, the cruel comments were occasional, but they were pretty much all I got. She made sure I was fed and clothed and educated (no small thing), and pretty much ignored me otherwise.

People cared for my mother, and the friends I brought home fell in love with her. She was genuinely kind, hospitable, and loving—particularly with young people, just not with me. I had friends weep upon leaving after a visit with her, but I always seemed to be outside of the warm circles she was capable of creating around herself.

*** * ***

My father was an excellent mechanic and maintained the bejesus out of our machinery, enabling some of those machines to last long enough to become almost members of the family. We drove our truck and our diesel tractor for thirty-five years until Father retired, and I do believe that both of those machines are still doing their job out there somewhere.

Our John Deere Model R diesel tractor came into my life in 1954, when I was ten years of age. The diesel became the workhorse of our little tractor stable and was what we used to pull all the heavier field equipment. We had over four hundred acres of summer fallow that had to be gone over two or three times a season to keep the weeds down, most of it up in the high and dry hills. Father did most of it until I was about thirteen and big enough to be trusted with the work (sort of). The wide-stance, muscle-bound tractor was often kept busy from dawn to dark and beyond. The pounding of the big diesel in the distance would precede the arrival of Father on the crest of the hill above the farm buildings, standing astride the green machine, one hand on the steering wheel, the other resting on his hip, his hat cocked slightly down over one eye, and a long day's dust covering him from head to toe. His sunburned flesh would glow dark red through its layer of dirt in the fire of the last rays of the setting sun as he casually wheeled the speeding machine down the driveway into the farmyard to park it beside the fuel tanks, a battered warrior returning home to his family from a long day's ordeal. As a child, I would watch him and yearn for the time when I could fight that battle in his stead, when I could casually charge down the driveway on that green steed in the last light of day.

When my time came to be up on the John Deere R, I never seemed to get enough of running that machine in its great oval circuits in the hills above the valley, pulling the tool carrier with its arrow-shaped shovels parting and turning the weed-grown and sun-bleached ground, tearing up the weeds and exposing the darker soil to the air even as it exposed earthworms and bugs to the predations of a flock of opportunistic seagulls that always seemed to know when to come up from the river bottoms to circle the dust cloud raised by my endless circling. Most of the fields that I worked seemed to have their own resident jackrabbit for me to haze back and forth across the field until I took my commotion elsewhere and left the rabbit to return to dig its hole back out in peace. I learned to watch the position of the sun, so I would know when to begin feeling hungry for the lunch that was usually brought out to me. After lunch, the combination of the heat and my full stomach would sometimes make me so sleepy that I would have to stop the tractor and take a short nap draped over the steering wheel, lulled by the heartbeat of the idling diesel, my back warmed by the sun. I loved being alone out in that landscape, whether I was on a tractor, on a horse, or on foot.

Running in my endless circles of turned earth, I would meditate from dawn to dark on the valley and its weather, marking the progress of a solitary cloud all the way across the otherwise empty sky as it led its shadow across the hills, bringing momentary relief from the summer sun to the landscape and its living things. When the fire of the day finally began sinking into the west, I would stop to retrieve my jug of drinking water from whatever shade I'd found for it, then leave the field, hitting the lever that raised the shovels out of the earth as I went, then kick the tractor into its road gear, take my charioteer's stance astride, cock my hat down a little over one eye, and make my run for home.

Most of the weather came from the west. We experienced a lot of violent hailstorms out there, and they would slide unbelievably quickly towards us from the horizon with their agitated swirling and wicked icy green-blue underbelly. When I saw one of those coming, I knew enough to be afraid. I knew that they could kill livestock, people, and crops. More than once, I saw the bleak expression on my father's face after hail had plowed a season's work back into the ground and stripped the leaves from the trees.

One hot August afternoon, when I was about twelve years old, one of those storms came up when Father was out in the south hills summer-fallowing and my mother was alone at home with us kids. When one of those storms threatened, everything had to be closed up and battened down against the violence of the winds that always accompanied it. Between taking care of that and making sure the children were all right, my mother had her hands full. However, someone had to go out and get Father because it was obvious from the speed of those clouds that he wasn't likely to get back to the house on that tractor before the storm hit. Mother couldn't drive the truck, and my uncle was not around, so I was elected, in spite of the fact that I barely knew how to shift the gears on the truck, much less drive it under adverse conditions. I remember my mother telling me that I would have to do it, looking at me doubtfully as though she knew she was putting her faith in a weak vessel—and she was right. The storm hit before I got out of the driveway, the hail and high winds hammered and buffeted the cab of the truck as I fumbled ineptly with the brakes and the clutch, and the dual tires skidded on the freshly slicked gumbo. Fear for my father, stubbornness, and desperation were the only things that kept that truck moving.

The hail was coming in on gusts of fierce wind, so there were breaks in the onslaught that enabled me to at least catch some glimpses of what was in front of me. I spotted our tractor in one of those breaks as I pulled in off on the dirt access road. Fifty years later, I still see that tractor sitting out in the middle of the field with no one on it— and feel the relief when my father crawled out from his shelter beneath the tractor to run through the ice and rain to join his somewhat overwhelmed son in the cab of the truck. I really, really wanted him to rescue me from my driving responsibilities, but I wasn't about to admit it and Father, as usual, was blind to my plight. Born competent, he sometimes forgot that I wasn't.

My father was focused on the struggle for survival, and taking time to teach me took time away from that struggle. He needed me to learn on my own, so I could perform when the need arose. Another lesson learned in the teeth of death and mayhem. Another day, another dollar on the Burgess ranch.

Both of my parents were tenderhearted, hard-working, and honest products of hard times. Alcoholic and abusive parents and the Great Depression left their minds and bodies wounded and scarred. They were two wounded birds engaged in a valiant but losing struggle to avoid passing on those wounds to their children and to shield their children from a world they couldn't shield themselves from.

I began to learn, even as a child, that authority figures had their limitations and weren't necessarily to be trusted or relied upon; that kindness, virtue, and hard work weren't necessarily rewarded; and that no one could really protect me. I was learning my role as a helpless witness to the suffering of others.

I was learning from my father that men are expendable protectors, gentle but built to take punishment. I was learning from my mother that there was something about me that was fundamentally unacceptable.

# CHAPTER 3

*THE NEIGHBORHOOD*

On a hill a mile or so west of our old ranch buildings, an isolated unmarked grave is nestled in an expanse of buffalo grass and protected by broken glass and rusty barbed wire. The legend is that it is the grave of a small boy, killed by the accidental discharge of a Sharps .50 buffalo gun in the hands of his older brother. The older brother then fled into the woods to live off roots and berries and evade searchers for two weeks until starvation drove him out. Soon thereafter, the father, who was one of the very early white settlers in the area, a widower, and a trapper by trade, disappeared with his one remaining son into what was left of the nineteenth century. I visit that grave once in a while and think about that older boy and the shock of that huge rifle's discharge and its consequences within the confines of that little cabin.

There were a dozen or so family ranches and farms in our farming and ranching community, most of whom had been there for a couple of generations, struggling to survive the weather, twenty years of the Great Depression, grasshopper infestations, alcoholism, mental illness, abusive patriarchs and matriarchs, laziness—and just plain bad luck. There was no electricity until the fifties, no television until the sixties, and no telephone service until the seventies. Medical care was a luxury, and what was available was mostly incompetent. There were no such things as social services or nursing homes.

Neighbors did not necessarily care much for one another, but they knew that ultimately, they had to depend upon one another at times, even for survival, and the struggle for survival can sometimes form bonds stronger than love or affection. Tolerance was part of our survival kit. We learned to avert our eyes from things we were powerless to change, to tolerate things that nowadays might seem to be intolerable.

The community in which we lived stretched about fifteen miles west into Montana from the North Dakota line, along the south side of the Missouri River. Rolling hills dropped precipitously down to flat rich valley land, interspersed with jagged confusions of buttes and badlands. Dryland ranches and farms shared bits and pieces of partially cleared bottom land, mostly used as hay meadows and pastures. Our gateway to the outside world was under the south end of a black, twin-towered railroad bridge that spanned the river and the small crossroads settlement of Nohly, which in the fifties consisted of a grain elevator, a post office, a schoolhouse, and a weathered old general store with a false front that had been converted into a carpentry shop with two rusted antique gas pumps standing out front. There was no plumbing of any kind in the buildings in that little crossroads settlement, except for a hand pump that drew water from a cistern into the school. Nohly had four outhouses and two permanent residents.

The only full-time residents of Nohly were a gentle old carpenter who lived in the rear of his shop and an Irish postmistress possessed of a vicious temper and a loud and foul mouth with few inhibitions about venting around anyone under any social circumstances, which sometimes made being around her a breathtaking and educational experience for a child. She had three rather notorious brothers, Lester, Tom, and Fred Reilly, three brawling drunks who owned a ranch in the hills adjacent to our place until Lester shot his younger brother Fred over bacon and eggs one morning when I was six or seven years old. I saw my first ambulance that morning.

Another neighbor family, the McCalls, lived in a house awkwardly perched on a high concrete foundation with a bare dirt yard overlooking a bend in the Missouri a few miles upriver from our place. Billy McCall's wife, Lottie, spent much of her day sitting at her kitchen table piecing together stories about her neighbors and writing them down on lined tablet paper. Every week she would send them in to the local newspaper, and every week her neighbors read the paper to find out what had been going on in their lives.

Lottie's columns used to be guilty of only occasional lapses, but as the years passed, she gained weight, the local party-line telephone system fell apart, it had become more difficult for her to get around, and the pursuit of truth simply became too strenuous for her. Most people didn't seem to mind reading a fictionalized version of their lives. Or at least, they didn't mind enough to risk getting her in trouble with the newspaper. People forgave Lottie's factual inaccuracies because they knew that she weighed three hundred pounds and was depressed—and because they knew she was married to Billy McCall, and the neighbor men were grateful to her because her sorry husband made the worst of the other local husbands look good. Once I heard my father say somewhat admiringly that a man could stay ahead of Billy McCall just by taking a bath and brushing his teeth once a month.

Billy McCall was scrawny, shabby, and dirty, had tobacco-stained, snaggly teeth, wore glasses that always seemed to be taped together and mashed down on his big, hooked nose, and had a nasal, high-pitched voice with which he loved to tell obscene jokes—especially when he was drinking, and that was often. Billy was what I once heard one neighbor call a "garden-variety ass-kisser." He spent almost as much time ingratiating himself with his neighbors as he spent working on his own place, certainly more time than he spent with his wife. His own ranch had been gradually declining over the years—buildings going unpainted, corrals withering and failing along with his marriage. Most of his friends were those few who were willing to take advantage of him. Too much of what little money he did have went to supporting his own drinking habits and those of others.

Every once in a while, Lottie had one of what the neighbors called her "nervous breakdowns," and someone would take her to Warm Springs Mental Hospital for a few weeks' vacation. No one ever told this child what it meant to have a nervous breakdown, which left me with the impression that it must be kind of like a tractor or a truck breaking down. My imagination stopped just sort of picturing someone fixing one of Lottie's body parts.

Often, when Lottie went away for one of her rests, the neighbor ladies would pick a day to get their gear together and go clean her house from top to bottom. Lottie was too overweight and usually too depressed to keep her house up very well. Billy had sense enough to make himself scarce during these cleaning sessions. Mother said the whole thing was good for everyone concerned because the neighbor women worked off a lot of steam cleaning up that filthy house and saying terrible things about Billy to one another that they might have wanted to say to their own husbands. I noticed that Mother always seemed to be in a good mood after a day spent cleaning Lottie's house. Billy wasn't the only husband to stay away from that place.

Somewhere in the 1970s, Lottie swallowed a can of Drano. She survived, but the doctors had to rebuild her esophagus. Unable to ingest solids for a prolonged period of time, she lost almost all her excess weight. The shock and stress of these developments caused Billy to have a heart attack and die a few weeks after Lottie had cleaned her pipes. The ranch was sold for a good price, and Lottie ended up happily ensconced in a comfortable nursing home.

Shortly after Billy died, I was home visiting, and Father asked me to drive him up to Billy's place to help him retrieve a farm implement that Billy had borrowed. The two of us hooked the tool carrier up to the old John Deere and paused afterward to take a cigarette break standing on the crest of a small rise looking out over what was left of the ranch buildings, the river, and the badlands beyond. Father finished tapping some Bull Durham tobacco into one of his scraggly roll-your-own cigarettes, lighting up as he contemplated what was left of the sorry McCall cattle empire. "Well, old Billy wasn't much … but he'll be missed." My father was a pistol.

# CHAPTER 4

*GOD'S DOG*

I grew up listening to bats rustling in the rafters of the attic, coyotes giggling and yipping at the northern lights, an old Hereford bull lowing in the moon shadow of a cottonwood tree, and the last steam locomotives wailing their siren's song to me as they fled their burden on the Great Northern line across the valley from us. These sounds filled and shaped me, just as I was filled and shaped by the sounds of my grandfather ranting hate from his deathbed, the song of meadowlarks piercing the air around the ranch buildings every summer morning, the hopeless weeping of my invalid mother from her bedroom, the strumming whisper of the breeze through the buffalo grass, the strange fluting tune played by the wind on the cemetery gate on the hill above the house, the exquisite eloquence of my father's silence—and the falling sigh of the hawk pulling my eye to the sky.

I was around four years old. The snow had melted off, but the ground was still saturated from the runoff; Everybody walked around with heavy scallops of mud attached to their overshoes, and cars and trucks slewed clumsily down the deeply rutted dirt and gravel roads. Mud was everywhere—in people's clothes, on the floorboards of vehicles, and the linoleum floors of every kitchen. It was a trying time for housewives.

A man who worked at the John Deere dealership in town, Dean Carlsen, had brought a litter of pups out to the farm for us children to choose from. I remember him squatting in the mud of our driveway, smiling at our delight over a cardboard carton full of the tiny little things. It might have been the first time any of us had seen recently born puppies. Somewhere, there is a photograph of my towheaded older sister, Sandra, holding one of them as she stood by our mud-spattered blue '47 Chevy, the family's first car.

We named the dog Rex, and he became a part of the family in a way I was never able to explain to outsiders, or to myself, for that matter. It could be fairly said that the dog received more affection by far than any of us children. Babies were babied, but once they stopped being babies and became children, the physical affection stopped. The occasions that my mother touched me were so rare that they confused and discomfited me when they did occur. I don't remember ever hugging or holding my baby brother. And later, when I visited my sister in New York after returning from Vietnam, she backed up one full step to avoid being hugged by me. Even in my father's old age, when I gutted up enough to put my arms around him, I had to resign myself to his inability to respond, although he was pretty good at shaking hands.

Never having learned to confide in humans, I learned to confide in Rex the Dog. Never having learned to touch humans, I lavished affection on him. I shed most of my tears on that poor dog.

All that hugging and petting didn't seem to stunt the dog's growth. He was some kind of shepherd/collie mix and, of course, turned out to be a wonder-dog. He seemed to be totally focused on the joys of adoring the family, keeping chickens out of the yard, and honing his skills at working sheep. Going near the cattle was a no-no, except for one occasion.

One summer, when I was about nine years old, a neighbor's Angus bull came to visit. The bull was a bit of a monster in size and had a reputation for being very aggressive. It was moving at a trot, its head up and swaying from side to side as though it were coming into a bullfight arena looking for something to kill, a huge black profile moving against the blue sky on the high hill above the ranch buildings. The menfolks were gone, and my mother immediately got us children into the house and locked the dog up in the back shed. Mother was a long way from being a shrinking violet, having grown up working cattle and horses, so we knew that this was serious. The bull was known for going on the prod in spectacular ways.

We were all in the living room watching the show through the front window when we heard a crash from the rear of the house. Rex had gone through the locked screen door, around to the front of the house and on up the hill, charging the bull from the side at a dead run with absolute intent, his shaggy white and gray fur flying as he leapt in to sink his teeth into the bull's muzzle. The bull responded by snapping his head away, violently separating Rex from his grip and hurling him through the air to the ground, where he rolled to his feet to return without pause to the fray, running and leaping for the bull's head to repeat his original tactic three or four times, until the bull's muzzle was a mangled mess and the animal finally turned to trot back up the hill where it had come from. Rex the Dog stood and watched the bull's retreat with fierce joyful eyes, his head and ears up, as though willing the bull to return and fight some more. Finally, when the bull had disappeared over the hill, the dog turned and pranced like an Arabian stud down the hill towards the house and his stunned audience, as though he had just fulfilled his destiny and found it good. I am Dog.

*** * ***

The Missouri River Valley runs generally west to east, but with a lot of deep curves, including an abrupt dogleg running almost directly north from where our ranch buildings stood on their shelf overlooking the valley. In summer evenings, the setting sun made this wall cast a long shadow over the hay meadows below our house. One evening, Rex the Dog and I went for a walk down through the elm grove immediately below the house on our way to cross the hay meadows towards the river. When we came to the fence line that separated the woods from the meadows, however, Rex sat down on his haunches and refused to go through the fence or accompany me any farther. He just sat there growling and staring at some shadowed haystacks that were almost invisible to my eyes, dazzled as they were by the setting sun. I was so surprised by Rex's uncharacteristic timidity that, at first, I focused solely on coaxing the dog to move without really considering the cause of his reluctance. Finally, giving up on convincing him, I shaded my eyes with my hand against the glare of the setting sun and was barely able to make out some large white splotches in one of the stacks, almost incandescent in the shadow cast by the valley wall.

Things became very quiet. Even Rex the Dog stopped his growling, though he still made no move to join me in my foray out into the hay meadow. I began walking slowly out across the sunlit hayfield towards the haystacks in the shadows, moving and feeling as though I were a participant in an unfamiliar religious ceremony. The stillness continued—no birdsong, no breeze, no nothing. The setting sun continued to partially blind me until I was about thirty feet from the nearest stack and had entered the shadow cast by the valley wall, where I stopped. There were a half dozen or more large white owls perched on the haystack with all of their bodies facing different directions but with all of their heads turned towards me. I stood there for some time without moving, submitting myself to the unsympathetic scrutiny of the church elders.

I experienced their gaze as a judgment and was left with a sense that my life was going to be both harsh and harshly judged. Those birds looked at me with hard eyes.

Later that same summer, perhaps in the fall, Rex the Dog came home from one of the solitary rambles he would sometime take around the ranch, more or less dragging his hindquarters, barely making it to our front porch, his body convulsing and out of control. He was obviously in agony, but it seemed to my twelve-year-old self that the dog's eyes were fixed on mine in mute apology in a way that broke my heart forever. Father had recently ordered some government trappers off our land, but he suspected that they had left some strychnine-laced carcasses along our property line as coyote bait and that Rex had given into temptation. They loaded the dog into a pickup and carried him off into the hills, but not so far away that I could not hear the gunshot.

There was a heavy rain shower later that afternoon, and afterwards raindrops hung from every leaf, every blade of grass, every point of every barb on the fences, shining like tiny quivering drops of sun-pierced crystal in the last light of day as I walked out into the bottomland pasture to bring the milk cows in. I was weeping with grief and anger, singing some made-up hymn to the damn dog as I stumbled along. Somewhere in the midst of all this emotional drama I informed my rigid Norwegian Lutheran god that if he wouldn't allow Rex the Dog into heaven, he could count me out, too. I was not optimistic concerning my powers of negotiation. I have stayed pretty much clear of both the god and the dog business ever since.

# CHAPTER 5

*BLIND MULES AND RED ROSES*

Early one morning, the old deuce-and-a-half Chevrolet truck sat in its accustomed snowbank, a white plume of exhaust percolating up from its tailpipe towards a sky still crowded with stars. The truck's battery had been brought inside the night before to keep it from freezing up. Father believed in properly maintained vehicles, ready to go at a moment's notice, particularly in the winter. There was no telephone to call for help in case of emergency, so he was right in being so conscientious, but he also hated the thought of his family getting into a cold vehicle. The truck had probably been idling in its snowbank since before breakfast. I swear, in the winter he burned more gas warming his vehicles up than he did driving them.

Of course, the drafty old truck cab was warmed more by Father's good intentions then it was by the decrepit heater. I sat all bundled up on the bench seat as the truck broke loose from the snowbank's icy hold to creak down the snow-packed track with the tire chains slapping at the wheel wells. My father's stolid, solid presence and the truck engine's faithful humming made me feel safe and adventuresome at the same time. The sleeping ranch houses we passed as we made our way down the frozen trail of a road were few and far apart. A full moon raced across the sky, pushing the dark shadows of dense, scattered clouds quickly across the snow-covered hills below. Large boulders rested out in the middle of a cow pasture, black in the moonlight like huge lumps of coal perched in nests of snow.

Father had never really gotten over horses, and the tire chains encouraged him to drive even slower than usual, so we cruised along the rough gravel road at a steady forty miles an hour for twenty minutes or so before we hit the pavement. A passenger train caught up with us just as we crossed the Yellowstone River. The lights in the dining car were on, and I could see waiters in immaculate white moving among the tables, preparing them for the breakfast rush. There were only a few early risers eating, so that, sitting on the worn truck seat in my shabby winter work clothes, I had a clear view of white linen, solitary red roses, and gleaming crystal moving away, leaving our farm truck to make its bumbling, solitary way through the dark white night.

We turned south after clearing the bridge to run along the base of the bluffs overlooking the Yellowstone valley until we came to a wide place in the road where we pulled over to park beneath the end of a set of narrow-gauge railroad tracks that protruded from a tunnel mouth in the hillside. Coal deposits were common in the badlands, and local ranchers would sometimes teach themselves to use dynamite and other mining tools to pick up a little pocket change during the winter when the coal was most in demand. This was such a place. I was looking forward to seeing the blind mule that the rancher/miner kept back in the tunnel during the winter, using it to pull a coal cart out to waiting customers.

I had somehow got it into my head that the mule lived in darkness all year around, exposed to the sun only for short intervals when it pulled the coal-filled cart out of the tunnel, and that the perpetual darkness it lived in had caused it to go blind in the first place. It was still dark, but the sky against the bluffs high over our heads was beginning to lighten with the coming day as the moon began to fade out down towards the western horizon. We were going to have to wait for a while. My father hated to waste perfectly good daylight working hours waiting in line, so we were there early to beat the line, wasting sleep time rather than work time. Father left the relative warmth of the cab to stretch his legs and roll a cigarette. I got out too and began clambering up the hillside.

The ground was very steep and broken, almost a cliff, and I had to pick my way carefully to avoid falling. There were patches of ice and crusted snow to make it even more interesting. I figured I wouldn't fall very far before hitting the frozen ground, but the hillside was steep enough to tumble me all the way to the bottom and break my neck about six times. Much of it was raw and barren, and the level places were soft and crumbly beneath the snow, with a fair amount of clay and shale mixed in, as though the bluff were slowly melting down towards the river bottom, which in fact it was. Up close, there was a fragile and temporary quality to many of those rugged, stark buttes and bluffs that appeared at a distance to be eternal.

I climbed doggedly up towards the sky, determined not to stop for breath and anticipating the feel of the sunlight on my chilled flesh. I finally stepped up and out from the shadow side of the hill onto its flat top just as the sun's fiery pink eye peeped out at me from a long narrow crack between the eastern horizon and a heavy layer of clouds. With miles of the dark Yellowstone valley spread out below me, I stood for a few minutes absorbing the mostly imaginary warmth of the first rays from the pink eye that flattened and spread out to become a long burning pink ribbon unspooling across the broken skyline as I watched.

Turning around, I looked back down at the mine entrance where Father had climbed back into the truck cab. A couple hundred feet down the road from him, the rancher and his hired hand were walking towards the mine, one of them with the mule's harness draped over his shoulder and the reins dragging along the snowy ground behind, throwing up little rooster tails of frozen sparks. I smiled in anticipation of the first moment of flight as I threw myself headlong off the top of the bluff, flying with long, giant steps down the rampart of eternally collapsing earth, leaping across crevasses, bounding back and forth from stone to earth, earth to stone, my legs trying to stay ahead of my plummeting trunk, trying desperately to keep me from the disaster I probably deserved. But I didn't fall. I still had a ways to go.

# CHAPTER 6

## *HIGHER AND LOWER LEARNING*

The grade school I attended stood out on a sagebrush flat on the edge of what was left of the tiny crossroads settlement of Nohly, one of three buildings still standing at the time. The view to the west was dominated by a bridge with twin soaring black towers that carried the Great Northern trains and vehicle traffic across the Missouri River. Its system of cables and weights was engineered so that a small kerosene engine could lift a massive span of the bridge straight up twenty feet or so into the air, enabling the riverboats with their tall smokestacks to pass under. It was a massive concrete and iron edifice, with towers that seemed to lean into the sky against the current of the river, and it was built out in the middle of nowhere by hundreds of workers who had lived in boxcars and tents north across the river, near the main Great Northern line. Unfortunately, the riverboats stopped running just after the bridge was finished in 1912.

The bridge's dramatic vertical black strokes stood in sharp contrast to the soft horizontal lines of the valley's landscape, and it made a marvelous jungle gym for us schoolchildren when we could get away with it, grade school kids clambering around a hundred feet in the air in the moonlight while our oblivious parents held their PTA meetings.

One night, as the grown-ups were having a meeting in the schoolhouse and the kids were running wild outside, I abandoned the hectic play of my schoolmates to walk alone over to the railroad bridge and clamber a hundred and some feet up the open ladder on the side of a dull-black tower to stand by the giant wheel at its very top. I kept a death grip on the iron railing while looking out over the valley with its wide river scalloped by the moon shadows of cottonwoods and willows, and the few widely scattered farmhouse lights. Someone might have looked up and seen my tiny silhouette against the stars where I stood and listened to the faint cries of playing children as they circled like moths in and out and around the schoolyard light far below.

I have often wondered at the freedom afforded me and the other children of that community, and what we did with that freedom. Their struggle for survival left our parents with little choice but to cast us children somewhat to the winds, letting us wander around that huge landscape on our own and trusting us to have enough common sense—and luck—to survive. The freedom we had as young children to get ourselves in and out of trouble was good training for what was, at times, rather premature adult responsibility. There were occasions when I would use a farm vehicle as though it were some kind of oversized Tonka toy. We were put behind the wheel of tractors and trucks just as soon as our legs were long enough to reach the pedals, and sometimes before. OSHA would have had a fit. We children loved it and thrived on it. A surprising number of us did survive.

This sort of thing also instilled a mindset that tended to make us easy pickings when our government came looking for quality cannon fodder. In a way, war was just another job that the adults were telling us needed to be done, and the farm and ranch boys tended to respond to it just as they would if their father had told them to head off a bunch quitter or clean out the chicken coop.

The country school that we attended had two classrooms, with a kitchenette and a tiny bedroom attached for the teachers to stay in during the week if they so chose (the schoolteachers were often house or ranch wives with permanent homes elsewhere in the county). In that time and place, it was possible to get a teacher's certificate after two years of college, and a ranch wife would often do so as a means to supplement the family income, or a young single woman would use teaching as a way of meeting lonely young farmers. Two of the young women who taught there during my time married locals. Consequent to all of this, the quality of the teaching was often, shall we say, a bit patchy.

The schoolhouse had two outdoor toilets and, as I mentioned earlier, a cistern with a hand pump inside the building. That cistern was filled with water taken directly from the river, and so much mud settled from it that the cistern had to be mucked out every year. Our drinking water was never treated or refrigerated, so the water we drank at school during the warm months was about as warm as the weather and sometimes a little chewy. Again, no one died.

\*\*\* \* \*\*\*

Television and telephones didn't come into our area until well into the 1960s and '70s to break into an isolation intensified by poverty and long bad winter roads. For the most part, we were a stolid and stoic lot, incapable of any real emotional accessibility or sharing of feelings—but that made casual conversation and social interaction with our neighbors even more important. We relied heavily on community gatherings for these contacts, and the small houses that most of us lived in made the schoolhouse the only logical gathering place for PTA meetings, pie socials, Christmas parties, card parties, etc. And *everyone* came to these gatherings. Families, widowers and widows, democrats, drunks, malcontents—they all came. And if someone didn't have a car, someone always was able to give them a ride.

There was something rather sweet about it all. Sharing a pie with a classmate's mother, playing whist as an eleven-year-old with a grizzled, intolerant, old card sharp glowering at me across the card table. Huddled in a white clapboard cave, sharing warmth and light against the harsh desolation of those snow-covered sagebrush flats, we had momentary shelter from the cold moon and the unacknowledged dark shadows and harshness of our daily lives.

At the time I attended grade school, about twenty students were in attendance representing a dozen or so families scattered along the Missouri River Valley for about fifteen miles. With so few students growing up together in that little white box, the school environment was one of enforced intimacy, a microcosm of the enforced intimacy of the larger community. We listened to one another's lessons, knew one another's clothes, smells, athletic and academic abilities, even one another's pets and farm vehicles. We played out our own crude versions of baseball, softball, football, and basketball during recesses with whatever equipment we could scratch together. With such a limited talent pool, everyone—small and tall, boy and girl—was pressured into participating. On the positive side, this meant that no one was excluded. On the negative side, it also meant that seven- and eight-year-old kids were going up against teenagers. Playing usually with very little, if any, adult supervision, things often got a little Darwinian out there. Except that in our schoolyard, the apes were the ones left standing. There was often a fair amount of bullying going on.

There were a lot of fights, and I got thumped on regularly during my first years in school. The other little kids learned quickly that some well-timed tears could usually end the fight. Unfortunately, my tendency was to struggle stoically, without sound, tears, or hope until the bigger kid got tired of thumping on me. Then I'd get up and throw a rock at my tormentor, which obliged him to begin the cycle all over again.

My temper did sometimes compensate for my lack of size and fighting skills in those schoolyard brawls. I gave the impression sometimes that I might be more interested in killing my adversary than in winning a fight. I wasn't so sure myself sometimes. This came to a head in the eighth grade when I caught a schoolmate pounding my little brother's head against a steel swing post. My rage was so intense that for a while there I was seeing the world through a red haze. I grabbed his throat and when I woke up from my bloody little dream, his face was beginning to turn blue. This flirtation with homicidal mania was sobering enough to end my fighting career, and I traded my rage in for a kind of low-grade chronic depression that pretty much got me through high school and into my freshman year of college without any more near-fatal incidents.

I had entered my little country grade school on familiar ground with a very small group of neighbor kids I had known all my life. High school, however, was a horse of a different color. It meant fifteen miles of bad road to a world of strangers, sidewalks, and telephones— where some men wore ties every day, in a town of almost a thousand people.

I went from three classmates to sixty, from a school of eighteen to a school of over 200. At thirteen, I had never been on anything resembling a date and had never used a telephone. Flush toilets were still a pretty exotic experience, and the combination lock on my school locker intimidated the hell out of me.

In a slightly demented attempt to broaden my horizons, and as part of my pattern of throwing myself into experiences without regard for my limitations or suitability, I went out for football in my sophomore year. I had never seen a football game or learned to hold a football. Plus I was a late bloomer and stood about five foot four inches and weighed perhaps 130 pounds. However, the one thing that I could do was endure pain and discomfort, so I gutted up and managed to get through the first and last season of my football career, but it was not a pretty sight.

Chronically shy, broke, carless, dateless, and clueless, I stumbled along towards graduation, mostly working fairly successfully at being invisible. I spent most of my time reading unassigned books, hanging out in the local pool hall, cruising the abbreviated main street of Fairview in friends' cars and watching other boys cruising with their girlfriends tucked into their armpit.

During most weekends and summer vacations, I was holed up out on the ranch, helping out with the cows and sheep, fencing, haying, watching the crops fail or not, and watching my father being worn down by it all like the broken brown hills that scalloped the horizon. As the years went by, Father, though unfailingly kind, became more and more preoccupied with my mother's moods and health, the financial situation, the work and the weather, and an unsupportive and unpleasant brother. Mother spent more and more time in bed.

I learned to be an easy keeper, to get by on the very least of attention, energy, and resources—for better and for worse. In certain respects, that little ranch of ours out there between the hills and the river was a refuge from the harshness of the modern world, but the weather, the place, and the people on it had their own brand of harshness. At times, it could be a kind of purgatory with a beautiful view. I began to go silent, on my way to becoming a very secretive adult.

My rapidly developing speed-reading skills did enable me to maintain a decent average in high school while doing little or no studying, and my extracurricular reading in literature and history began nudging my grades upward a little from their mediocre base. I was becoming more and more interested in the written word and, in my senior year, I was exposed for the first time to someone who loved the English language, a greenhorn English teacher who informed me that I was a poet.

My parents were throwbacks to a time when people built schools with their own hands, determined to get their children educated, desperately wanting us out of the trap they saw themselves in. They couldn't help me financially, but their focused willpower was almost enough in itself to levitate me through to a college degree. I remember Mother toiling through the paperwork as she stubbornly sought out grants and loans to help with my tuition.

As for myself, I had no ambition, only a secret, absolute determination to go wandering, alone and unencumbered by possessions, out into the world to see what would happen to me. Distracted by their struggle for survival, my parents had little time or energy to devote to helping me develop good study habits, and I was a hard customer, preferring to daydream, observe, and bide my time. However, I was just wise enough to suspect that an education might come in handy, even to a wanderer. The only input I got from my high school teachers was given to me by two rookie teachers who took me aside in my senior year and lectured me on the waste of time and money it would be for the likes of me to attempt going to college.

*** * ***

I arrived by train in Moorhead, Minnesota, in the fall of 1962, wearing Richland County's cheapest suit, with fifty dollars in cash and an unbelievably flimsy set of tin luggage with which to confront the ivy-festooned stone walls of Concordia College. I had never been on a college campus before in my life or seen stone walls with ivy climbing up them. Busts of dour bald-headed Norwegians were scattered around campus, and it seemed that everyone but me was wearing tweed, driving a convertible, and had graduated valedictorian from some high school in Minnesota or North Dakota or Iowa. There must have been someone with a sense of humor working in the admissions office the day my application went through.

Instead of tweeds, I got to wear a little yellow beanie and cheap corduroys for the entirety of my freshman year. Attendance at daily chapel services was mandatory, freshmen were required to live on campus, and there were curfews for all the dormitories. Religion, yellow beanies, virginity, and academics were all taken very seriously on Concordia's campus. Again, everybody around me seemed to be playing a game that just stymied the bejesus out of me, whether that game consisted of trying to get into the Lutheran heaven or achieving academic success. I spent most of my freshman year trying to overcome my inhibitions with women and telephones, socializing mostly with other men whose academic futures were as doubtful as mine, washing dishes in the campus cafeteria, watching *Bonanza* on Sunday nights, and doing enough homework to avoid getting kicked out—with a little shoplifting on the side.

The problem was that I lacked any real sense of academic purpose or ambition, and that I was simply too relaxed. The shoplifting was my way of flirting with the devil and sticking it in the eye of the smugly righteous powers-that-be on campus. The tensions of the family situation and the confinement of life on the ranch seemed far away on that campus.

My college freshman year was a busy year. I kissed my first girl. I had my first encounter with racism (no one else would room with a black man), and my first encounter with sexual confusion and homosexuality (a good friend was molested and the experience left him confused about his sexuality). Concerning the latter, I suspect that my complete naiveté enabled me to be somewhat matter-of-fact about the whole affair and be a pretty good friend. Our conversations about the issue sort of faded away, as did our friendship.

By the time we were seniors, my friend was going steady with a girl, and, though still on friendly terms with me, he showed little interest in continuing our friendship. Ah, well. We both did the best we could. As far as the black roommate was concerned, he turned out to be quiet, popular, extremely studious, well-dressed, and fastidious in his personal habits. I, too, was fairly quiet. He came out of his freshmen year at Concordia with something close to straight As and disappeared without explanation in the general direction of Oklahoma while I came back to my sophomore year on both academic and disciplinary probation.

I had to poor-boy my way through college sans cash and scholarships, but I still lived better than I ever had at home. Sharing a room with only one roommate? A telephone on the wall outside my door and a bathroom across the hall? High cotton.

I settled in academically during my sophomore year, in part because the fact that I was placed on academic and disciplinary probation (a kegger got busted and I had flunked a five-credit French course) had finally gotten my attention. I was indifferent to academic competition and success, but I was quietly determined to graduate, and I realized that it was time to clamp down. This realization finally ended my career as a petty criminal. If I'd ever been caught stealing on that good Christian campus, they probably would have ridden me out of town on a rail, expunged my academic records, and sowed my dormitory bed with salt.

A friend who lived in a basement apartment had recently installed one of those huge stereo systems that started to come on the market during the early sixties. He'd apparently been bragging on it to his landlord, a WWII veteran, and the old man had come downstairs to look at it. My friend was putting on a stereo demonstration record and, while he was fiddling around with the still unfamiliar equipment, the landlord and I stood around in front of the speakers, chatting about something or another. My friend and I were both horrified and guilt-stricken when the screaming dive of a fighter plane suddenly filled the room, moving down and left to right, from one stereo speaker to the other, inspiring the old man to take a diving leap into the space between the sofa and the wall.

There was also a WWI veteran who worked in the college cafeteria as a janitor. He was very thin and trembly, with deep-set eyes that always seemed to be staring at something only he could see. Someone told me that he was shell-shocked. I didn't know quite what that term meant at the time, but I would find out later. In the meantime, the faces of these two old veterans would be among the first installations in my memory gallery of walking wounded warriors.

*** * ***

In the fall of my sophomore year, I sat in English class and listened to Dr. Walther G. Prausnitz read an excerpt from Chaucer's *Canterbury Tales* aloud to the class in the original archaic English dialect. Dr. Prausnitz was a short, pudgy, balding, sallow-complexioned man with a beak of a nose and a reputation both for being brilliant and for breaking students' balls. He referred to me in class as "the Montana sheepherder." Well, that's what I was. I liked him and assumed that the so-called "ball-breaking" that intimidated so many students was really his maladroit attempt at teasing. Anyway, that's the way I chose to take him, and it seemed to work for both of us. On that particular day, he stood with his ancient, scuffed-up, enormous black wing tips illuminated by golden fall light streaming in through the window of the basement classroom as he began to read from Chaucer. As I listened to his somewhat nasal but resonant voice and watched his thin, beak-like lips shape themselves lovingly around each syllable, I understood for the first time the sensuality inherent in the English language. I stayed in touch with that man until he died, sometime in the 1990s.

*** * ***

In the winter of 1965, I was a college senior and there was some thinking to be done, mostly decisions to be made about the Vietnam War and the draft. I came back to campus early from Christmas vacation to attend a friend's wedding and spent most of the rest of the time holed up in my dorm room, writing a grim little short story about a wounded soldier dying a slow miserable death alone in the jungle, drifting in and out of a dream of dying on a hillside beneath the stars back home. I entered it in a rather prestigious all-campus writing contest—running as a dark horse, to say the least. I don't know what got into me. To my complete amazement, I ended up winning the contest and, along with it, the only academic recognition of my entire college career. To enhance my moment of glory, someone in the English department had noticed my short story and submitted it to some obscure magazine without my knowledge and came the day I opened my mailbox to find a copy of the magazine with my story in it and a check for fifty dollars, which I promptly spent on a beautiful pair of cowboy boots. Somewhere along the way, I lost both my copy of the magazine and the boots. I still miss the boots.

Some rather despairing impulse towards normalcy caused me to propose marriage at the end of Christmas vacation to a classmate I was dating at the time. She demonstrated her good sense by smiling and gently suggesting that I wasn't demonstrating any. I had met her in one of my English classes during my junior year. She was cute, smart, liked me a lot, and was absolutely determined to hold onto her virginity until she had a husband. I do believe that she also had a sneaking suspicion all along that I was not really a prime candidate for that position. In some respects, it was the teenage romance I'd never had. We had a wonderful time, but in both our hearts, we knew that even if I survived the war, my restlessness and recklessness would survive with me, making me an extremely unlikely companion for her dreams of family and domesticity. Our goodbyes were gentle.

When I had written my short story about Vietnam, I hadn't written it in a vacuum, of course. It was coming into 1966, and the Vietnam War was beginning to seem a lot more real to many Americans, including myself, what with the draft heating up and all. McNamara and LBJ had decided to lower the standards for the draft to make sure that the not-so-smart and not-so-lucky got their opportunity to see exotic places—and to protect the smarter and luckier middle-class college kids from the draft as much as possible. The truth is, we were mostly a bunch of scared and confused adolescents having to make decisions we weren't really qualified to make, all because the adults were immobilized by their own confusion. It's just that some of us paid a bigger price for that confusion than others. And so, the politicians fiddled while McNamara's Band burned.

Still, even amongst the sheltered brick and ivy environment of our little Christian college in 1966, the middle-class young were beginning to feel the heat. I listened to the talk, did some reading, and concluded that our country's leaders were at least as confused as I was concerning the war. My doubts were not strong enough to push me into the anti-war camp or into dodging the draft, which would have required a kind of cowardice or courage of which I was not capable, anyway. It all boiled down to whether I could allow someone else to do the dirty work and the bleeding in my stead. Actually, I suspect that everything was settled for me that long-ago fall afternoon when my father had me kill those kittens. Someone always has to kill the kittens.

*** * ***

I was twenty-one in the spring of 1966 when my father and mother drove five hundred miles to watch my sister and me graduate from college, the longest trip they'd made in their lives, and afterwards my father announced that he was going to buy me a beer. He didn't ask me how his underage son knew which bar would make him comfortable. We stood for a while sipping our first Budweiser together and beginning a tradition that would continue for the rest of his life. I chose the occasion of our first beer together to tell him that I'd be enlisting in the army in a few weeks, with plans to volunteer for Vietnam. A lifelong Republican, he had nothing to say at the time, but a week later he took me aside and offered to sign over his half of the home place, everything he owned in the world, if I wanted to apply for a farm deferment. That was the only thing he ever had to say to me about the war. My daddy was a pistol.

In a later life, I would come to know many Vietnam veterans, most of them draftees, and many of them understandably bitter about being forced to fight a war and then despised for having fought it. I didn't blame them, but my father's offer denied me the role of victim and the sour refuge of bitterness and allowed me to make my decision free of any fear of the draft.

After completing basic training in Fort Jackson, South Carolina, I was given an unexpected two weeks' leave. I was broke and there was an airline strike going on, so I had to borrow money from a friend to buy a bus ticket home. It turned into a trip from hell with everyone in the country trying to get on a Greyhound. Every bus station had standing room only and every bus was running hours late. I finally gave up in Minneapolis. I walked out of that town lugging my duffel bag, a tired, sweaty, and rumpled sad sack of a greenhorn soldier. I had run out of eating money, and if I were going to starve to death, I preferred to do it along the freeway somewhere than sitting in a bus station.

One of my rides dropped me off outside Moorhead, Minnesota, where I had attended college, so I decided to drop in and say hello to an English professor, a Dr. Hoppe, who had been both my teacher and academic counselor while I was in college.

Dr. Hoppe was a confirmed bachelor and lived in an apartment near campus where he would often hold court with favored students, mostly men from upper-middle-class backgrounds, English and philosophy majors with a taste for pipes and tweed sports coats. Nice enough guys, for the most part, but a little bit pretentious and self-consciously intellectual. I hadn't owned a tweed sport coat, nor had I rated myself as an intellectual, but even I had been dork enough to have smoked a pipe for a while, and I had been good enough at what I did as an English major to marginally qualify for Dr. Hoppe's inner sanctum, comfortable with dropping in now and then at these little gatherings.

I strolled through the campus on my way to Professor Hoppe's apartment and rang the doorbell a few times until Dr. Hoppe opened the door.

"Hello, Dr. Hoppe."

The professor obviously recognized me, but he just as obviously had no intention of inviting me in. With his eyes fixed on my sorry excuse for a uniform, Dr. Hoppe stepped out on the porch with me, carefully closing his apartment door behind him, and proceeded to read me the riot act.

It seemed that one of my classmates had fled to Canada to avoid the draft. I remembered him. I hadn't known him well, but he'd seemed a nice person, one of the tweed-jacketed pipe smokers who'd been one of Dr. Hoppe's favorites. His father had been the head of the music department at Concordia, if I remember correctly.

Looking at me expressionlessly, Dr. Hoppe informed me that he thought that I was a coward for wearing a uniform and that it took real courage for my classmate to flee to Canada. With that, my erstwhile mentor turned on his heel and reentered his apartment, closing the door in my face. I remained standing there for a moment before stepping off the porch to begin making my way back to the freeway. This time, I avoided the campus.

It was the summer of 1966, and the drab green cocoon of military training had made me oblivious to many of the changes that were occurring in the country. I had grown up where and when soldiering was still considered, at worst, an acceptable rite of passage for a young man. It had never occurred to me that the uniform might upset some people—nor had it occurred to me that courage had anything to do with any of this.

# CHAPTER 7

*PREPARING TO SEE THE ELEPHANT*

It was April of 1968, Martin Luther King Jr. was dead, and I had $900 in a silver money clip and forty days to drive across America with my army officer's cap perched in the back window of a blue 1964 Chevy—forty days before I climbed aboard a silver bird and went to Vietnam. I wanted to have at least a taste of wandering before going overseas. It's not that I was having a lot of dark, melodramatic thoughts about the possibility of coming back from Vietnam in a silver box. It was just that for two years I'd spent a lot of time with young infantry officers-in-training, a few of them already marked by a combat tour. The best of them seemed to have come to a quiet acceptance of their own expendability with few illusions about the enterprise. It was what I had signed up for.

Besides, I knew that I was probably destined for a desk job. I had begun my training at Fort Benning Officer Candidate School in Fort Benning, Georgia, with the vague and naive belief that if I did my job right, I could keep my men alive. During the intervening months, however, it had finally sunk in that part of my job of an infantry officer was to give orders that got men killed. I wasn't sure I could live with asking men to die for a cause that I had growing doubts about. This was no longer a theoretical situation for me. The rubber was about to hit the road.

However, the same stubbornness that enabled me to complete a masochistic high school football season was driving me to complete Infantry Officer Candidate School and blinding me to the cold reality that my ambivalence made me a potential danger to myself and my men. Instead, I cast my fate to the winds—along with the fate of the men I might have endangered in combat if things had gone differently.

My eyesight was very bad, and I'd had to sign a waiver to get into the infantry. Now an army eye doctor determined that there were further problems with my eyes and that I would have to sign another waiver to continue with the infantry. I refused and branch transferred out of the infantry into the Adjutant General Corps.

To this day, I suspect that the doctor picked up on my ambivalence and decided to save me (and my men) from myself by falsifying the results of my exam, enabling me to avoid my fate as a combat platoon leader. Regardless, by the time I took my first civilian eye exam, the problem had disappeared. I've always wondered how much I and the men I *didn't* lead in combat owe to the compassion of that army doctor. God takes care of drunks and fools.

So, in the spring of 1968, my blue Chevy and I took Route 76 west out of Washington, DC, headed for Texas. I drove straight through except for a few brief naps in the back seat of the Chevy until I came to Galveston and the Gulf of Mexico, where I took a sharp right to drive along shining water until I came to Corpus Christi. I spent a day there, tentatively immersing myself in the Gulf, drinking tequila, and gorging on fresh seafood. In the late afternoon, as I cruised slowly along Padre Island, sipping on a beer and looking for a place to stop and watch the sunset, a kangaroo bounded out from behind a small sand dune and began racing alongside the car between the highway and the sun-reddened water.

The next evening, coming north out of Laredo, I picked up a hitchhiker who turned out to be just out of the navy. The sailor was a couple years younger than me, just wandering around the country getting rid of his sea legs. I stopped to fuel up and buy a case of beer, and we wandered off into the sunset up Route 83 onto Route 90, in the general direction of Arizona. We were doing a pretty good job on the Budweiser, and I began honking on my harmonica to entertain my new friend, who was drunk enough to appreciate the entertainment. The rain quickly became a real gully-washer, falling so hard that it seemed to bend down the ends of the windshield wipers. After a while, I really wasn't seeing the road much anymore, but it didn't seem to concern the sailor any more than it did me, so I kept on driving, playing my harp to the beat of the cowering windshield wipers and downing those Budweisers, trying to keep an eye on that white line.

When I woke up, I was sprawled out across the front seat, it was broad daylight, and there was a beautiful desert view staring at me through the windshield. I thought about this for a moment before turning around to find my back seat filled with a snoring sailor—and another beautiful view of the desert through the rear window. No road in sight. I woke the sailor, and we got out to have a pee and a cigarette and discuss our situation.

The rain had washed away all traces of our back trail. All we knew for sure was that we were somewhere in Texas and that the car was pointed pretty much west. The sailor and I looked at the road map and agreed that the best we could probably do was head north and trust our luck. The Chevy did all right going cross-country as long as I took it very slowly, and we managed to pick our way across a quarter mile or so of desert before we came to a fence and a barrow pit separating us from Highway 90. I thanked my lucky stars that I had refueled when I had and that the desert shed rainfall so quickly. I steered the car away from the morning sun, working my way along the fence line until I came to a cattle guard and an approach road that got us back onto the pavement. Eventually, I aimed the Chevy at Pecos, and the two of us toasted our luck, the still half-full gas tank, and the faithful old Chevrolet with our last two warm Budweisers.

We spent the next few days meandering across extremely arid real estate towards the Grand Canyon, which seemed as good a destination as any other, stopping in numerous small-town bars and coffee shops as we made our way across Texas, New Mexico, and Arizona doing our best imitation of out-of-work cowhands.

We eventually did get to the Grand Canyon, and I had a difficult time getting any kind of perspective on the immensity of the place. It was a little like being suspended out in space somewhere, trying to judge distance and size without anything for comparison. I was finally provided that perspective by an unfriendly and disbelieving park ranger who came up on me while I was occupied with throwing some pebbles down into the abyss:

"Do you see that little chain of dots way down there on that ledge where you were throwing your rocks?"

"Yes, sir."

"Those dots are mules with tourists sitting on them."

"Yes, sir."

"Their guide radioed park headquarters that falling rocks were spooking his mules."

"Yes, sir."

"Not to mention his tourists."

"Yes, sir."

The park ranger suggested that the sailor and I remove ourselves quickly from his jurisdiction, and we did. I had been traveling in mostly desert now for over a week, and I was experiencing a profound yearning for water, so we drove 150 miles straight through to Page, Arizona, including a swing through the Painted Desert. It was stunningly beautiful, I was certain, to someone—but the only effect it had on me at that moment was to make me hot, thirsty, and bored. I had had just about enough of the desert. We pulled into Page and were amazed by our first sight of the Glen Canyon Dam reservoir. The sky was almost cloudless, and the still surface of the lake was a mirror to the sky and the landscape, two identical inverted universes.

We rented a small unpretentious cabin near the water with the intention of going swimming right away, but instead we were almost immediately overwhelmed by the air conditioning in our room (and two days of drinking too much beer) and ended up falling asleep. When we awoke it was dark and, we realized, Saturday night. Instead of taking a swim, we headed for a nearby bar, figuring that cold was cold and wet was wet. The place was hospitable, busy, and comfortably redneck. The only two open seats were at the bar, one on each side of a nice-looking older Indian lady, who seemed to be on her own and totally oblivious to our foolishness. Because the sailor and I were in the middle of a conversation as we came in the door, we remained standing, drinking our beer, smoking, and talking a mile a minute directly over the head of the Indian woman who seemed to be completely absorbed in her own meditation with her cigarettes, her drink, and the back bar mirror. Occasionally, I would hear her humming to herself. It sounded vaguely familiar, some kind of Hawaiian music, but I couldn't place it.

About midnight, the sailor entered a plea for mercy, and we decided to call it a night. I was pretty tired myself, but at least I was no longer thirsty. The sailor started to walk out of the joint, but as I was turning away from the bar to follow him, I impulsively bent down and, for the first time that evening, caught the eye of the little Indian female Buddha who had been sitting between us.

"Ma'am, may I go home with you?"

"Sure," she said, giving me nothing more, not even a twinkle in her eye.

We caught up with the sailor just outside the door, and I handed my car keys to him.

"Why don't you pick me up at that Esso station we drove by on the south side of town, around nine in the morning?"

He seemed a little confused by this sudden development but nodded and walked away.

The lady lived in what looked to be an almost brand-new double-wide trailer. As we pulled into the driveway, another set of headlights pulled up right behind us. I had a bad moment there, wondering just what I'd gotten myself into.

She must have sensed my sudden wariness, reaching up to touch me reassuringly on the forearm. "I hope you don't mind a little company. She's a good friend of mine, and they don't have any other place to go."

I wasn't exactly sure what *that* meant or where this was all headed, but I figured I could always run for it and hoof it back to our cabin if things started getting out of hand. After all, I hadn't signed up to have sex so much as I had signed up to see what would happen.

Everyone got out of their respective cars and introductions were made on the porch beneath a full desert moon by our hostess as she fumbled with her key in the door lock. The lights went on, and the four of us filed into the living room, which was rather sparsely furnished with inexpensive but new-looking furniture. There were a lot of dolls, however: tiny little dolls wearing what looked like handmade costumes—swimsuits, formal dresses, cowgirl outfits, etc.—dolls on shelves, dolls on the television set, dolls on the table, dolls everywhere.

Our hostess brought drinks out from the kitchen—mixed drinks for her and her other friends and a Budweiser for me. She'd been paying more attention than she'd let on. After serving the drinks, she turned on the stereo before coming over to sit on the sofa next to me. She still seemed to be avoiding eye contact with me, but the back of her hand touched mine where it lay on the sofa cushions. The music kicked in, and I recognized the tune that she had been humming in the bar: Don Ho singing "Tiny Bubbles." Uh-oh. The Indian lady and her girlfriend did the talking while the other man and I did most of the drinking, occasionally nodding and smiling across the room at one another in mute commentary on our mutual irrelevance.

By the end of the next two hours, I had become a little desperate, not to mention drunk and exhausted. My hostess apparently had every record that Don Ho had ever recorded and didn't at all mind listening to a lot of them twice. My head kept falling over. It was almost three in the morning when I finally found myself naked under the covers, watching with numb appreciation as the Indian lady undressed. She was cute as a button and I liked her a lot, but it had been a long, long day and I felt just about as lustful as a dead tomcat. She stripped down and walked straight at me. It occurred to me that the lady had said only one short sentence to me throughout the entire evening and was still showing no interest in opening up a dialogue. She flipped the covers back and smiled forgivingly down at my inattentive penis before lying down beside me and immediately falling asleep, snoring like a little rabbit against my shoulder.

When I woke up, the sun was peeping over the windowsill, my companion was still snoring like a little rabbit, and my body seemed to be a lot more interested in her than it had been the evening before. I lay there for a few minutes, my thoughts drifting around the events of the previous evening, the musical legacy of Don Ho, and the attractive and extremely naked Indian lady I was cuddled with. She was really, really sound asleep.

And she was still sleeping when I rolled out of the bedroom window to plant the riding heels of my cowboy boots firmly amongst her freshly blossoming petunias or whatever the hell they were, and the early morning sun was casting long shadows across the empty small-town street. I clomped down the middle of the road towards the Esso station, whistling "Tiny Bubbles" until someone's radio somewhere came on to interrupt my serenade with Johnny Cash. I leaned up against a gas pump, feeling every one of my twenty-three years, lit up a cigarette, and listened to Page, Arizona, resist Sunday morning with competing country and western stations. After a while, I saw a pillar of dust rising from behind a certain blue '64 Chevy coming towards me down the road. The sailor reached over to open the passenger door for me as he pulled up next to me.

"You crazy booger."

*** * ***

A week and a half later, I was standing in my second lieutenant's uniform on the tarmac of a little airport forty miles or so downriver from the home place. I was suntanned, shaggier, and a little thinner than I'd been when I left Washington, DC, thirty-nine days before. The Chevy was parked behind the shop back on the ranch, with an empty silver money-clip in its glove compartment. I had given the keys to Father, telling him to do anything he wanted to with the car, probably scaring the hell out of him. It wasn't that I believed I wasn't going to come back. It was simply that I had been so focused on Vietnam for so long and so intently that life beyond it almost didn't exist for me. The car had become irrelevant.

The weather was hot and dry for the middle of May, and the grass on Sitting Bull's hills looked more like midsummer than mid-spring. My mother was weeping, apparently out of concern for me, and that was a bit outside the realm of my experience. In our stoic Scottish Norwegian little corner of the universe, it was often rather difficult to tell the difference between hostility, indifference, and love. Father was staring off over the river and working his jaw, which was about as emotional as things ever got for him.

I thought about Sitting Bull riding out of those brown hills, coming down from Canada to surrender what was left of his half-starved tribe, his half-starved horses, and the last of his guns and ammo to the Union soldiers at Fort Buford. There had never been enough guns—or Sioux, for that matter—except on the occasion of that heady little encounter with Custer on the Little Big Horn River. Coming down out of the hills to the fort, Sitting Bull had known that it was his last day of freedom, must have known that things were going to keep getting worse. He might have been dreaming his own death song as his pony carried him down from the brown hills into this valley where the fort and the soldiers waited. On the other hand, he might have been just feeling tired. I would come to know that feeling.

# CHAPTER 8

*A BLIND MAN SEES THE ELEPHANT*

I woke to find myself down on my knees, scraping at the concrete floor with my fingernails and the butt of my .45. My brain was rattling against my skull as if someone had just sucker-punched me in the head. There was a metallic clattering and tinkling overhead accompanied by large nearby explosions, incoming rockets impacting around me, shrapnel slicing in through opposite walls of my hooch to collide overhead. Someone was screaming nearby, and I low-crawled over to peep out the door. A soldier I didn't recognize was dancing around in circles, his half-naked body lit by flames from burning hooches, holding what seemed at first to be a bundle of dark-red rags against his stomach. Then I realized that he was holding his intestines in as he danced and screamed "incoming, incoming, incoming." I knelt there with a loaded and cocked .45 clutched uselessly in my hand, watching the wounded soldier's white and red butt bobbing in the firelight, and I laughed.

The next morning, I stood on a side-hill just outside of Long Bien with a pair of binoculars in my hands. I had an excellent view of a mountain that was, at that moment, the center of a great deal of attention by a fair number of America's fighting men. It was really not much of a mountain, just a large, deforested hill with a flattened top that was slightly tipped in my direction so that I had a fairly good view of it. A single observation helicopter was circling high overhead.

Colonel Patton's tanks had surrounded the mountain before advancing to form a line just short of its lower slopes, where they had stopped while continuing to walk their cannon fire ahead of the grunts making their way up the mountain side. The ground pounders were taking their time and not firing their rifles much, leaving most of the gunplay to the tank cannon, which was so intense that the American soldiers appeared to be walking across freshly plowed ground, weary bird hunters picking their way across a field at the end of a long and fruitless day.

However, I was not paying too much attention to the American troops. Instead, I kept the binoculars trained on the thirty or so little men in black pajamas ahead of them who were clambering up the mountain like crazed and exhausted wild horses being hazed by shell fire instead of cowboys. Some of the VC still had their weapons but were mostly using them like walking sticks instead of guns, glancing back now and then with the eyes of children trapped in a house fire. There were a few walking wounded among them, stumbling and being pushed along by their comrades. One of them stopped, shrugged off a restraining hand, and turned to walk back down the mountain into the wall of shell fire.

The survivors spilled up over onto the flat top of the mountain like ants swarming on top of a burning ant hill as artillery and tank rounds began dropping among and around them. Did I see one of the VC shoot a comrade before throwing his weapon down and some of them beginning to tear their clothes off? Did I see another turn to stare calmly down the twin tunnels of my binoculars at me and tear clumps of sweat-slick, raven-black hair out of his head? I cannot help but question some of my memories of Vietnam, like a recovered lunatic might question some of the more bizarre memories of his incarceration.

*** * ***

In Vietnam, it seemed that I was always wet with either sweat, humidity, or rain. The downpour paused as I stepped down out of the open cycle-cab onto a solitary slab of broken pavement, a gleaming, black ice floe floating in a shallow river of mud. The little back street was quietly waiting for the pedestrians to come back out from where they had taken shelter in the open shop fronts. The momentary lull made me touch the .45 on my hip even though this was supposedly a secure area, meaning that no American had been shot at lately.

Coming to keep a promise, I stepped from the street into a tiny courtyard, taking a deep breath when I saw the woman standing with her back to me working over her little charcoal stove. I moved silently up behind her and touched her shoulder. She whirled and began to squeal, laughing and jumping up and down at the sight of me. Covering her tears with both hands, she ran out of the courtyard and down the alley, leaving me standing there with my hands on my hips, smiling at her fleeing back. It had been a while since anyone had seemed particularly glad to see me. She returned in a few minutes with her arms full of beer bottles. The exercise seemed to have settled her down a bit.

When I had last seen her, a few months before, I had told her that I would see her again, and she had reproached me, telling me that it was wrong to make promises like that in a place and time of war. I was young and dumb, and she was right, of course, but her reproach had made me determined to keep the promise that she had refused. And so, I reached out to touch the only Vietnamese face I would ever touch. She stood passively for a moment as I traced with outstretched fingers the marks left by the years, the hard times, and her chronic belly laughs that tolled like raucous church bells. It was like touching the blues. The night slowed while we ate, drank our beer, and babbled like two thieves who had stolen something precious from the devil. Late in the night, we lay down on her sleeping pallet and held one another. There was a moment in the late hours when I, half-asleep, began to stroke her back in a different way, but she stopped me, telling me that her body was unworthy of me. Not knowing exactly what she meant by this and being too young to know how to respond to her closed sadness, I at least knew enough to still myself—and to carry her words with me to my grave.

Later, the woman watched from her pallet as I strapped my gun belt back on. I stepped over to touch her face once more, then walked out to where the downpour had resumed. I would never see her again and would forget her name as I forgot all the names of the few I had allowed myself to care for in that place. But I would remember the face. I remember faces.

# CHAPTER 9

*MY FREEDOM BIRD*

Ninetieth Replacement was where most military personnel were being processed both in and out of the country. We sat on wooden benches beneath an open sky like any commuters waiting for a bus back home, short-timers waiting for transport to the airfield and their freedom birds, and FNGs awaiting transport to their assigned units, The short-timers in faded fatigues looking a little blank and hungover, haunted by their confiscated weapons, the FNGs in brand-new fatigues waiting a little wide-eyed for their first glimpse of the elephant, glancing sideways at us short-timers as though we held secrets to this dangerous new world that we might be willing to share.

I had been finding it increasingly difficult to believe that I was going to get out of Vietnam alive, and being without a weapon made me feel even less optimistic as I sat on a bench with the rest, waiting for the buses and trucks that would take some of us into trouble and some of us out. One very young nurse sitting next to me tried to begin a conversation with me that I resisted at first, as a child might resist being awakened from a deep sleep. However, she was young and pretty, and I found myself, like a damn fool, trying to reassure her that the bad things she anticipated weren't, in fact, going to be all that bad, as though stupid reassurances were going to protect her somehow. I don't know what I was thinking.

That is when the .45 semiautomatic went off about thirty feet away from us and, for a moment, I knew that my bullet had finally caught up with me. When I came back to myself, most of the other short-timers were also stirring themselves, blinking as though someone had just turned the lights on. The young nurse was staring at me, appalled. So much for reassurance. It turned out that some fool had accidentally fired a .45. Somewhere, that bullet wanders the universe looking for me, and it is not my enemy or my friend.

The air terminal the army bus brought us to was essentially a steel umbrella with open sides supported by massive steel beams. We sat in a block of plastic seats reserved for the homeward bound and, right next to it, an empty block of seats reserved for our replacements. We would be leaving on the same freedom bird they had arrived on. As the newcomers filed into their seats, a shout went up from the more sensitive souls among us, "You'll be sorry!" And they would be.

Waiting for takeoff, our cold silver tunnel was very quiet. These same unarmed and mute men now seated in air-conditioned rows being waited on by stewardesses had just finished carrying weapons with dangerous intent for a year, busting up ambushes and bars and burning down some villes, burning shit and diesel fuel, getting in fistfights in beer-soaked red clay, writing home every day, ingesting massive amounts of cheap pure heroin shipped in courtesy of Uncle Sam, driving tanks, manning twin .50s and M-60s, fragging a few clueless and luckless officers, flying helicopters up the moonlit Mekong, pimping whores in Saigon, pounding typewriters down into gray desks, screwing every whore they could scrape up five or fifteen dollars for, cutting off surprisingly delicate ears, writing home every day, crying tears soaked into red clay over the loss of one too many friends, sending marijuana home in the hollow bellies of ceramic elephants, sending home half their pay to Momma or a wife, writing home every day. American soldiers in Vietnam tended to live for their mail, but I had preferred to live as though nothing and nobody existed outside of Vietnam. To this day, I don't like opening mail.

Now I watched these clean and orderly if somewhat weathered and fatigued-looking young gentlemen offering polite thanks as they accepted the frozen towels considerately handed to them by stewardesses wearing their lipstick a little too brightly. I sat in that giant, winged aluminum box and watched from my window seat as they finished loading small wingless aluminum boxes into the cargo hold below. I was tired. Sitting Bull and me.

TWA flight number 406 lifted off like a bat out of hell, burning out its tubes for altitude because Charlie liked to take parting shots when he could, a potshot or two with a mortar or rocket, once a fifty cal., usually just tearing up the tarmac a little, though once they had found a bullet hole in one of those aluminum coffins down below. "No one hurt, though," a stewardess said, then caught herself. "I mean, no one who wasn't already—" She heard herself again and then gave it up, turning red and away from me, trotting down the aisle to comfort someone else. I watched her walk away, thinking that American girls' butts are built different from those of Vietnamese girls.

I sat safely buckled into my seat, Mantovani's "Love Is Blue" flooding into my ears from the headphones as the blue-black jungle disappeared beneath the wing to be immediately replaced by blue sky and blue-green ocean. It was as though I'd been color-blind for a year. This hardened combat veteran sighed as he settled into a lifetime of being the only Mantovani fan in the universe. I felt the sudden urge to take a leak, but there was a long line of similarly motivated troops standing in the aisle, so I drifted off to sleep instead and dreamed of an Italian fountain with a non-peeing cherub as its centerpiece.

I dozed on and off as the plane soared over the Pacific with the sun sliding across its back. We made a two-hour fueling stop in Hawaii, where military police prevented any of us dangerous men from leaving the boarding area and raping and pillaging the tourists. There were, however, a dozen or so young officer's wives selling raffle tickets at a table who were apparently not afraid of being raped and pillaged. Dressed in extremely low-cut dresses, they were charging twenty-five bucks a throw for a shot at a new car and a glance at tender white tit as they leaned obligingly down over the table to take our money and give us our receipts. The plane was delayed for half an hour when one GI turned up missing. The MPs found him unconscious on the floor of an airport men's room with a lump on his head and his billfold missing.

I remained dully wakeful for the remainder of the trip. Eventually, our freedom bird came tearing into San Francisco at low altitude with the setting sun's dying red explosion brushing the tips of the waves beneath us with dancing points of fire, with the filigreed Golden Gate Bridge glowing red before us against a background of low-hanging rain clouds.

We landed in Oakland and were taken across town to Travis Air Force Base for processing in a bus that did not have wire mesh across the windows to keep hand grenades out. I saw a white Cadillac convertible pulling out of a McDonald's parking lot, driven by a blond woman wearing a fur coat that cost more than they paid a grunt for a year of carrying a gun. I saw a gigantic red horse flying over a gas station; I saw longhairs toking up in a park. I saw a lot of people having a lot of fun.

I had somehow expected to see America mourning her dead, tearing her hair out in frustration and grief, slashing at her arm with a knife like an old-time Cheyenne woman who'd lost a loved one in battle. But America was not slashing her arms. America was not mourning anyone. America was not interested.

*** * ***

At Travis Air Force Base, they informed me and the rest of the weary planeload of prodigals that those who were being processed out of the service would have to stay over until the next day, so I dropped off what little I was carrying at my room, took a shower, and headed for the officers' club, where I contemplated with great reverence a frozen stein filled with honest-to-god Heineken beer sitting next to a shot glass of fine bourbon on an honest-to-god hardwood bar.

I had spent two years of my young life preparing to spend a third year in one mess of a war. They'd killed MLK Jr. while I was in Panama attending jungle school. Two weeks later, they put me in charge of a riot control company in Washington, DC, telling me that the Commies were plotting to take over the nation's capital. They'd killed Bobby Kennedy a couple of months later, shortly after my arrival in-country, and then things had gotten a little worse for me and a lot worse for some others. My war had consisted mostly of long boring periods of pushing a desk around, dealing with drunk and/or morally corrupt superior officers, with a few brief intervals of *Lord of the Flies*. I hoped that the devil had reserved a nice little corner in hell where Johnson, McNamara, Nixon, and Kissinger would spend an eternity explaining themselves to the war dead of the ages.

I sat staring over the top of my upscale bourbon and beer into that back bar mirror, contemplating the strong possibility that no matter what else happened to me in this life, I would not die in Vietnam. Then I heard my name spoken quietly by someone standing just behind me. In the mirror, I saw a grinning first lieutenant who had graduated from Fort Benning with me, one of the good ones. In Officer Candidate School, there had been, among the usual mix of the good, the incompetent, and the crazy, a few golden boys. I would always think of these as among the very best men I have ever known. Intelligent, athletic, virtuous, and competent. Star quarterbacks stepping back, hawk-eyeing for a receiver, calmly facing McNamara's meat grinder without the benefit of a cheerleading squad.

Two of these golden-auraed men had been in my training company, and the officer in the mirror was one of them. He and I hadn't been particularly close during our training, having been in different platoons, but it was sweet to see him alive. At first, it was like two college alumni meeting accidentally in an airport lounge and killing a little time and a few too many drinks while waiting for their respective flights. But then we began the inevitable game of recalling classmates from the old OCS company and realizing that a good number of them were dead or seriously messed up only two years after graduation. I don't remember much of the rest of that evening, but what I do remember seemed to have involved broken glass, overturned furniture, some yelling, and even possibly some tears.

The next morning, someone stuck a finger up my ass, someone else gave me $3,500 in back pay, and I caught a flight home to Montana. As I sat in my seat waiting for takeoff, wearing my army uniform for the last time, I wondered if anyone could pay me enough to make me look up hundreds of assholes every day. On the other hand, I guess that they had.

# CHAPTER 10

## *ON THE ROAD*

I woke up slowly in the spare bedroom with the song of a meadowlark outside my window greeting me like an old friend after a long absence. Father was rummaging around in the kitchen, cussing at the cat, turning on the radio for the morning market report. The morning sounds of home.

I had flown into the same little one-horse airport I had flown out of when I left home for Vietnam. My parents weren't expecting me because unexpected delays (some of them permanent) were known to happen, and I didn't want them suffering unnecessary confusion and anxiety. In fact, there *had* been a last-minute problem, and my departure from Vietnam had been delayed two weeks. The plan that I had been carrying around in my head for months was to rent a nice car and surprise them with a grand entrance. The returning war hero. Right.

I had walked up to the Hertz counter dressed in all my returning war hero splendor and told the young woman there that I wanted the fastest car they had. She pleasantly informed me that I was too young to rent a car. I just as pleasantly responded that I wasn't leaving without a car. She looked at me for a moment, then excused herself to retreat behind a closed door to talk to her boss. In a minute or so, the door reopened just enough for me to see a man's eyeball staring out at me, then closed again. The young woman came out to hand me the keys to a huge brand-new 1969 army-green Plymouth, just like the cars they used in Vietnam to cart around senior army officers. Jeez.

However, I figured I might be pushing my luck if I were too particular, so I made my exit with keys in hand. Besides, that ugly Plymouth, whatever its aesthetic shortcomings, did have one huge V-

8 engine in it. The sixty-mile drive home on mostly gravel roads was a little breathtaking at times because of my insistence upon keeping the speedometer needle hovering around ninety a good deal of the way and also because of the fact that I'd done so little driving in Vietnam. Driving that Plymouth was like riding a clumsy, giant tiger.

On the afternoon I arrived back at the ranch in that spring of 1969, my father was out summer fallowing in the south hills, and I was watching out the front window when he came charging down the hill on the big John Deere, looking askance at the huge Plymouth parked in the driveway. His son had finally gotten his own green machine.

Father never asked about Vietnam or made any comments about it. A couple of weeks after my return, he did observe wonderingly, apropos of nothing, that the heart fibrillations he had been experiencing during my absence had ceased upon my return. That was as close as he ever got to telling me that he loved me.

*** * ***

A couple weeks later, I swung out of the bed, got into a pair of clean jeans and a new blue-checkered Western shirt, and moved out of the bedroom to join my father in the kitchen. I'd been home for a month, mostly working with my father during the day and drinking too much and driving too fast at night. I had woken to the sound of rain on the roof during the night, so I knew that there probably would be no work to be done. After breakfast, I backed my resurrected old blue Chevy up to the gravity fuel tank and, leaving the car door open, stood and let the gas run, listening to Ray Price singing "The Night Life" on the radio and looking out over the valley.

I was not the first of my extended family to go off to war. My father's kid brother worked as a company clerk in England for the duration. My mother's two brothers followed General Patton across North Africa and Europe. One brother had come out of his hard war pretty well, but the other had spent most of his war collecting bodies and body parts, and he never recovered.

Post-World War II America had difficulty understanding or respecting psychological war wounds. Men had their dreams interrupted by war, assuming that, if they survived, they could resume their dreams afterward. Instead, many of them came back to find their dreams had become meaningless and replaced by nightmares—and a country that required them to act as though the nightmares had never occurred, as though their hearts had not been wounded.

My uncle was not a good enough actor, so, like a lot of other WWII veterans of that era, he took his wounds on the road. I have often wondered whether that hobo who came off Snowden Bridge that day and inspired me was a war veteran. What role did my own war play in putting me out on the road? I don't know. Probably not much because I had always planned on going out there, but I do know that the war left me feeling distrustful of society. It made it more difficult for me to get *off* the road: off to what?

And so, in the spring of 1969, I finished fueling up my Chevy, drove into town, and walked into the Albert Hotel Bar. Bill Dunn, the owner of the place and a WWII veteran, was sitting at a table having an eye-opener. I didn't know Bill very well, but he always seemed to give me the benefit of the doubt, probably just for being my father's son. Bill was a big, florid man who always wore dark dress slacks and a starched and ironed plain white shirt, and he kept his thick brown hair in a Vaseline-slicked pompadour with white sidewalls and a perfect part on the left. He gestured for me to share his table and bought me my first drink of the day. I'd left home with fifty dollars in my pocket, and I woke up twenty-four hours later in the back seat of my car with the fifty dollars still in my pocket and no memory of anything after that first drink. I sat up into blinding sunshine to find myself parked in a wide spot in the road about halfway home with my watch pointing out that it was almost ten o'clock in the morning. I knew that if there were any justice, I would have been yearning for death's mercy, but I had never felt better in my life. I knew that it was time.

I fired up the blue Chevy and made my run down the remaining ten miles of dusty road to the home place to announce to my folks that I was leaving. In hindsight, dropping this on them was cruel, especially considering my mother's brother's disappearance after WWII. Here I was, apparently following in his footsteps. I wasn't trying to be secretive or cruel. A lot of questions weren't asked in our family, mostly because we were afraid of the answers. We were experts at suffering in silence. Even when I told my parents that I was going to take off hitchhiking in the middle of the night without explanation or destination, there were no questions or concerns expressed. I had no idea how to explain myself and it never occurred to me to try. This would not be the last time my silence would hurt those I loved.

I asked my youngest brother, Steve, to drive me seventy five miles out into the hills later in the evening to a spot that I had in mind for my departure. I was already packed and ready to go. And, once again, I left no instructions as to what I wanted done with the blue Chevy.

I had hitchhiked that five-hundred-mile stretch across North Dakota once or twice a year during my four years of college, and it had been a foretaste of adventure, but now, driving through the night with my brother at the wheel of my old blue Chevy in the spring of 1969, I was getting ready for the real thing, for everything I'd dreamed of since I was a child. There were no houses or yard lights in sight, just a low cloud cover and a brisk, chilly breeze coming in from the west. I got out and stood next to my pack on the shoulder of the road and watched the taillights of the Chevy disappear over the crest of the next hill then reappear as the car climbed up the next higher hill, repeating until they finally disappeared over a distant ridge, leaving me with darkness and the cold wind nudging at my back. I had paid for and I had waited for this moment, but the waiting and the paying made the moment that much sweeter. I slung my pack on my back and started running down the middle of the deserted road away from the vanished car lights, yelling into the darkness and the overcast sky.

# CHAPTER 11

*COLLATERAL DAMAGE*

Over the years of hitching the highways of North America and Europe, I developed a kind of paternal attitude towards the drivers who shared the road with me, whether they picked me up or not. Standing there next to my pack with my thumb out, I felt as though God was watching my reflection in the glinting windshields of passing Chevrolets, Fords, and Kenworths. I stood on a dusty, gusty stage, acting out and dressing for the role of a romantic hero—a fairly reckless and overly proud young man, though I believe that my pride was sometimes all that enabled me to survive. Over the years my traveling clothes evolved into Levi's as clean as I could keep them, an open-necked shirt, a bright-colored neck scarf, a wide-brimmed hat with silver conchos, and a pair of Western-style boots. Once in a while, a member of the audience would give me a ride. In return, I gave them the company of the last free man. Anyway, I thought so.

A week after watching the blue Chevy's taillights disappear, I sat on a plush suede leather couch, feeling out of place after only a year's absence. The last time I had sat there, I'd been a sheepherder's son disguised as a lover and an officer and a gentleman. I was no longer disguised. Dressed in my traveling clothes, I was beginning to look like the pilgrim I really was, a pilgrim who did not belong on that fancy couch anymore. The lady sitting facing me had never disguised herself.

"I'd try to be with other men, then I'd say your name at the wrong moment."

She was twenty years older and the first woman to have opened both her body and heart to me. I knew nothing yet about the stone-grinding world of broken hearts, loneliness, despair, desperation, snot, and tears—the world of being broken. Older and absolutely aware of her vulnerability, with visible fault lines where old fractures had reopened and others opened for the first time, she knew what she had to lose. I did not know that I had anything to lose. She held her hands out to me, and I responded automatically by reaching out to take them, only to have her turn them to reveal the ragged scars on her wrists, wide streaks of mottled and angry red.

My only excuse, really, was that I'd meant no harm. She was my first lover, and I'd been so stunned by her availability to me that I'd just plunged headlong into the experience, loving her but with nothing to offer her. She had written to me a few times while I was in Vietnam, but nothing she had said had even hinted that there was anything wrong. If she had been trying to protect her young lover from her suffering, she had succeeded. Until now, anyway, when the source of her pain had shown up on her doorstep to stare blankly at her scars. I knew that something more was required of me, that she needed something from me, but I couldn't even begin to imagine what it was, and she wasn't about to ask.

*** * ***

I left Washington, DC, just a couple of days later, taking a bus to New York City. The truth was that I was still taking care of unfinished business. Carrying the burden of guilt and inadequacy that the fiasco with my ex-lover in DC had left me with, I went on to New York to say goodbye to my sister Sandra and my brother Terry. I hadn't seen either one of them for several years. Terry had settled in Queens a year or so before, after getting out of the army, and was working at some sort of electronics gig. Sandra was teaching at one of those terrible underfunded ghetto schools. I felt that I should at least touch base with them before stepping off completely into the unknown.

Neither one of them seemed particularly relieved to know that I had survived my little war, although their share of the family stoicism made it hard to tell. God forbid that any of us would acknowledge being glad to see another family member. It was slipping from May into early June by the time I walked up the Manhattan sidewalk towards my sister Sandra's apartment. I'd left my gear in my brother's apartment, so my steps felt light and bouncy walking through spring in Manhattan after spending an hour or two lost on the subway. It was my first experience of New York. It was spring, and the leaves were coming out on the trees just as the spring dresses were coming out on all the beautiful women. New York dressing up for the season.

I pushed the button that buzzed Sandra's apartment, as per her instructions over the phone on the previous evening, and in a few minutes, she came out onto the front steps to greet me. My sister looked as she had always looked, somehow robust and fragile at the same time. Smiling a little too brightly at me as she came out the door, she stood with her arms folded under her breasts and a certain tightness around her eyes. I supposed that it was because we hadn't seen one another in two and a half years. When I reached out to put my arms around her, she took one full step backwards before holding her ground. No hugs today. Or ever, as it turned out.

I spent a week wandering around New York City, sleeping on the sofa in my brother's apartment, watching first-run movies (*McCabe and Mrs. Miller* marked me forever, the bumbling loser winning at last, then dying alone in the snow) in the luxurious theaters which I remember as being sort of clustered around Times Square, and wandering around on the subway system, which fascinated me. I loved riding those sliding steel snakes aimlessly through their labyrinth. Buddha would have loved New York subway trains.

On my last night in town, I took Sandra out to dinner and afterwards we walked together watching the upper towers of the city gleaming in evening light, and by some miracle ended up holding hands for a little while, for the first and last time in our lives. I took from that visit to New York a memory of my sister Sandra trusting me enough to take my hand, just that once. I had seen the first signs of her slide into schizophrenia, but I didn't know it.

My childhood on the ranch and my military experience had taught me the assassin's art of acting without feeling once a course of action was decided upon. I don't believe that there was anything that anyone could have said that could have turned me from my wandering. I could see the suffering: Mother's invalidism, Father's mute pain, Sandra's fragility, and my lover's physical and emotional wounds, but I felt absolutely helpless to do anything about any of it, and I was sick of being a helpless witness to the suffering of others. It hurt me to see it, but they were all on their own. I was standing in the shadow of the girders on the old Snowden Bridge, the rails were vibrating, and I was going to ride.

# CHAPTER 12

---

## *GONE*

I made a run by Greyhound bus up the asphalt trail of Highway 95 to Boston, where I went back to hitchhiking until I ended up out on the fishing islands off Brunswick, Maine. My last ride offered me room and board in return for doing some repair and maintenance work on his house, and I took him up on it. Two days after I moved into a room in his big barn of a house, I went down to the Brunswick employment office where I told the man that I wanted to draw unemployment compensation, but I wasn't interested in a job. The paper-trail-worn bureaucrat raised an eyebrow at me, looked over my discharge papers, signed me up for an electrical engineer position, and promised not to call me in for a job interview.

I bought a fire-orange Honda CB750 motorcycle with just a few miles on it, using up most of what was left of my discharge pay. Every morning, I would rise early, go run a few miles, take a shower, and then ride the bike down to the harbor where there was a small working man's diner out on the dock. I sat there for a couple of hours almost every morning throughout the summer, watching water, fishermen, tourists, and sky, eavesdropping on conversations, smoking cigarettes, drinking coffee, scribbling bad poetry, reading books, and paying attention, watching to see what might happen next. One morning, someone played Johnny Cash's "I Never Picked Cotton" on the jukebox. I knew that I'd picked a little cotton but, by god, sitting in that little diner watching water dance in the sunlight made up for lot of cotton-picking.

I had absolutely no experience with motorcycles, so I had to resort to on-the-job training before beginning my career as a motorcycle outlaw. The bike was hot as a pistol, which made for an interesting learning process. When I rode the motorcycle out of the dealership, I wobbled a little at first, then overdid the acceleration and lifted the front wheel up off the ground. My life experience had not prepared me for this situation. I disappeared over the hill almost prone on the motorcycle with my legs extended back behind me, straddling the rear wheel. Later on, someone told me that the crew at the motorcycle shop thought that I was putting on a show for their benefit. I hope that they were more entertained than I was.

There was a sheltered cove out on the island that the locals used as a public beach, and on one of those first days when I was out riding on my bike, I decided to visit it. Unfortunately, it didn't occur to me that turning off hard pavement onto a soft gravel surface at any kind of speed might have a dramatic negative effect on the Honda's handling characteristics. I skidded in the loose gravel, missed the turn and slammed into a split rail fence, hitting the fence close by a post, so that the rails popped out without breaking, allowing me to plunge through a tall privacy hedge to find a woman sunbathing in the nude directly in my path. I managed to avoid leaving tread marks on her suntanned bottom and chose to flee around the house and out through an open gate, leaving my victim apparently believing that she had just been harassed by a crazed Hell's Angel. The woman's version of events made the rounds and, when combined with a certain motorcycle salesman's description of my dramatic departure from his dealership, started me down the path towards a certain notoriety within the small community. I was becoming Hell on Wheels.

Black granite ridges shielded the little public beach from the wind and the open ocean. When swimming there, I preferred to sunbathe up on the granite shelf rather than down on the beach itself. I liked the almost painful feel of the black sandy stone pressing into the naked flesh of my back and the crusty feel of dried salt. I would lie there and watch the sky and the sea and people on the little beach snuggled deeply into harsh black granite.

One day, three blond women walked down off a little access trail onto the sand, wearing modest swimsuits and carrying beach bags. One of them was strikingly handsome with a little gray in her hair, and the two younger and more slender women were obviously her daughters. They were a fine-looking trio. I found myself focusing on the older of the daughters. Her almost-white hair was very long, while her sister and mother both had shorter, more practical haircuts. All three women spoke with faint European accents.

I was never much good at approaching women I was attracted to. My sexual and social life would always have a strong tendency to rely more on the bad taste, kindness, and courage/recklessness of women than on any social skill of my own. Regardless, two hours later, the oldest daughter, whose name was Frannie, was on the back of my 750, her arms clasped around my waist.

It turned out that the mother was a Dutch woman who had starved through the German occupation of Holland during WWII. She had married the girls' father, a Belgian restaurateur, after the war, divorcing him sometime in the late fifties after having Frannie and her sister. She ended up remarrying a Maine lobsterman, of all things, and Frannie, her sister, and their mother found themselves rather exotic transplants living on an island off the coast of Maine. The two daughters spent many of their summer vacations in southern Belgium with their father.

We spent the summer roaring around southern Maine on my motorcycle, swimming in the inlets and back bays, fishing, going to dances and making love—sort of. Things weren't right for me, and my ignorance and anxiety were not helpful. Fortunately, Frannie's patience and good humor helped prevent my sexual unreliability from overriding my intense and pure enjoyment of my freedom, her company, the fishing islands, the ocean, and the motorcycle. Years later, I would find out that temporary impotence wasn't an uncommon phenomenon amongst returning veterans. It would have been helpful if someone had broken that news to me a little earlier.

*** * ***

There came a day in late August when she and I were on the beach together sunbathing. My eyes were closed but I was awake, listening to the faint sound of Frannie's breathing, a few seagulls, and surf in the distance, feeling chips of ancient granite pressing into my back. My mind was drifting through the past few months of Atlantic tides and late-night motorcycle rides, of standing upright on the foot-pegs screaming into the wind with Frannie kissing my back. Suddenly, I heard her breathing change, and I opened my eyes to see her shoulders shaking. She was struggling to stifle the sounds of her own weeping.

"What's wrong, Frannie?"

"Something happened last night."

She explained that shortly before we met, she had broken up with a local boat captain's son whom she'd dated through the last year and a half of high school. The boy had apparently been a pretty sensitive soul who hadn't fit in very well with the local high school's fisherman/jock culture. The father was determined to make a "man" out of him, and the ongoing and rather one-sided battle of the wills between the boy and his father apparently had had a serious effect on the boy's mental health and his relationship with Frannie. He became emotionally dependent on her to the point of obsession, and there had been a few episodes of sexual violence. She had ended the relationship in early summer. The boy's father had succeeded in bullying him into enrolling in Annapolis Naval Academy, where he had lasted two weeks before running away and returning home to the island on the previous night to beg her to run off with him. She had refused, and they had found him dead just that morning, lying in the surf next to his father's recently discharged hunting rifle.

I lay there in the sun for a few moments without commenting.

"Why didn't you tell me about any of this before?"

"I didn't want to spoil this. I didn't want it to have anything to do with us."

Suddenly, the sun's warmth on my body and the sharp blue of the ocean seemed like cheap thrills. I reached out and placed my hand on her forearm. I thought about a nineteen-year-old young woman who had played and laughed all summer, carrying those secret shadows without faltering.

Inevitably, September rolled around, the leaves began to change, and Frannie and I talked things through. We both understood and accepted that she needed to go off on her own to begin her college experience, and that I needed to be alone on the road. Our parting was a gentle one of acceptance and understanding. I wanted her to have her freedom, and she wanted me to have mine. We should have left it at that.

# CHAPTER 13

*A WALK IN THE PARK*

Somewhere in eastern Pennsylvania late at night, it had been raining for the past hour, and I'd had about enough of the motorcycle for the day. Four hundred miles or so since morning on two wheels didn't require much rain to turn a night ride on an unfamiliar two-lane road into a fairly edgy proposition. It was with a profound sense of having found refuge that I pulled into an island of neon and wet gleaming chrome, an art déco diner sitting out in the middle of nowhere with at least a dozen cars clustered around it, one of them a reincarnated 1959 DeSoto with swept-back, pointed fins, vivid salmon and white marbled by the neon light. I peeled my legs off the bike and the silver helmet off my head, lit up a cigarette, and shuffled around the bike for a few moments, working the shakiness out of my legs as I peered up through a crack in the rain-laden cloud cover at the stars beyond.

Inside the crowded diner was a Saturday night, die-hard, after-hours crowd eating their bacon and eggs and drinking coffee. They were all a little stoned, convivial, warm and dry. I was not. I took my BLT and coffee at the counter and sat for a while with my back to the crowd, watching the mirrors and soaking up the warmth of the place. I was never all that comfortable around people who were drunker than I was, but these people seemed to be more genuinely cheerful than they were drunk.

I had a second cup of coffee as an excuse to be warm and dry a while longer, and one happy lady decided that I was Michael Landon traveling incognito. I could understand her confusion. Landon was short, dark, and handsome, and I was not. She spent quite some time gently trying to convince me of my celebrity status, refusing to believe that I was about as close to being a nobody as anyone she was ever going to meet.

It was getting on to two in the morning when I finally left the diner, and the rain had almost stopped, just an occasional drop rippling the gleaming, rough, wet mirror of the parking lot as I made my way across it to my machine. I idled the bike down the highway for a few miles, looking for a place to camp for the night. I was very tired, and I wanted off the wet night road. I spotted an approach leading down into what looked like an overgrown pasture and decided that this was probably as good as it was going to get. I parked behind a little copse of trees where the motorcycle couldn't be seen from the road, spread out my bedroll under a sheltering tree, and sat for a while smoking and listening to the rain dripping from the leaves and making little popping noises on my tarp. The highway quieted for the night, and, putting out my cigarette in the wet grass beside me, I covered my head with canvas and followed suit.

Around ten the next morning, I cruised through the town of Gettysburg. I had been driving beneath gray skies through occasional misty rain for three hours or so, and it showed no sign of breaking up. Not wet enough to turn motorcycling into a hardship, but wet enough to take most of the fun out of it. I was a little wet and chilled and a lot hungry, but mild discomfort and harshness seemed appropriate conditions for visiting the scene of Bobby Lee's bloody folly.

The fall leaves were holding on well despite the rain, still as spectacularly beautiful as they'd been all the way down from Maine, but the tourist season was over, and it was the middle of the week, so the battlefield park was almost completely deserted. The wet weather probably didn't encourage the tourist traffic much, either. I was relieved to have my solitude in this place. I wasn't in much of a mood to share the old battlefield with crowds of people in Bermuda shorts and carrying cameras.

I putted the bike slowly along the Confederate lines on Seminary Ridge, stopping now and then to walk around and read the various signs and monuments, but thinking specifically of Pickett's charge and Lee's apology to the survivors of the battle. I'd always been a little impatient with the idea of glorifying a man who committed treason and insisted on romanticizing and fighting for a cause that defended slavery, but at the same time I couldn't be too hard on a general who had enough heart in him to apologize to his men after a battle. We could have used some apologies in Vietnam. When I thought of Lee in those moments, I thought of him as weeping, his tears losing themselves in the raindrops sliding down his face as he wept in front of his men for his own foolishness, for those who lay bleeding out in the rain.

I stood near where Pickett was supposed to have addressed his men prior to launching their suicidal stroll across the broad rising meadow that must have seemed endless—and was endless for many of them. The light rain continued to fall as I stood looking out over the killing ground surrounded by deep wet fall fires and mist, the gleaming candy-orange and chrome motorcycle waiting patiently behind me.

Suddenly a voice rang out over the meadow, the trumpet-like tones of an officer addressing a military formation on a parade ground. I looked over to my right beyond a little point of broken reeds that extended out into the battlefield and saw a small group of men dressed in gray officers' uniforms standing in formation, all facing over towards my right and beyond the outcropping of reeds. The mist and the distance made it a little difficult to pick out the details, but a man who seemed to be a high-ranking officer stood with his back to the other officers, speaking in stentorian tones as though he were addressing a hidden military audience off to my right.

I realized that I was watching a reenactment, possibly of Pickett's pre-battle speech to his troops. I moved down the path to my right, leaving my motorcycle behind, thinking that moving to the other side of the reeds would give me a better view of the proceedings, but when I got there and looked out to where the reenactors had stood, there was nothing to block my view of the rain-darkened reds and oranges on the far side of the meadow, nothing to break the silence except the drip of rain.

I stood there for a while before turning away to return to my motorcycle. I kicked it into life, its muffled pounding spreading out in flat concentric circles beneath the weight of the misting rain. Here and there along the ridge were paved footpaths that branched off from the main road that usually ran through areas where some specific army unit, Confederate or Union, had fought or had formed up before joining the fight, and were lined with monuments and plaques to the units, their men, and their leaders. There were little signs at the beginning of each path indicating its destination. Most of them seemed to dead-end, requiring the tourists to turn around eventually and return the same way they had come.

I stopped at the beginning of one of these paths. Craving silence and wanting to walk off the strange, disconnected mood I found myself in, I turned off the motorcycle and struck out along the path, glancing perfunctorily at the monuments and plaques along the way, feeling a little disoriented and weightless, as though I might float away. As I walked, there were fewer and fewer monuments, and the pavement gradually deteriorated into a dirt trail before disappearing altogether. When I turned around to retrace my footsteps, there was no path to retrace and there were no monuments. When I bushwhacked my way back to the little parking lot, my motorcycle was still there, but there was no sign or path in sight.

At the far end of the battlefield, the Confederate and Union lines draw gradually almost together, the terrain growing higher and rougher until it forms a hollow that had come to be called the Devil's Cauldron. There was a visitor center nearby with a large parking lot. A big tour bus was sitting in it when I pulled in, and on the far side of the bus a tour guide was lecturing a group of tourists. A man who was obviously the driver was leaning against the other side of the bus, smoking a cigarette and paying no attention to a lecture he had probably heard a thousand times. I shut the bike down and moseyed over to say hello.

"Uh, are they having any reenactments today?"

"Nope, they're done for the season."

"Do they ever have a reenactment of Pickett's talk to his troops before they began their charge?"

"Nope, nothing like that. Why?"

I told the man what I'd seen earlier. The bus driver smiled a wisp of an ironic smile at me.

"Congratulations. Every once in a while, someone sees something."

# CHAPTER 14

## *SOUTHERN HOSPITALITY*

The last time I cruised into Fort Meade, Maryland, I was stationed there and driving the blue Chevy with an officer's decal on the bumper that had warranted a salute as I drove through the gate. This time, I was a shaggy gypsy on a hot-rod motorcycle taking a little detour down memory lane, and I was not saluted.

Doing my best to prepare myself for shipping out for Vietnam, I'd attended Jungle Survival School in late March and early April of 1968. We'd been out in the Panamanian jungle for days with little green fanged snakes jumping out of trees at us, sleeping where we fell on the jungle floor, so exhausted we didn't care if something did want to chew on us, and moving a lot at night under triple-canopied jungle so thick that at times I forgot that there was a sky, until one night I came out from profound darkness onto a high ridge to be stunned by a full moon. I enjoyed every minute of it. I mean, no one was shooting at us. It was like an extremely intense and strenuous Boy Scout camping trip.

My team successfully completed the course and crowded into the arms room to turn in our weapons. The shock of our combined stench in that confined space made me realize just how filthy we all were. I retreated to my barracks, hacked the legs off a pair of jungle-ruined fatigues with my knife, put them on and walked out of the barracks door to dive into the ocean that was just a few yards away. It felt unspeakably good, and I plunged around in the shallows like a mortally wounded seal for twenty minutes or so until I saw three familiar-looking figures dressed in officer's summer khakis coming down the walk from the direction of the barracks.

Recognizing the three men as former OCS classmates, I waded out of the surf, all skinny, sunburned, and ragged, to greet them.

"Hey, it's me, Burgess!"

The three of them stopped in their tracks, their mouths hanging open. I swear to god, one of them turned white.

"We'd heard that you were dead!"

Somehow, word had gone out on the Fort Benning Officer School for Boys alumni gossip network that I had gone to Vietnam and been killed. I wonder how many of my old classmates went to the Wall in Washington, DC, expecting to find my name. I'm not sure just how that makes me feel.

*** * ***

After finishing the survival course, we were bused into Cólon for the evening, where we were warned to watch our backs and to go about our sin business in pairs. The next day, our jungle- and hangover-worn crew was flown into Charleston, South Carolina, on a military flight, arriving under a pinkish-red evening sky that seeped into the ocean like watery blood. I grabbed a taxi at the airport and found a motel room downtown. It was Friday night, but the place seemed strangely subdued, almost physically flattened beneath the weight of the pale pink twilight. I asked the cab driver, who was black, about it, and the man stalled a bit before telling me that they'd just gotten the word that MLK Jr. had been killed. I told the cab driver that I was sorry, but he didn't have much to say to a white man wearing an army officer's uniform on April 5, 1968.

After cleaning up and putting on a fresh uniform, I stepped across the street to a bar-restaurant for a drink and a meal. It was fairly crowded with a bunch of scared white people who immediately started buying me drinks, apparently seeing me as the war hero come to save them from the hordes of vengeful blacks. I took the coward's way out and drank their money up for a while. Luckily, there were no riots in the streets of Charleston for me to put down that night—just one somewhat jungle-beaten and inebriated twenty-three-year-old army officer stumbling across a late-night avenue on his way to a bed.

The next morning, the Charleston air terminal was overrun by frustrated and edgy white-bread humanity fleeing the upcoming slave insurrection, and I knew that I was going to be a long time catching a standby flight. However, I also knew that Southerners tended to believe that army officers were, in fact, gentlemen, so I walked over to hang out near the long ticket lines and look for likely prospects. I spotted a distinguished middle-aged couple accompanying another army lieutenant away from the ticket area. I used my spiffy little gold bars to insinuate myself into their company. It turned out that they lived a little north of Charleston, and, having given up on the flying situation, were going to drive their son to Washington, DC, instead. When I mentioned offhandedly that I was trying to get there too, they responded with typical Southern generosity and invited me to come along. When you're hot, you're hot.

My hosts fit my eastern Montana ranch kid fantasy of old-money Southern gentry: soft-spoken, handsome, cultured, with instinctive good manners. We cruised sedately out of Charleston in an immaculate old Mercedes sedan with the son at the wheel, the mother riding shotgun, and the father sitting across from me in the back seat. The father was dressed in almost shabby tweeds, and back home in Montana, the mother would have been dressed appropriately for Easter Sunday church. The smell of old leather, a faint aroma of pipe smoke, a whiff of perfume. I was extremely impressed.

We drove through a spring-greening, Southern countryside for a half hour or so before stopping for a late lunch at their home, which was comfortably spacious with an air of slightly worn elegance. The three of them were consistently loving and gentle with one another and seemed to include me effortlessly in their little circle of warmth, even taking me into the kitchen to introduce me to their black cook, who had perfect roast beef sandwiches, potato salad, and lemonade waiting for us, all obviously prepared from scratch. I was in high cotton.

After lunch we resumed our journey north, another four hundred miles or so to Washington, DC. An hour and a half from our destination as the light began to fade, the son turned on the radio with some comment about wanting to hear the news. It hadn't occurred to me until that moment that the four of us had gotten through almost the entire journey without anyone mentioning King's assassination or anything else to do with the ongoing racial unrest. The news commentator was discussing the garbagemen's strike in Memphis when the son interrupted in his gentle, cultured Southern drawl, "If I were driving one of those garbage trucks, and some of those n-------s lay down in front of me, I would simply drive over them."

I glanced over at the young officer's mother for her reaction, and she was nodding, looking at her son with eyes shining with approval and maternal pride. She had been sitting with her arm extended along the back of the front seat, so that she didn't have to move her hand very much to pat him gently on the shoulder. That's my boy.

Later, the four of us stood behind her son's red Ford Thunderbird where it was parked in the shadows of the late evening airport parking lot. It was time for a parting of the ways, and the mother graciously extended her hand to me, almost as though she were expecting me to kiss it. Unable to touch her and unable to explain myself, I turned away to walk towards the terminal. I'd carry the image of that suspended right hand with me for fifty years and counting.

*** * ***

As I finished my little patrol down memory lane at Fort Meade, I passed by a meadow, or a drill field, that I remembered very well from a time when it had had a bunch of deuce-and-a-halves filled with kids armed with M-16 rifles and wearing gas masks, and me standing by my jeep's radio waiting for the word to go into Washington, DC, to keep the Commies from taking over the city—at least, that's what the FBI had told us. My men and I were to ride shotgun on the fire trucks when they went out on calls during the riots. However, we would have live ammunition "only if and when President Nixon declared a national emergency." After that briefing, my first sergeant wondered aloud just when an attempt by Communist hordes to take over the nation's capital became a national emergency.

# CHAPTER 15

---

## *BIKER HEAVEN*

The Blue Ridge Parkway runs south for 469 miles from Washington, DC, mostly through national parks, down into North Carolina, almost into Georgia. I and my candy-orange bike caught it in the fall of 1969, running down miles and miles of near-empty curving road along mountain ridges covered with turning leaves, low-hanging clouds of fire guiding us most of the way down the coast.

On the first afternoon out of DC, I pulled into a turnout that looked out over the Shenandoah Valley. I killed the bike and leaned back on the sleeping roll I kept strapped to the bike's sissy bar, lit up a cigarette, and basked in sunlight that tasted of a coming winter but that was still warm enough to touch my flesh with the sweetness of a tentative kiss.

In a little while, two cars, a Volvo and an old Porsche, pulled off the highway to join me for the view. Two elderly couples got out and eventually strolled over to introduce themselves, one of the men with a couple of exotic, short-haired hunting dogs on leash. I gave them enough to take the edge off their curiosity before they meandered away. The old man with the dogs hung back for a moment, took another long look at me and the bike, then said quietly, "Don't let anything stop you," and walked off to rejoin his friends.

That night, I pulled into a campground with just enough daylight left in which to scratch up wood for a few hours of fire. There was a free-standing water spigot nearby, and I had the place to myself, so after I got the fire going, I stripped and stood naked beneath the fall-fired trees, scrubbing down goose-bumped flesh in the fading gold and red light. I'd forgotten to pick up any groceries, so I just lay down on my open bedroll to watch the fire and daydream for a while, smoking a few cigarettes for nourishment.

I stubbed out my last cigarette for the evening, grinning at the protests of my empty stomach as I watched the fire fading into glowing coals and thinking about maybe getting out my harmonica when two cars pulled in, making their way through the campground to take the camping spot next to mine. The nearest vehicle was an old Volkswagen van. I experienced a twinge of resentment at the unnecessary invasion of my privacy before I realized that my motorcycle and I were almost invisible in what little light was provided by the dying embers of the fire.

There were two young couples, and they immediately fanned out to stumble around among the trees looking for firewood in the inadequate light of their high beams. It was way late to be setting up camp and they were acting a bit like tired and grumpy children trying their best not to be tired and grumpy, so I called over and offered them the use of my still-smoldering fire and remaining wood. I ended up getting a big baked potato lathered with butter and a piece of home-made pie out of the deal. After the meal, we all sat easy and comfortable around the fire for a while, passing a joint and a few words around, but it was late and everybody was tired and the four visitors soon faded back towards their cars to get some sleep.

Drugs, rock and roll, and easy sex were part of the sixties and seventies landscape, especially on the road. To a lesser degree, that landscape was a milder version of the moral landscape that I had traversed in Vietnam. Of course, now I wasn't carrying a gun, and I usually didn't have much money, but as a gypsy I was freer than most to do damage and walk away without facing consequences.

I had picked up four commandments growing up and in Vietnam that stood me in good stead on the road: (1) Be wary of drugs and alcohol, (2) Be wary of bad company, (3) Be wary of accepting too much hospitality, and (4) Do no harm. Of course, I broke all these rules at one time or another, but just trying to observe them helped keep me alive and/or out of jail. The most difficult rule to keep was the fourth one: Do no harm.

I lay on my bedroll for a while, blowing quietly on my harmonica and watching the light from the dying fire play on my motorcycle's candy-orange flanks. Spotting a shadow moving towards me from the direction of the cars, I stopped playing, but the shadow asked me to keep playing. So I did, eventually forgetting about the shadow in the tree line. When I finally put the harp up, the shadow was no longer there. I played a fairly rough harmonica, but a quiet night by a campfire on the side of a mountain can make almost anything sound good, I guess.

*** * ***

Dropping down out from the Great Smoky Mountains into Georgia, as I brought the bike out of a deep, fast curve into a straightaway, I saw a crew of men, mostly black, working along the highway, watched over by uniformed white men on horseback with lever-action rifles aimed in the general direction of their charges. I came out of a long run in mountain shadows into the glare of an afternoon sun that lit up the clearing and the men in it like a giant flashbulb going off. The Honda hit seventy mph before diving back into shadow, leaving the tableau burned into my mind like the negative of a photograph. The convicts and the guards must have seen something like an orange and chrome comet streaking by with a silver-helmeted longhair aboard flashing a peace sign at them. It was the best that I could come up with, given the short notice.

The next afternoon, I parked the bike in front of a cafe in Waycross, Georgia. The place was busy, and I drank my coffee at the counter, hitched around on my stool so that I could keep an eye on my bike through the large plate-glass windows. I didn't have much, but what I had was on those two wheels. A boy, maybe fifteen or sixteen years old, pulled his 350 Honda motorcycle in next to mine and sat on it for a moment, eyeballing the 750 before coming into the restaurant. He looked the crowd over for a moment, spotted me as the most likely-looking motorcycle outlaw in the joint, and came over, grinning a little self-consciously, knowing that I had caught him ogling my motorcycle.

"Sir, is that your bike with the Montana plates?"

"Yup."

The boy's name was Sam, and he turned out to be quite a motorcycle enthusiast and a romantic. In 1969, there weren't many people traveling on motorcycles, and the few that were out there tended to travel in packs. A lone biker traveling with out-of-state plates was a rare sight. This was before television and movies began to romanticize the loner-on-a-motorcycle bit. During that entire trip down the Eastern seaboard, I never saw another person traveling alone on a motorcycle, which was just fine with me. So, with my longish blond hair blowing around a silver helmet, my suede leather jacket, and the candy-orange Honda, I was a bit of an exotic. It was a small miracle that someone didn't take their twelve-gauge out and blow me off that bike, just to have a trophy to take home to their momma.

Sam and I talked for quite a while, until I mentioned that I needed to start looking for a place to camp for the night. The boy's response was to suggest that I go home with him. When I suggested in turn that the boy's parents might have a problem with a strange barbarian showing up at the gate with their favorite son, Sam assured me that his parents were the most hospitable people in the county. I wasn't sure whether Sam was kidding himself or what about his parents' generosity, but I decided to take a chance on it. I could always run for my life. I guess that I had the image in my head of a little trailer-house stuck out in the piney woods somewhere.

Sam's family, as it turned out, did not live in a trailer-house. I followed my new young friend into a large oval turnaround at the top end of which was a large brick home, almost a mansion, with a lot of white rail fence around a huge yard. As far as I could tell, neither of the boy's parents skipped a beat upon seeing what the cat had dragged home. We all ended up drinking iced lemonade out on the patio. They like their lemonade in the South.

I was invited to stash my gear in the guest room. The father said that he and his wife were a little embarrassed about not being able to offer me a home-cooked dinner. "We've been invited out to eat at the home of some friends, so why don't the two of you just go into town and have something to eat—our treat."

There was an unfamiliar soft Southern night sky above us with a clean quarter moon. We ran side by side, taking our time, our bikes dancing effortlessly through the meticulously banked two-lane country curves. Sam had a particular drive-in in mind where, it turned out, he knew most of the customers and all the teenaged carhops. He obviously felt cocky showing his captive motorcycle gypsy off to his friends and acquaintances while the two of us leaned against our machines and ate our burgers and fries. I found myself enjoying a little hero worship.

Young Sam was feeling talkative when we got back to the house, and I ended up on the carpet next to the boy's bed using one of his pillows and listening to Sam's tender night noises for a while before drifting off. The next day we went into town together after eating breakfast with the parents. The last time I saw my young Waycross friend, Sam was sitting on his motorcycle in the high school parking lot, watching me fire up the 750 and roar out onto the highway, headed south. I know why I remember him. I wonder what he remembers of me. I wonder what his parents saw in me that made them trust me with something precious.

# CHAPTER 16

---

## *GONE TO BE A SAILOR*

When I got into Orlando, I called up two friends from college days, a married couple, and they seemed delighted to see me, inviting me to stay with them and their two little kids for a while. However, it was as though the comfort in that house had a kind of kryptonite effect on me, draining my energy and confidence, and making me reluctant to go back out and face some of the harsher aspects of my gypsy world. Lapsing into a sort of lethargy, I ended up hanging around their house for a week or so until Jake, the husband, gutted up and gently let me know that things were getting a trifle crowded. I was terribly embarrassed, knowing that it had hurt both Jack and Jake to ask me to leave (Rule No. 3!). This gypsy business was turning out to be more complicated than I had thought. I had expected being on the road would lead to situations where I would have to protect myself from predators. Instead, more often than not, I had to protect other people from their own generous impulses and from my own moments of weakness and neediness. Again, Rule No. 3. It wouldn't be the last time I violated it.

I wheeled out to Tarpon Springs on the Gulf Coast. I had never had much to do with the sea, and the only fishing I had ever done was ice fishing on the Missouri River. I had a feeling they didn't do much of that kind of fishing out of Tarpon Springs.

I made camp on a sandspit on the southern edge of town and spent a couple of days hanging out in the bars and restaurants around the docks, asking questions about fishing boats and fishing captains. I drove the bike too fast along the beaches, watched sunsets, and fed the sand fleas at night. My sleeping bag was far too warm for the weather, but if I lay on top of it, the sand fleas would have at me. So, I spent my nights crawling in and out of my sleeping bag, alternating between sweating and being chewed on.

On the third morning, I walked out onto one of the main docks looking for a boat called the Sidewinder, a name whose significance would become clear to me later on. I'd been told that its captain, Jerry Spaulding, was one of the very best commercial fishing captains around—and an honest one. These fishing crews were all paid on shares by the owners, depending entirely on the size of the catch for their pay—and on the individual captain's honest accounting of the catch size and the profits.

The man who turned out to be Jerry Spaulding was sitting on the dock by his boat in the early morning sunshine, working on some kind of netting. *The Old Man and the Sea*. As I walked towards him, I wondered if that's what they caught fish with. I had no idea. Nets? Hooks? Their hands? Worms? Jerry looked to be in his late sixties, sitting there peering over the top of his reading glasses at me as though I were some fish to either be kept or thrown back in the water. I introduced myself and said that I'd heard he was hiring a fishing crew.

"Yep. Going out tomorrow morning with a short crew. Mostly to break in a new captain. You fished for grouper before?"

"No. But I don't mind learning."

I liked the way Jerry Spaulding was checking me out. The wise old man of the sea was polite enough about it and didn't ask a lot of questions, but he was finding out what he needed to know even as his eyes continued to twinkle at me over those half-glasses. At least, he thought that he was learning what he needed to know about me.

"Well, son, why don't you be down here at the boat at six tomorrow morning? We'll stock up on provisions, eat breakfast, and get out of here."

I was greatly relieved. I was running seriously low on funds and also getting really sick of sand fleas. I discovered that Florida wasn't a great place to be poor. I spent one more night with the sand fleas and was down at the dock at six in the morning, my motorcycle stashed safely behind a nearby cafe, with the owner's permission. My new boss told me that he usually went out with a six-man crew.

"I'm getting ready to retire, so it's going to be just me and you and the new captain. He and I are kind of checking one another out, and he's familiarizing himself with the boat before he has to deal with a full crew."

The three of us jumped in Jerry's pickup and went to get groceries. I was impressed. There were a lot of steaks, bacon, eggs, and beer. We were going to be eating like kings—well, two of us were, anyway, as it turned out. After we'd stowed the groceries and other supplies on board the Sidewinder, I'd figured we'd be going out to sea but, instead, our captain took us to a restaurant and treated us to a tremendous breakfast and started buying us drinks. I was game. A couple of boilermakers had me just about convinced that I was a real sailor.

We didn't cast off until one in the afternoon. I was still feeling a little stoned, but there was nothing for me to do but go along for the ride. The two captains were focusing on one another and the boat, so I crawled up into the crow's nest and watched the harbor and then the shore slip away. The weather was calm and clear, and I stood for hours watching from my perch as the sun dropped through the darkening steely sky down towards the ocean ahead until a perfect moment when the sky and the sea became the same soft lavender, just as the colors of the evening winter sky would sometimes meld into the color of the snow-covered high plains of my childhood. The Montana sheepherder goes to sea.

I slept without dreams that night until two in the morning when Jerry woke me to take the morning watch. The Sidewinder was on automatic pilot heading out into the Gulf of Mexico, and it was my job to watch for hazards in the water, such as a log or another ship or a sudden change in the weather. Jerry seemed to assume that I knew what I was doing. The weather was still clear, with a half-moon out, and the sea was as calm as winter ice. There was nothing between the ship and the horizon but sea and stars. The diesel engine throbbed like an immense heart, seducing my pulse into synchronicity.

I woke the next morning with no memory of being relieved from my watch or of climbing into my bunk. I did awake, however, with extreme nausea and an appreciation for the appropriateness of the name Sidewinder. I also noticed a newfound sensitivity on my part to the odors of diesel fuel and fish that permeated my cabin. I forced myself out of my bunk, staggered to the ladder and somehow got up and out onto the deck and fresh air, only to end up draped over the railing, purging the toxins from my soul into an unsympathetic sea.

Which pretty much established the pattern for the next five mornings, except for the second morning when I found myself unable to walk to the railing and was forced to maneuver on all fours. These expeditions were intended more as a penance and a demonstration to Jerry of my good intentions than out of any real belief that I might be able stay on deck and do any fishing. My suffering lasted for six days and nights and was intensified by the knowledge that each one of those six days was taking me farther away from blessed solid land.

The odors in my cabin told me more than I wanted to know about the activities of the other two men on board. Towards the end of the first full day at sea, the fish smell became stronger and fresher and, later in the evening, was joined by the smell of broiling steaks. None of these developments brought any relief to my condition.

On the seventh morning, however, I woke with a sense of perfect well-being and lightness due, in part, to the fact that I hadn't eaten for almost six days. I was so hungry that I could have almost eaten fish for breakfast. Steak and eggs were fine. There were only two days of fishing left, and I threw myself into it even though I knew that it was too late for me to earn a share of the profits. My presence on that boat was costing Jerry, and it was money that I couldn't possibly make up in the two days remaining. All I could do about it was work hard and enjoy myself for the remainder of the trip. Which I set out to do.

The weather remained calm, and the fishing went well. The Sidewinder was a 55-foot-long steel boat with eight fishing poles in permanent slots around the outside of the deck. The fishing poles were more flexible versions of the steel leaves that make up the springs of an older car or truck. The fishing lines were of lightweight steel cable with electric winches that raised and lowered the weighted hooks with their bait. There was a radar screen in the wheelhouse that located and identified the fish hanging out below the boat.

We kept our hands on the fishing lines and could tell (at least, Jerry and his new captain could tell) by the vibration and movement of the line when a fish was hooked. When that happened, a button was pushed, and the line was automatically reeled in. Knowing how to read that vibration was the key to being a good fisherman. Otherwise, five minutes might be wasted pulling a fishless hook up, or a hook might be left hanging down there with a fish on it, a hook that could have been pulled up, defished, rebaited, and sent down to go back to work.

Just about when I started getting the hang of fishing for grouper, it was time to head back into Tarpon Springs. I climbed up in the crow's nest again when we got in sight of the shoreline and stayed up there as the boat came into harbor, a lean, suntanned, shaggy blond fisherman being photographed by tourists standing on the dock as we pulled in. A lean and tanned motorcycle bum who had just spent a week out at sea throwing up and wishing that he were dead. I imagined photo albums on coffee tables across the land with pictures in them labeled "Tarpon Springs Fisherman Coming into Harbor." It was all right by me.

There was some hard work left to do unloading the fish and cleaning the boat up from one end to the other, but finally, the three of us were standing in the wheelhouse together. Jerry was having a hard time making eye contact with me, and I had a pretty good idea why but decided to let him suffer with it for a while. Finally, he cleared his throat and said, "Philip, you understand you didn't earn any wages on this trip. The fact is, having you along cost me money."

"Jerry, I didn't figure on getting paid. I'm just sorry I was such deadweight most of the time. I feel like I got a helluva free boat ride out of the deal."

"You're the sorriest fisherman I've ever had out on a boat with me, but you're also the gutsiest. If you're ever in back in Tarpon, give me a call and we'll try her again."

"What?! I wouldn't hire me!"

He handed me a check for twenty-five dollars and twinkled at me over the top of those damn reading glasses.

"Nobody who gets as sick as you got ever gets seasick again."

Maybe so, but it would be a while before I'd be ready to test that theory voluntarily. I walked off the dock, wheeled the 750 out from behind the little cafe, and got back on the road, feeling pretty good about things until I noticed that the motorcycle couldn't make up its mind which side of the road to stay on.

I finally realized that I'd developed sea legs. I managed to get to the edge of town before I had to give up and sleep it off in a motel room—that cost me twenty-five dollars.

# CHAPTER 17

*SWAMP RAT*

I rolled into Orlando, Florida, in the fall of 1969, just a few days after Jack Kerouac had died puking blood and booze in nearby St. Petersburg, unbeknownst to me. I had managed to get through the sixties without even hearing of the man. The construction of Disney World was just getting under way, and Disney's people had put the word out that they were hiring all crafts. Of course, they weren't, so Orlando was overflowing with cheap labor, mostly construction workers fleeing a recession, some of whom had traveled hundreds of miles to get on Mickey Mouse's payroll only to find out that they had been conned. Consequently, aging carpenters and chubby plumbers were being forced to take work as laborers. Hundreds of working men looking for work needing a cheap place to stay, needing refuge.

As flophouses go, The Devil's Inn was a bit of a gem. In fact, it was more of a residential hotel, and someone obviously took a lot of pride in the place. Three floors, with a lobby downstairs, a small cafe up front, and a bar in back. Everything painted either off-white or hospital green and kept clean. One large bathroom, including two shower stalls, on every floor. Rent was paid by the week, in advance. I got a room on the second floor at the head of the stairway. My only complaint was that I felt a little uncomfortable using the common bathroom late at night, though you might think that army life would have inured me to a lack of privacy.

I never saw any women in the place except for employees, even in the bar. Some of the residents at the hotel were long-term—mostly tired or retired older working guys, some with disabilities, trying to live off their Social Security, watching soap operas and game shows on the black-and-white television in the lobby, taking their walks, nursing their one beer a night in the bar, smoking their cigarette ration, and wryly observing the mostly younger newcomers, short on cash but long on hope, still very much on the move and in the game. The younger men tended to treat the longtime residents like elder statesmen, buying them an occasional drink or offering a cigarette, courteously hearing out their stories and advice. In its own way, The Devil's Inn was very cool, including its name.

I had discovered a place somewhere between hunger and starvation that was actually rather pleasant, a little like being stoned. In this semi-hallucinatory state, colors were more vivid, shapes more defined, and I felt very much alive. I was running low on money and having an address and being able to stay clean were essential to finding a job, more important than keeping my belly full. Every morning I'd buy a cup of coffee at the hotel's cafe, and stir it thick with cream, sugar, and catsup. The waitress was nice enough to pretend that she didn't notice, keeping me in free refills, even slipping me some crackers now and then. I kept a case of beans under my bed and, lacking a stove, ate them cold for my evening meal with some of the crackers saved from the cafe. Lunch was a luxury I couldn't afford. I found that keeping on the move helped me ignore the hunger pangs, and so I did a lot of walking. Of course, a lot of walking increased the hunger pangs.

The hotel stood near the not so invisible line that separated white Orlando from black Orlando, and I often found myself wandering around the black part of town. Little Stevie Wonder was coming to town, and it was as though every black man's little brother had gone out into the world and was coming home in triumph to sing his miraculously retained innocence. I made my undernourished and somewhat lightheaded way along ghetto sidewalks, floating in a blind black child's music that seemed to pour from every open window and door. However, I knew that I was walking on thinner and thinner ice, so when someone gave me the name and telephone number of an outfit that was supposedly doing some hiring out on the Disney World site, I figured that it was a long shot, but what the hell. I called and, blow me down, got an appointment to see a man about a job late Monday morning.

\*\*\* \* \*\*\*

The road into the construction site wound through tracts of scrub brush and sand dotted with the occasional isolated cottage of some retired couple who'd come to Florida with dreams of palm trees and green ocean and found themselves living as economic exiles in shabby little houses miles from the nearest beach. Suddenly, a dump truck came booming at me from around a curve, well over into my lane. I reflexively swerved the 750 off the pavement into the ditch where it partially buried its front wheel in the soft sand, throwing me forward in a somersault which might have turned out to be somewhat graceful if it hadn't been interrupted by a face plant in the side of the ditch.

I was quiet for a moment or two, lying there with the dust settling around me. The truck hadn't stopped. I eventually got up and pulled the bike out of the hole it had dug for itself, manhandling it up from the ditch back onto the road. It was drivable, but there was enough damage to the front end to rule out any long trips for a while. I stood astride the battered bike for a few moments, trying to get my brains unscrambled, before dazedly noticing that there were some fresh blood splatters on the gas tank and that there was no one standing around bleeding but me. I looked in a rearview mirror and saw that a fair amount of hide had been scraped off my nose, left cheekbone, and forehead, leaving a gritty mixture of sand and blood in its stead.

I was dazed and shook up, but I knew I wasn't seriously hurt, so I wheeled the bike back down the road to the last house I had passed on my way in. An elderly couple answered my knock, initially amazed to have visitors, but quick to respond to my situation. I ended up sitting on a toilet stool, with the old man picking sand out of my face with tweezers and the old lady behind us giving instructions. I was looking good for a job interview, all right. Not even my shirt had been spared.

It's a wonder the sight of me on their doorstep hadn't caused the sweet old couple to have simultaneous heart attacks. They wanted me to stay and rest a bit, but I was obsessed about finding work, so off I went on the motorcycle. The bent front fork made my bike run a little sideways, like a hound dog running down the road with his back end trying to pass his front end.

I got the job all right, much to my surprise, although it might have had something to do with a couple of photographs on the wall of the contractor on a full-dress Harley-Davidson. It didn't occur to me until later that the dump truck that had left me eating sand in the ditch probably belonged to the contractor, and that I might have asked for some compensation for the damage to my motorcycle. The contractor told me to report for work the following Monday, which was a full week away and said that I'd get my first paycheck two weeks later. Again, it didn't occur to me to ask for an advance that might have saved me from another three weeks of semistarvation.

That evening back in Orlando, sitting on a picnic bench behind the hotel, contemplating the damage to my bike and feeling the aches in my battered body, it seemed to me that the day had been pretty much of a wash. On the upside, I had a job, I was still alive, and the motorcycle was still drivable. On the downside, my face was looking pretty ugly, the motorcycle repairs were going to cost me money that I didn't have, I might starve to death before I got my first paycheck, and I had ruined my only good shirt. I was sitting there smoking a cigarette and thinking that I was glad I had a sense of humor when a Triumph motorcycle pulled into the parking lot and stopped alongside. He pulled off his helmet and nodded at the 750.

"Nice-looking machine—your bike?"

We started talking about motorcycles, and I offered a cigarette to the newcomer. Ken had just pulled into town from someplace in northwestern Georgia and was looking for work and a place to stay. I excused myself to step into the hotel bar, returning with a couple of beers, and we sat there talking and watching it grow dark for a couple of hours. We ended up hustling the hotel clerk into stretching the rules a little bit, and, in return for a few extra dollars increase in the weekly rate, Ken ended up rolling out his sleeping bag on the floor of my room.

He was about the same age as I was and was also an army veteran, although he had never got to Vietnam. He was on the run from a marital train wreck back in Georgia and, like his new roommate, didn't have too much of a plan. A couple of days after Ken arrived, the two of us managed to bluff our way into evening jobs working in the kitchen of a big local seafood restaurant. Again, it would be a while before we saw our first paycheck. However, the free evening meal they gave us at the restaurant would go a long way towards helping me survive until the money began to come in. Ken immediately began to address his marital issues by setting out to screw his way through the entire waitressing staff.

*** * ***

It was a half-hour run on backwoods roads to the Disney World worksite, and work began at eight, so I'd get up at six, dress, and have my morning mixture of coffee, catsup, sugar, and cream at the hotel cafe before taking off. It was winter and there was often a lot of rain and the fog had a propensity for ambushing me. I'd come cruising over the top of a hill and drop abruptly into a wall of billowing moisture which would immediately fog up my face shield, leaving me wobbling blindly down the road for a few moments until the fog cleared.

Most of the work consisted of digging deep trenches in the sandy soil and building oddly shaped concrete forms in them. The pay was low because Disney had the unions in hand. In addition to this, we got rained out a lot. Eventually, I started getting some paychecks and eating better, even getting the cash together to patch up the 750.

I continued to work nights at the restaurant with Ken, but even working at two jobs, I was finding it difficult to get a traveling stake together and was feeling a little more beat up every day. I was on my feet so much that I had to slash my fancy boots with a knife to get them on my swollen feet in the morning. This turned out to serve a double purpose because we were working in damp soil and mud a lot, and the slashes served to drain the water and give my feet a chance to dry out a little during the day. Jungle rot in Disney World.

During my first days on the job, I would drift away from the rest of the crew at lunchtime, usually out to the parking lot to sit on my bike and quell the hunger pangs with a cigarette. At the end of the first week, the foreman, a middle-aged, sun-dried redneck, came up to me where I was helping set up for a concrete pour just before noon and took me aside to ask me where the hell I've been going during my lunch breaks.

"I just like eating alone, Charlie."

Avoiding eye contact, he handed me a folded-up five-dollar bill.

"Get your ass down to the corner store and get yourself something to eat."

He turned on his heel and walked away. I did as I was told. From that day on until my first payday, someone on the crew always had an extra sandwich or something for me.

The Disney World project was situated on gently rolling terrain with a lot of scrub brush and small trees that were being systemically torn out by Caterpillar tractors pulling huge, studded rollers behind them that pulverized everything in their path, reminiscent of similar machines used in Vietnam to create clearings in the jungle for American base camps and landing strips.

One Monday, when our crew showed up to begin the work week, a fifty-foot hill had appeared, overlooking our worksite. During the week, a helicopter landing pad was built on top of the hill, and a huge Mickey Mouse balloon floated high above the hill and the platform. Over the next weekend, the pile of dirt and the platform disappeared, leaving the giant Mickey Mouse balloon in place to stand vigil over Uncle Walt's wet dream. Someone told us later that the hill and platform had been built for an hour-long visit by Walt Disney's widow. General Westmoreland would have loved it.

*** * ***

I was beginning to wonder why anyone would want to winter in Florida. Most days were clear, once the sun burned the fog off. But sometimes that took until noon, and it tended to rain a lot at night, flooding the concrete forms that were being built in the deep ditches. The sandy soil would drain the water off quickly, but it always left deposits of sand in the forms that would have to be removed before concrete could be poured. That meant we had to get in there with little scrapers and brushes and clean the sand out from around the elaborate rebar constructions that the steelworkers had bent and wired into place.

I was getting skinnier, and my feet hurt all the time. However, I was getting along pretty well with my roommate, in spite of the fact that Ken seemed to be enjoying himself more than I was. One night, he took a little time off from his Lobster Palace harem and invited me to join him for a couple of beers in the hotel bar after work. The place was busy, but most days it was that way any time after noon. Worn-out old men and restless young. It was like being in the middle of a small-time gold rush.

We bought our beers and found a corner table and somewhere in there, Ken began to tell me his story. He had been an Army Ranger assigned as an instructor in a survival course in the Everglades of southern Florida. One day as he was working as an aggressor in an exercise, he'd captured one of the student-soldiers going through the course. I'd been through some of that stuff, and I knew how intense and realistic some of those courses could get. People got hurt and sometimes got killed. It was easy to forget sometimes that it was just an exercise. That's apparently what had happened to Ken's "captive." He'd gone after Ken, his "captor," with a bayonet.

As an instructor, Ken had been carrying a .45 pistol loaded with live ammo in the event one of the larger predators that inhabited that swamp got feisty. No one had mentioned to Ken the possibility that the "larger predator" might turn out to be a fellow soldier. When the "captive" took a second swipe at his "captor" with his bayonet, Ken lost faith in his powers of verbal persuasion and managed to center-punch his assailant with a .45 round.

"I was watching his eyes the whole time," he said. "They were crazy afraid and angry before I shot him, then they turned sad and confused, as though he were moving from one bad dream to another."

Ken had been in the pipeline for Vietnam, but war games and war kind of lost their charm for him after the shooting incident.

"I was in the chute for Vietnam. Nobody ever talked to me about it, but I was a mess, and there's no doubt in my military mind that someone decided that I was in no shape to do a combat tour. I had sense enough by that time to be sort of glad that I didn't have to go, but the idea that killing a confused kid would save me from combat? I didn't know how to feel good about it. I still don't."

He had gotten out of the army two years before our encounter, returning home to Georgia with his honorable discharge to marry his fiancée and settle down to a job selling farm equipment. However, the wife and the farm equipment didn't stop the nightmares and the night sweats. He'd started drinking too much, and found himself fighting a lot with his wife, even came close once to hurting her—which is why he'd finally left. It had been somehow easier to leave her than to tell her what was going on with him. Which was how he ended up in Orlando screwing women in uniform.

The next afternoon, when I came in from mucking around in the swamps, Ken wasn't around, but I didn't think too much about it. We weren't exactly tied to one another's apron strings. However, I never saw him again.

\*\*\* \* \*\*\*

Florida had turned out to be a little too much for me. I knew that I really should just tough it out there until spring and get a decent traveling stake together, but I was beginning to feel as though every dollar I saved was being taken out of my hide. I was tired of having sore feet, tired of wading around in Disney's mud, and tired of being tired. So I decided to leave.

There weren't too many good omens for a road trip. A longhaired member of my Disney World work crew was heading for Dallas also, and in a moment of weakness I let myself be talked into lending him forty dollars with the promise that the guy's sister in Dallas would repay me when I got into town. Then the motorcycle mechanic who had done the work on my bike refused to repay the fifty dollars left over from an advance I had given him for motorcycle parts. No receipt, of course. Consequently, I was a long, long way from having a decent traveling stake. Besides that, it was still winter, and it was still cold and wet.

In that time and place, fifty dollars was big money for me. Twenty dollars' worth of gasoline had taken me from Maine to Florida. I had counted on that fifty to buy a heavy leather jacket and gloves, which I would need for a winter trip along the Gulf Coast. Now I was going to be making that thousand-mile winter trip wearing canvas work gloves and a rain jacket over my light leather coat. I was going to be a pretty chilly motorcycle outlaw by the time I got to Texas, and I was going to be depending a lot on a stranger to pay me the forty dollars that I was owed. I should have known better. But I was worn out and burned out on Florida and feeling terribly restless.

On my last day working under the giant Mickey Mouse balloon, it was raining again, although not quite enough to shut us down. My guardian angel foreman, Charlie, took me aside again and stood next to me with his arms folded across his chest, still avoiding eye contact.

"Burgess, how long has it been since you talked to your daddy?"

"It's been a while, Charlie."

"Don't let it go too long, son. You never know what might happen."

And with that he turned and walked out of my life. I drove away from beneath the eye of that giant Mickey Mouse balloon on my candy-orange motorcycle, singing the Mickey Mouse theme song to myself. In Vietnam, the senior officers and NCOs hated it when their men sang that song. So, of course, they sang it a lot.

# CHAPTER 18

---

## *GONE TO TEXAS*

Coming north through Inverness, Florida, on Highway 41, the 750 died. I shut it down at a gas station and it refused to start up again. I am one of those people who tends to rely on the kindness and skill of strangers when it comes to mechanical things, but being a man and being almost broke besides, I had to at least put on a show of tinkering with it, trying to convince myself that there was some simple and inexpensive solution. Which is what I was doing when a big swarthy, unshaven man in his early forties wearing motorcycle leathers came out of the gas station to watch. I didn't like people watching me when I didn't know what I was doing, so I stopped doing it and wheeled the bike a safe distance away from the gas pumps before lighting up a cigarette. The big guy walked over, eying the Honda's Montana license plate.

"You're a long way from home, bub."

"That's just how I feel."

Deadpan, the biker walked over and nudged the back tire with the toe of his boot. It didn't seem to help much. We talked a bit and came up with a tentative diagnosis of electrical system problems, though the stranger, Dwayne, admitted to not being much of a mechanic, either. He offered to give me a ride over to a nearby Harley-Davidson dealership whose mechanics would work on anything with two wheels and an engine.

"They'll come and pick your bike up and take it into their shop and work on it, but they probably won't get it done today. You can bunk out at my place tonight, if you need to."

Dwayne was one of those big, ugly, gruff guys to whom dogs and children instinctively gravitate, and it never occurred to me to distrust his intentions. He had a big Harley-Davidson Electra Glide, and sitting up on that thing behind Dwayne made me feel like someone's kid brother. I couldn't even see over the guy's shoulder. It was the first time I'd ever ridden up behind someone on a motorcycle, and I couldn't imagine why anyone would want to do it unless they were in love with the driver—which I wasn't.

It turned out to be a terminally dead battery on the Honda. The bike shop was in the process of closing up for the night when we got there, but Dwayne was an old customer of theirs and they stayed open long enough to retrieve my bike from the gas station, promising to get a new battery in it first thing in the morning. I wasn't particularly happy at the prospect of the unexpected expense, but I knew that it could have been worse.

Dwayne hadn't smiled yet that I had noticed, but I was beginning to realize that he just wasn't much for smiling. I found myself sitting up again behind the big man, cruising along Florida back roads on one big hunk of thundering chrome and steel, peering out from around Dwayne's shoulder at a countryside ragged with Spanish moss.

Dwayne lived alone in a small house on a secluded ten-acre farmstead. He bustled around the kitchen fixing dinner while Hank Snow played on the stereo and the two of us worked on a couple of beers. For a muscle-bound biker with a few days' accumulation of whiskers on his face, Dwayne seemed to have a bit of a maternal streak in him. He still hadn't smiled or shown much interest in conversation, but I didn't mind. Being my father's son had trained me to be comfortable in the company of silent men.

After dinner, Dwayne took me for a short walking tour of his little place, picking up pieces of moss that had fallen from the trees as we went. He had a dozen or so milking goats in a pasture and a small hayfield, but that seemed to be the extent of his farming activities. Next to the barn, there was an early 1950s International semitruck tractor rusting into the weeds. After a while, we went back into the house and opened a couple more beers. Dwayne got a beat-up old guitar out, put one ponderous engineer-booted foot up on a chair and began to strum and sing little segments of country songs. I got the impression that the man wasn't doing this for my entertainment, but rather that it was a regular evening ritual for him, a daily practice session or something. Dwayne wasn't much of a musician, but he was obviously dead serious about the enterprise, and I wasn't about to raise any objections.

While Dwayne was working on his guitar licks, I snooped around the kitchen and the living room area, looking at books, magazines, and photographs. I found a whole shelf of pictures of Dwayne and what looked to be a son at various stages of growing up, including two of the boy in an army uniform but with no mother in sight. A few did show the adult son with a young Asian woman, possibly a girlfriend or wife.

When Dwayne seemed to have worked the guitar playing out of his system for a while, I asked him about the photographs and the young man. He turned away from me to go into the kitchen, returning with a couple of fresh beers and handing one to me.

"That's my son and his wife."

Dwayne put his beer down in a handy spot and got himself back into playing position with the guitar, as though he was going to start singing again. Instead, he just strummed little random chords and talked, like maybe he needed accompaniment. Talking blues. Dwayne had been born and raised in a small town in western Pennsylvania. The Korean War began shortly after he got out of high school, and he almost immediately received his draft notice. His first response was to propose to his girlfriend, who already had a baby born out of wedlock to another man.

"Well, you know, you're young, scared, and horny, and at the same time it's a little like you're starring in a movie. Getting married made it perfect. Besides, she needed a father for her kid."

So, Dwayne spent two years trying to think of things to say to his wife in letters while he learned to drive trucks with bullet holes in them. There were a few occasions when he got caught in the wrong place at the wrong time and he had to get down in the mud with the rest of them and fight for his life.

"I spent most of my time driving like hell, terrified, and trying my best to stay alive and unfrozen"—and sending letters home to his wife full of reassuring jokes and lies.

After his discharge, he came home to his wife and a three-year-old stepson and started long-haul truck-driving, making a good down payment on a secondhand International semitruck (the one sitting out in the yard) with his discharge pay. They did all right. Dwayne made good money, they were able to have a nice home and car, and the wife was free to stay at home and be a good momma. For a while.

"It was too easy, really. It was too easy for me to spend more and more time away from home. That truck cab became my real home. I could have my bad dreams in it without anyone asking questions or being afraid of me—hell, I was afraid of me sometimes. I guess that I thought I was protecting them—and I was making good money—so I had all kinds of excuses. We were both too young and I was too crazy."

For two years, Dwayne pushed that red International up and down the Eastern Seaboard, listening to country music on his radio, smoking too many cigarettes, catching the occasional glimpse of winged red horses against the skyline, flirting with waitresses who called him honey, and getting drunk now and then when the nightmares got too bad, though he wasn't very much for the bottle. When he was at home, he spent a lot of time playing with his stepson, going fishing with friends he didn't know very well anymore or sitting in the living room, staring at the wall—and not talking to his wife.

"I can't blame her for what happened, though I did blame her at the time. She was twenty-two years old, for god's sake, and already living as though her life was over. Except for the kid, she was alone when I was gone, and alone when I was home. Neither of us being able to even say that something was wrong. How many times did she see me crawl up into that truck cab, knowing that I was relieved to get away from her, and not knowing why. I mean, I wasn't really glad to get away from her, I just wanted to get away from whatever the hell it was that we couldn't say."

In the spring of 1954, Dwayne made a run down to Winston-Salem that went better than he expected. The turnaround went so well, in fact, that he pulled into his home yard a day early. The car was in the driveway, but his wife was gone, and the boy was locked in his room. Dwayne went into their bedroom and read the signs that told him if he waited around for her to return there might be a homicide. He took the car to a dealer and sold it at a loss, then cleaned out their bank account, figuring she could have the house. He loaded every bit of kid food and kid clothes he could find, along with the kid, into the sleeper of his International truck-cab and pulled out of the driveway, headed south. That was it for her. He never saw her or talked to her again. They never did get a divorce.

Dwayne ran that International tractor-trailer rig easy and empty a thousand miles south along the Eastern Seaboard through Pennsylvania, Virginia, and the Carolinas, all places he'd seen many times before but all somehow looking fresh and different now. The boy seemed to take to long-haul trucking just fine, sleeping a lot, eating everything put in front of him, and doing pretty well at holding his water between rest stops.

They wound up in Inverness, Florida, for no reason in particular.

"I got into this place pretty reasonable. Real estate was pretty cheap around here then. The kid and I did a lot of long hauling, along the Gulf mostly, back and forth as far west as Houston, Texas, for a year or so. I put off putting him in school as long as I could. Taught him myself to play the guitar and read. I parked the International out by the barn the day he entered school and haven't moved it since. I'd pretty much drove the wheels off it by then, anyway. It had earned a rest. I started driving for local outfits while he was going to school, mostly nine-to-five. Even drove a Pepsi truck for a while."

His son quit high school in his senior year to enlist and ended up in Vietnam. It was a bad spell for Dwayne, calling up some of his old nightmares, but they both got through it alive. The boy ended up spending a couple of months recuperating from wounds in a hospital in Japan and came home with a Japanese wife and a plan for a career in the army.

"All that kind of blindsided me, but I was sure glad to see him in one piece, and the two of them seem to be doing all right. We had a good time together while they were home, even taped some songs together."

He went over and punched a button on his big tape deck, and I heard Dwayne's cracked baritone doing rough harmony with a younger tenor, and a childlike woman's voice lisping in on the chorus: "Pwaise the lord, I sawr the wight."

\*\*\* \* \*\*\*

I had known my share of fifty-below weather up in Montana, but I'd never been so cold in my life as I was herding that motorcycle through Mississippi and Louisiana in February of 1970, underdressed and underfed. Because of the cold and my cash shortage, I decided to just gut up and get through it, swinging north from Mobile up through

Jackson and Vicksburg instead of stopping over in New Orleans for the Mardi Gras. I was in no mood for Mardi Gras, and I doubted that New Orleans was in any mood for a broke biker with Montana plates.

*** * ***

So late one cold, foggy, rain-threatening evening, I turned the 750 into the entrance to the Vicksburg National Military Park and found myself in the middle of rows of tombstones and monuments, broken ranks of stone soldiers gazing out west across the Mississippi River. I had the place to myself, so I parked the bike and wandered around on foot for a while, shivering and tired, yet somehow reluctant to leave. I finally compromised by laying myself down by one of the headstones and falling asleep with bits of icy mist beading on my clothes and my face. That night, I dreamed of winter camp with Little Wolf and the Northern Cheyenne in the Sandhills of Nebraska, with Yankee and Reb soldiers standing watch over tired Indians and me.

I have no idea how long I slept, but it was still dark when I woke up, and I was even colder and wetter than I'd been when I first lay down. I ran in place for a few minutes to get my blood going again, wondering whether I was desecrating the place with my antics. However, I reckoned that most of them probably knew a little about trying to stay warm on cold, wet nights.

Coming off the west end of the steel bridge across the Mississippi River, just across from Vicksburg, I ran a gauntlet of unpainted shacks lining both sides of the road, with a few black kids playing in the yards despite the weather. It occurred to me that the dead soldiers looking down on this from the cemetery probably still didn't know which side had won their war.

*** * ***

The hippie kid who'd borrowed the forty from me had told me to collect it from his sister when I got into Dallas. Predictably enough, when I presented myself on her doorstep, she had no idea who I was, much less anything about money owed. Well, I had enough money to pay rent for a few weeks before I had to have a paycheck. Looked like coffee and catsup might be on my menu again for a while, though.

# CHAPTER 19

## *THE EYES OF TEXAS ARE UPON YOU*

I lay in my bed listening through the wall to the shuffling noises of Mrs. Willet making her nightly rounds. Shuffle—bump, shuffle—bump. I had found a cheap and comfortable place to stay through the hippie network, a room in a little brick private home in a slightly rundown neighborhood, and my guess was that it was a converted master bedroom. My landlady, Mrs. Willet, was a widow lady in her fifties who had had polio when she was younger and needed a walker to get around. She seemed to be a bit of restless soul, and, though I never saw her outside, she remained active, pushing her walker from room to room throughout her house for what seemed to be twenty-four hours a day, shuffle—bump, shuffle—bump. The house was built solidly enough, so that I generally heard her only when she came near the wall by my bed at night.

But I was just glad to have a safe, clean, and warm place to stay, and this sure beat the flophouse in Orlando. I even had a black-and-white television to myself. I didn't really mind being awakened occasionally by her shuffling noises, and she seemed to be a pretty sweet old lady.

On my first Dallas Sunday afternoon, I cruised over to Robert E. Lee Park and found hundreds of mostly young people swarming around Lee's statue playing Frisbee, flirting, playing music, drinking wine, and eating (and smoking a lot of dope). There were tables where donated food was available for anyone to eat who wanted it. Homemade cake and pie, fried chicken, bread and rolls, etc. There was a stage set up where some sort of open-ended rock-and-roll jam session seemed to be going on, and there was a suspicious-smelling blue haze hanging over everything, roiling in and out of the tree leaves.

I wondered what General Lee was making of all this. It was only seven years since John F. Kennedy had been assassinated on a Dallas street, and it seemed to have left Dallas frightened of her own young, these longhaired dope-smokers who talked wildly about revolution and free sex, danced barefooted in the streets, drove Volkswagens with peace signs stamped on their bumpers, and demonstrated against the war in a city that had never seen a war it didn't like.

I realized that I had graduated from being a baby-killer to being an enemy of the republic one Sunday afternoon when two motorcycle cops pulled me over, ordered me off my bike, and told me to stand with my hands on top of my head while one jittery cop body-searched me and another jittery cop stood there with his hand on the butt of his pistol. The two cops finally left without comment or explanation, and I realized that searching without cause might be routine procedure for them. They had been polite enough about violating my civil rights.

Growing up on an isolated, rural ranch without telephones or running water and attending a little two-room country school until I began high school, I had grown up with a strong sense of myself as an outsider, and even though I enlisted in the US Army, I had gone in with a fairly healthy outsider's wariness of both my government and that government's little "hearts and minds" project in Vietnam, even while holding onto at least remnants of a belief in the basic fairness of the system. My military experience taught me that when the crunch comes, we are quite willing and able to sacrifice our young, and that, consequently, the young are quite justified in keeping a wary eye on their elders.

So, although the methods and style of the antiwar counterculture movement seemed strange, undisciplined, and rather obnoxious to me, I had been very glad that at least someone was objecting to the slaughter. And now, even though I still felt very much an outsider there, I found the generosity, acceptance, and playfulness of Sundays at Robert E. Lee Park to be comforting, and I returned there to bask in it almost every weekend while I was in Dallas. At least the hippies weren't body-searching me, and no one objected to my appearance or my motorcycle. In Robert E. Lee Park in Dallas, Texas, in 1970, with my long hair and motorcycle, I could make like Mao and swim with the fishes.

I sat with my bare back pressed against a tree trunk, thinking that I was probably experiencing a contact high. A beautiful young woman with a butterfly tattooed just below the cheek of her beshorted ass sprinted in pursuit of a Frisbee. A blood-red horse flew through a cloudless sky. A column of grim-faced motorcycle cops cruised around the park looking like old newsreel footage of MPs escorting General Patton and his armored units on parade. A young mother held her baby to a naked breast while singing along with a woman who was playing a guitar. Two crew-cut undercover cops, wearing carefully creased Levi's, penny loafers, and shoulder holsters under Hawaiian shirts, stood eyeing the crowd and eating chocolate cake from one of the free-food tables, the frosting of which I happened to know was laced with LSD.

*** * ***

Two weeks after I hit Dallas, I got a job through the laborers union hall only a few days after I had resumed my coffee and catsup breakfast regimen. I celebrated by gorging on bacon and eggs and hash browns on the morning of my first day's work—and four cups of coffee with no catsup. The jobsite had a brand-new small factory and showroom going up on it, along with a fair-sized warehouse. The superintendent who was in charge of building the entire complex was my boss, a man I remember only as Jackman. The project was almost completed when he hired me to clean up and help put some finishing touches to the place, such as putting up guardrails all around the large parking lot.

Jackman was a small, trim, balding guy who always seemed to be suntanned despite his mostly indoor job, and who dressed redneck dapper—late-model work boots and chinos, and Pendleton shirts. He worked as a kind of hotshot troubleshooter for a large regional construction firm with its headquarters in Houston. Apparently, they had run into some difficulties in completing this project and had sent Jackman in to put the wheels back on the wagon. He kept a fancy red Ford pickup on the worksite but commuted to work in a brand-new Lincoln Continental.

Jackman apparently hadn't absorbed too much of the typical Texas fear/anger/hate attitude towards longhairs because he and I got along just fine. Part of this was because I was a bit of a working fool and had learned that most working-class bias against longhairs could be overcome simply by demonstrating a capacity for responsibility and hard work, given the opportunity.

*** * ***

On a Sunday afternoon in May, on or about the first anniversary of my return from Vietnam, I was on my motorcycle headed for Denton, Texas, which was about an hour's run north of Dallas. I was wearing a brand-new, heavy leather jacket, I had $200 stashed in my room, the 750 was running fine, it was spring, and I was getting ready to leave for California at the end of the month. I'd found out through his sister that the kid I'd loaned money to in Orlando was living in Denton, and I was going there in the faint hope that I might collect the forty dollars. What the hell, it was a great day for a motorcycle ride.

Springs in Texas were early and sweet, compared to Montana, where the season can be wonderful but has a nasty habit of not arriving until June, and no one I knew was getting killed. I was cruising along up the interstate like Sunday going to meeting, heading a convoy of four or five cars up the slow lane across the steel bridge that spans Lake Dallas. Doing the speed limit and getting ready to pass a semi-rig, I flipped on my turn signal and paused for a second or so, keeping one eye on my mirror even as I made my move. Driving a motorcycle a lot has a tendency to either turn you into a very conservative driver or get you killed—or both. I had learned that paranoid bikers tend to live longer.

I seemed to be asleep and fading in and out of a dream that involved a series of truck axles flickering by overhead, the sound of a motorcycle engine revving up, then choking into silence in mid-scream. At some level, I recognized the sound as signifying the death throes of the 750, and even in my dream I grieved. I woke with my head hanging over the edge of the bridge, looking down into the waters of Lake Dallas.

I went away again and woke to face a ring of eyes staring down at me with a mixture of compassion, fascination, and distaste. I went back to sleep.

Later the Texas Highway Patrol told me that a carload of drunks doing ninety mph had hit me from behind, and the impact had thrown me forward and up under the tractor of the semi I was passing. I slid for 350 feet on the corrugated surface of the bridge, finally coming to rest on its outside edge.

I don't know if I was in shock, but I was in an extremely numb and passive state, in part a result of the painkillers in my system, I suppose, although I wasn't seriously hurt. Even though the back of my helmet was crushed and there was a lot of blood and shredded leather, and I was indeed a mess, it was a mostly cosmetic mess.

I remember staring at the roof of the ambulance, drifting in and out of a bad dream. I was beginning to realize that what I had experienced as a dream was, in fact, reality, and that my candy-orange bike was dead. Almost a half-century down the road, and I still remember with great clarity the dying scream of the 750, even as I slid down that bridge back into the dark.

The announcement in the hospital by this shaggy motorcycle outlaw of his humble financial situation and lack of insurance seemed to cast a certain pall over the proceedings. They cut away what was left of my clothing, and a doctor looked me over before having an x-ray taken of my left leg and pronouncing it broken. A sizeable chunk of flesh had been torn out of my butt.

The next thing I knew, I was dressed in a pair of hospital jammies and flip-flops and standing on the steps in front of the hospital with a patched-up behind, a pair of antique wooden crutches, and nary a clue as to how I was going to travel the fifty miles back to Dallas and my rented room. They had taken my last dollar to pay for the ambulance. A combination of painkillers and/or shock kept me from caring too much. It was still a beautiful day. I vaguely assumed that something was probably going to have to happen next, but I had no idea what that something might be.

A young male attendant who had been a witness to some of the proceedings came out and sat down on the steps next to where I was leaning on my crutches. I gratefully accepted his offer of a cigarette, and the two of us smoked for a while in companionable silence. Eventually, the attendant asked me if I was waiting for a ride home. I told him rather dreamily that I had no idea how I was going to get home, which seemed to upset the guy. I hoped that I hadn't said anything wrong.

"They can't get away with this. Wait right here."

I wasn't experiencing the slightest inclination to go anywhere. The sunlit steps seemed just hunky-dory to me. I couldn't sit down because of the condition of my butt, but I felt fine standing there, leaning on my crutches. It was rather on the warm side, but there was a breeze stirring just enough to keep it comfortable.

In about ten minutes, the attendant returned with two young nurses in tow who had got off duty and were headed home to Dallas. He slipped me a sample bottle of painkillers, and I found myself reclining carefully on my side in the seriously duct-taped back seat of a rusted-out, hot-rod, '59 Chevy headed south on its enormous battered wings like some faltering old goose bound not to perish in frostbitten climes.

The two nurses were kind to me, even helping me make my way into my room and knocking on my landlady's front door to tell her what had happened to me. After they left, I immediately called Jackman at his home to tell him that I wouldn't be coming in to work the next day.

"Why not?"

"I got in an accident on the road to Denton and broke my leg."

"How is your motorcycle?"

"Pretty bad."

"*Where* is it?"

"I don't know. I was kind of confused. Still am, I guess. The highway patrol probably knows."

"I'll skip work tomorrow and we'll take the truck to Denton and get it. They'll have it in storage somewhere."

I still wasn't tracking too well, but later on when my head cleared, my memory of this conversation would endear Jackman to me forever. After we got through talking, I looked at the bottle of painkillers they'd given me and went to sleep instead. I would weaken later in the night.

The next morning, bright and early, Jackman came by in his fancy red Ford truck and took me out to breakfast before heading for Denton, which was fine with me because I'd begun to come out of my post-accident daze and was realizing that my situation not too promising. I had no idea how long it would be before I could work or travel again, and the $200 I had in the kitty wouldn't last that long living in Dallas. Not to mention what it might take to fix up the motorcycle.

"They didn't put a cast on the leg?"

"No, I didn't have enough cash on me to pay for it."

"You should call your union. Their insurance should cover you. You got anything put aside?"

"I'm okay for a while." I had forgotten that as a union member I automatically had medical insurance.

When the two of us walked into the Texas Highway Patrol headquarters outside of Denton, we must have been quite a sight for redneck eyes. Dapper Jackman with crew-cut hair segueing neatly into his bald spot, freshly ironed shirt, chinos, and polished boots walking next to a long-haired me looking a little worse for wear, on crutches with a purple foot sticking out of a pants leg split halfway up to the knee. Jackman peeled off to take a seat in the waiting room and look at old magazines while I pursued a quest for knowledge and understanding with the receptionist, who told me that the 750 had been hauled to a junkyard. She gave me a receipt with which to reclaim it, then waved me over to the desk of a highway patrol captain.

The captain was polite enough and confirmed the story that I had been told in the ambulance, telling me that the car that hit me was doing twenty-five miles per hour over the speed limit, and that the driver, who was black, had been drunk and driving without a license. Still being polite and soft-spoken, the officer informed me with excellent eye contact that no charges were going to be made against the drunk driver, and that if I took it to court, the investigating officer would testify that I was at fault.

I was still a little dazed by recent events, and by the painkillers I had finally sought refuge in.

"Just exactly what am I supposed to do about all of this then?"

"Get out of Texas, boy."

They probably paid a bounty to the other driver for nailing me. I guess that I was lucky. Being a Yankee Vietnam veteran with long hair on a candy-orange motorcycle in Texas in 1970 was probably enough to get me shot. It never occurred to me at the time to seek legal recourse. I existed in a world which did not provide recourse. What made it even more interesting, if not ironic, was the fact that the drunk men in the car that had hit me were black. These events created an insecurity in me concerning my civil rights that I've carried with me into my old age. A part of me is always waiting for them to be taken away again.

I don't remember leaving the highway patrol station, but we went to pick up the motorcycle—we almost needed a shovel— and on our way back to Dallas, Jackman suggested that because I really didn't have a place to store what was left of my bike, he would be willing to store it on the jobsite for a while. I agreed. I really hadn't thought any of this through yet, and neither had I faced the fact that the 750 had been transformed into a worthless pile of broken metal and that paying to remove it from the junkyard had not been a rational act. Nor did Jackman point this out to me, out of compassion, I'm sure.

That night I ran a ridgeline in the broken hills above the Missouri River Valley of my childhood. It was a cloudless night and though a half-moon almost filled my eyes and darkened the shadows, I saw every rabbit crouched in those shadows and heard the sleeping sweet breath of every blacktail deer curled up in the coulee bottoms. My nostrils sampled the wind, identifying the various scents like a connoisseur separates and identifies the sources of different wines, yet there was no bloodlust in me, just the lust for running full out along the ridge, for raising my scruffy nose to that moon. Breathing in, breathing out.

*** * ***

I lay in bed for two days, never sleeping for more than an hour or two at a time, barely moving except to go to the bathroom. I kept the black-and-white television on twenty-four hours a day and resorted to that little bottle of pain pills every once in a while. The pain wasn't so bad, but my ass bled a little through the bandages every time I moved, leaving little red roses on the sheets. On the second day, I called up the union hall to ask about my insurance and was told that some technicality made me ineligible for compensation. It didn't occur to me to fight that, any more than it had occurred to me to fight the highway patrol.

On the third day, I got out of bed, took a shower, and walked an uncomfortable fifteen blocks to a nearby hospital, not thinking to call ahead. They rebandaged my butt and x-rayed my leg again, the doctor telling me that my leg was indeed broken and to come back in two days to have a cast put on it. Someone else pointed out that this was going to cost me sixty-five dollars. Suddenly I realized that I was a damn fool for even coming to the hospital in the first place. I couldn't afford medical treatment, to say the least. It was as though all my survival instincts had gone to sleep or something. It occurred to me that it must have taken quite a shot to the head to smash that helmet the way it did. The doctor slipped me a sample pack of painkillers as he left.

That night my landlady brought over a scorched TV dinner for me, sitting down in the extra chair to watch me eat it. "I never did like cooking, and I guess it shows," she said to me, grimacing at the little piles of slightly blackened food. I smiled and told her that I was in no position to pass judgment.

"Now we've both got gimped up left legs, but yours is still beautiful."

For a moment, the two of us gazed at my bunged-up, bare leg sticking out of its seam-slashed pants leg. It had never occurred to me before that someone might see any part of my body as being beautiful. Then it occurred to me that she probably saw all healthy legs as beautiful, broken or otherwise. Our mutual assessment of our respective maimed limbs was interrupted by the ringing of my telephone. It was Jackman to tell me that some guy wanted to buy what was left of the 750 from me for fifty bucks. I had been thinking a little better the last day or two, and the foolishness of hauling that motorcycle back to Dallas had begun to sink in, so I didn't hesitate to agree to the sale. I thanked Jackman again, and he told me that he'd send me a personal check in the mail because the guy was paying for the motorcycle with cash.

"Philip, I need you to make me a promise."

"Sure, Jackman."

"I need you to promise me that you won't leave town without giving me a call first."

I promised. It occurred to me long afterwards to doubt that anyone had made an offer on that motorcycle, but I was feeling a little too bunged-up, broke, and vulnerable at the time to question it, even to myself.

*** * ***

I didn't think of myself at that time as being a veteran, much less as being entitled to any benefits. To me, veterans were middle-aged guys who had served in WWII and hung out in American Legion bars. I had no intention of ever hanging out in an American Legion bar. I was just a man who had lived through a prolonged and unpleasant experience that was now over. However, it did finally occur to me that veterans hospitals were created for veterans, that I was one, and that there was a veterans hospital in Dallas.

The next morning as I was getting ready to leave for that hospital, the radio announced that there were tornado warnings out for the Dallas area, with high winds already kicking in. There were two bus changes to make on my way to the VA hospital, and the idea of negotiating these changes in high winds and rain on crutches with an unprotected broken leg gave me serious pause. However, I was even more afraid of what could happen to that leg if I didn't get some protection on it pretty soon, so I headed on out the door without giving myself a chance to change my mind. It was a strange and humbling experience for me to doubt my own ability to take care of myself, to see my body as vulnerable and inadequate to the tasks at hand.

This time, they put me in a wheelchair instead of on a wheeled cart, but the drill was about the same. The nurse, an older man, pushed me from room to room and the dressings on my ass were changed before they x-rayed my leg once again—and told me to come back in four days to get a cast put on it. I was beginning to consider the possibility of radiation poisoning. I leaned on my crutches for a while in front of a plate-glass window in the reception area and watched the tree branches whipping around in the rising wind and near-horizontal rain. The storm had brought a premature nightfall with it. I was beginning to feel a bit worn down by circumstances.

Making my way over to the admissions desk, I asked the lady there if I could get a bed for the night, telling her that I was afraid of being out in the storm with a broken leg. She looked at me pretty much the same way the highway patrol captain had looked at me, informing me that although there were beds available, it was against policy to allow non-patients to stay overnight. I then asked her if it would be possible for me to sleep on one of the couches in the large reception area and she, obviously surprised by my request, gave me the go-ahead. I got the distinct impression that she regretted giving permission almost before the words got out of her mouth. By now I had become vaguely aware that I was not welcome in that place, and I was feeling a little confused by the undercurrent of hostility.

I had a candy bar from a vending machine for dinner and stayed awake as long as I could, reading magazines and watching the storm outside, but it had been a long day and eventually I had to lie down in one of the five-foot-long vinyl and steel couches provided for the veterans' comfort in the lounge. It turned out to be an even longer night. Every time I moved, the leg and/or my butt protested, but the rigid discomfort of the couch made it impossible to lie still for very long. At one point, I opened my eyes to the sound of voices nearby and saw a doctor standing at the lounge entrance talking to the orderly who had wheeled me around the hospital.

"What's the story on the freak sleeping on the couch?"

"Oh, he smashed himself up in a motorcycle accident, doctor."

"Well, good. That should keep him out of trouble for a while."

They turned and walked off together down the hallway, their voices fading into the distance while I lay there contemplating my introduction to the joys of veterans' benefits.

*** * ***

I was alone in a speeding jeep with an M-16 upright in its bracket beside me and a beat-up old Gladstone bag jammed partway under the shotgun seat, a rooster tail of red dust shooting high in the air behind my little vehicle as it jostled down the road through the skeleton of a derelict plantation, the ruined rubber trees on both sides of the road looking like defoliant had been used on them recently, like a forest in a scary fairy tale where the evil magician had won a terrible battle. I'd been told that the defoliant being used was harmless to human beings, but I remembered my father refusing to let me take a job hand-spraying weeds in a neighbor's cow pasture.

At the end of the road, where I'd half expected to see an old French plantation house, there was a little cottage that looked from the outside as though it had only two or three rooms. There was a larger, fire-blackened foundation off to the right. The bigger buildings were probably bombed or burned out in some ancient firefight. This country was littered with such sites, memorials to forgotten little skirmishes important only to those who died there, their spirits wandering off with memories of some pockmarked masonry wall or rubber tree framed by personal muzzle flashes.

I wheeled the jeep to a stop some distance back from the front of the house and stepped down rather delicately, out of consideration for the paranoia I assumed to run rampant in all Vietnamese civilians carrying AK-47's, such as the nasty-looking little boogers who were standing guard by the front door of the house. I pulled the Gladstone bag out of the jeep, leaving the rifle in its mount, figuring that if they wanted to kill me, I was already dead. I had my .45 to keep up appearances with, but I figured my best bet was to appear as harmless and oblivious as possible. I gave the guard a half-wave, half-salute and my best clueless American grin as I passed by him. God. How they must have hated us.

I stepped into sudden darkness, pausing a moment just inside the door to adjust my vision from the white light outside. A skinny, old man was sitting behind a small table in the middle of the room looking at me with anthracite eyes. He was flanked by two bodyguards holding AK-47s that were not quite aimed at me as I stepped deliberately forward as though I were approaching an altar and placed the Gladstone bag on the table in front of him, bending down to snap it open before stepping back. The evil old magician still regarded me as though assessing my edibility, not even glancing down into the open bag. I gave another wave/salute, turned, and managed to make my way out the door as though it had never occurred to me that I might not be allowed to leave.

Hearts and Minds.

*** * ***

I managed all right for a while after getting a cast put on the leg. There was a grocery store within walking distance of my little apartment, and I'd trek down there every other day for supplies, moving slowly, what with the crutches and all. My landlady was sweet, continuing to bring me scorched TV dinners now and then. But I knew that I had a situation. I was going to run out of money before the leg was healed. I could live a lot cheaper out on the road, but I figured that the cast would make it difficult to get rides and impossible to get work. So, a week or so after the accident and just a week after the cast was put on, I sat down in my driveway and pounded the cast off with a stray brick.

Remembering my promise to Jackman, I called the number he had given me, and his wife (whom I had never met) answered the phone to tell me that her husband was out of town for a few days. I gave her my name and asked her to tell Jackman goodbye for me. She was silent for a moment, then, her voice breaking into sobs, asked me if I'd mind her saying a prayer for me. What in the world had Jackman told her about me? But by this time, I at least knew better than to refuse a prayer said in my behalf, so I acquiesced, and she began praying to her Mormon god for me then and there. And so I left Dallas, Texas, in the spring of 1970, with a strange woman blessing me and weeping for me and my road over the telephone.

# CHAPTER 20

*TO HELL IN A HANDBASKET*

Outside Tucson, Arizona, the cotton rows stretched out a quarter of a mile towards the edge of a sky without clouds, so I had to hoe a half mile of double-rowed cotton to get back to the water jug. During the day, the temperatures ran from the upper nineties into the hundreds, and by the time I made the turnaround and began working my way back towards the water, the broken leg was usually beginning to fail a bit. It didn't hurt that much, but it seemed to tire easily. Mostly I worried that I might fall or something and bung the leg up permanently, but I saw nothing for it but to keep going until it either healed or didn't.

It was hard for me to trust my own judgment regarding the condition of the leg. Every afternoon around three, a small single-engine racing-green airplane flew overhead and released a glider to float free and soar off following the whimsy of the updrafts across the desert, up and away from me as I paused to watch and rest the leg.

*** * ***

A week out of Tucson, I lay on a blanket in a city park in suburban Albuquerque, New Mexico. It was Saturday, and the park was crowded with mostly young Chicanos playing softball, picnicking, and generally having a good time. I daydreamed, watched the few clouds parade across the sky, and soaked up the innocent and playful sounds of the crowd. Two young Chicano women approached me and asked me to play Frisbee with them. I thanked them, saying I'd love to play if they didn't mind watching me make a fool of myself on a gimpy leg. I'd learned that I could make short sprints hopping on one leg, my momentum holding me upright as long as I kept up speed and accepted the inevitable headlong fall at the end of each run. I managed these falls by tucking and rolling. Sometimes I even managed to bounce back up on my one good leg. It worked pretty well most of the time.

So, the three of us formed a triangle and began throwing the Frisbee back and forth. I was having the best time I'd had in more than a month, but after a while I noticed two young Chicano men seated on the grass near where we were playing, making what seemed to be unpleasant comments in Spanish to the girls. I didn't know much Spanish, but it didn't take a linguist to understand that their comments were upsetting the young women.

Finally, one girl let the flying Frisbee get through her hands and it sailed within reach of one of her tormentors, who grabbed it, then held it out as though offering it to her. When she reached for it, however, he whipped the Frisbee behind his back, taunting her with it as she stood there with her hand extended, and saying one of the few Spanish words that I understood. "Hey, *puta*. Hey, *puta*."

I bounded like a one-legged kangaroo over to the scene and grabbed the Frisbee out of his hands before he could get up, somehow managing to keep my feet at the end of my awkward, hopping charge.

I stood balancing myself on my one good leg and venting some heartfelt sentiments at the two startled Chicanos. I'm not at all sure just how I had intended to carry out my threat of double homicide with one broken leg and no weapons, but my intentions were sincere at the time. Apparently, the two hoods were convinced of the sincerity of my intentions, at least for the moment, because they got up and left, probably because they weren't quite prepared to beat up a cripple in front of their peers.

My Frisbee partners and I moved away from the scene of the fracas and began throwing the Frisbee again, but the lightness was gone. Some minutes later, just as I was thinking about quitting, there was a sharp blow from behind to my kidney which knocked me off my feet, or foot, as it were. Even as I was going down, I realized that I was in the middle of a mob fight that was apparently bent on my destruction. I instinctively curled myself into a ball as I fell, wrapping my arms around both my legs to protect the broken one, preparing to take whatever came my way and thinking that I probably deserved it. I had completely let my guard down. Sunday in the park.

I took a couple of hard kicks in the side, and someone sort of stepped on my head, but it was nothing like the punishment I'd been expecting when I hit the ground. It was over in a few seconds, and I cautiously opened my eyes to find that I was no longer the center of attention. Instead, some of the crowd was administering a few parting licks to the toughs who had blindsided me. The two finally broke free and ran for the tree line. It seemed to me as though everyone in the park stood staring after them for a moment before shrugging their shoulders and turning to pick up on the fun where they'd left off.

After a few moments, my two Frisbee partners came over and helped me to my feet, even escorting me back to my blanket. I thanked them, reassuring them that I looked a lot worse than I felt and that I'd be all right on my own. One of the girls patted me on the head, and they walked off to find new playmates. The truth was that I wasn't feeling so good. I lay down and promptly fell asleep in the midst of the skylarking crowd, soothed by the occasional waft of marijuana on the sun-warmed air.

*** * ***

When I awoke, the park was empty as far as I could tell, except for me and a few empty beer cans scattered here and there. The sun was gone, and the park was slowly beginning to sink into shadows. I dozed off again briefly, only to be reawakened by the sound of nearby voices. I opened my eyes to the sight of seven tough-looking Chicanos approaching out of the darker shadows of the nearby parking lot. Two of them were the pair who had jumped me earlier. I got up slowly, thinking that this time the jig was really up. It was too late to run even if there had been a place to run to, and I couldn't run anyway.

It had been a long day. I felt tired, stiff, sore, a little lonely, and unable to drum up any crazed kamikaze adrenalin for the occasion, not even fear. I stood as they all lined up in a semicircle facing me, effectively cutting me off from any possible retreat to the parking lot. One of them was wearing a sleeveless T-shirt, displaying an intricate system of tattoos that made his arms look almost black in the failing light. The others seemed to be deferring to him as they stood there leering at me.

"You the *gringo* who likes to hassle Chicano girls?"

Uh-oh.

"No, but you've got two friends there who do."

The leader glanced at his two compadres out of the corner of his eye, and they immediately began making loud, indignant protests. I suspected that my two accusers didn't have a lot of credibility with Mr. Tattoo, but it didn't matter. It was now a matter of face. Mr. Tattoo was not in the mood for a formal investigation, and he was going to take the easy way out, and the easy way out was over my bruised white-bread body, soon to receive a new crop of bruises—if I were lucky, unless they were dealing with guns or knives. I wasn't certain just how serious these people were, but I was hoping for guns. Knives give me the heebie-jeebies.

Right then, protecting the leg seemed more important than survival. I couldn't bring myself to ask them directly to have mercy on a cripple, but I couldn't resist bringing my disadvantage to their attention. Mercy seemed a long shot, considering the circumstances, but it was the only shot I had.

"You need to ask yourself why a white guy with a broken leg would hassle two Chicano girls in the middle of a park full of Chicanos."

"You gotta broken leg?"

"Yup."

I pointed at my left leg where it protruded out of a jean leg still ripped along the seam from when it had a cast.

"Bullshit."

This from one of the two punks who had jumped me earlier in the day. I was wishing that I had enough juice left in me to bound into the gang and take a shot at getting my hands on the little booger, but just as I was savoring this stupid revenge fantasy, everything was brought to a halt by the sound of a car horn from the direction of the parking lot.

There was a limousine gleaming in the dim yellow glow of the parking lot's single streetlight. A small slender man in a dark suit got out of the back seat and strolled across the lawn towards us, his open-collared white shirt luminescent in the night. He motioned briefly with his hand, apparently signaling the gang leader to come to him because Mr. Tattoo immediately strode off towards the newcomer while the gang held their formation and entertained themselves by glaring at me. There was a brief businesslike consultation between the two before the newcomer turned to motion me towards him. I couldn't see how things could get any worse, so I obeyed, gimping over to follow the elegant little Mafioso—or whatever the hell he was—back over to the limo. His driver was standing next to the open door of the car, and the two of us got into the back seat and were driven off.

Some unfamiliar Latin-sounding music played quietly on the sound system. There was a nice little bar in there, and we rode in companionable silence for a while, sipping some fine brandy, smoking cigarettes, and watching Saturday night Albuquerque go by the open windows. I didn't have anything to say or any questions to ask, thinking that my afternoon was certainly having its up and downs. My young Chicano savior finally broke the silence without looking away from the window.

"I've got to be somewhere. I think you should stay with the car for a while. The driver will drop you off at nine anywhere you need to be. You probably shouldn't hang around town any longer than you have to."

The long car pulled over to the curb, and the dapper Chicano reached over to gently shake my hand before stepping out of the car to stroll across the sidewalk into a side entrance of a posh-looking hotel.

I had stashed my pack downtown at the city's little hippie resource center, and they had directed me to a house, really a converted church building, that was open for the night to anyone who was willing to sleep on the floor. However, the place wasn't open for crashing until after midnight, so I had some time to kill. I cruised around in the limo until just before nine, then had the driver swing by the center and wait for me while I retrieved my pack. My wildly upscale arrival and departure made quite an impact on the counterculture denizens who were hanging around the entrance.

I had the limo driver drop me off at another city park that I had spotted earlier, smaller and closer to downtown than the other. It was crowded with hippies smoking dope, listening to rock music on their boom boxes, and just hanging out. I settled in on a park bench and listened for three hours to the music and the clink of steel against glass from a little pavilion nearby where a group of longhairs were apparently exploring the darker side of the drug culture.

*** * ***

Someone was muttering, "Harry, Harry, where the hell are you?" I woke at some strange hour in the morning in my sleeping bag on the floor of what must have been the choir loft of the old church before it had begun its present incarnation as an activity center and huge crash pad for young America on the move. There were a dozen or so other people sleeping scattered across the floor. The searcher for Harry had just stepped across me and was methodically checking the faces of all the other sleepers. The lad seemed somewhat agitated and had what appeared to be a large, sharpened screwdriver in his hand.

It occurred to me that it might be just about the right time to leave Albuquerque. Two o'clock in the morning found me out under an overpass, standing in a cold wind with a half-dozen other travelers huddled around the light of a single candle, trying to convince ourselves that we were being warmed by it. Perhaps we were.

*** * ***

Late spring of 1970 in Denver brought in hard showers and sometimes downpours every other day or so. It was ten in the morning, and I was downtown methodically knocking on every door that had a business sign on it, every place that looked remotely like it might have a job for a gimped-up ex-motorcycle bum. Door to door, block to block. I was going to have a job before it got dark or began to rain again, whichever came first. That was the deal I'd made with myself. I didn't have enough money for a room, and there wasn't much cash left for food. And it looked as though those clouds were going to bust loose before lunchtime.

I walked onto a construction site past a sign that announced that they were building a new municipal library. I was willing to bet that this was a union job, and I'd had to quit paying my union dues two months before, but part of the deal I'd made was to leave no stone unturned. So, I asked for the foreman and found that gentleman yelling at a man who appeared to be a union representative. I knew enough to keep my mouth shut until he'd finished running the guy off.

"What's with the limp, son?"

I didn't see any way out of lying. "I've got one leg just a tad shorter than the other, but it doesn't slow me down."

"This is a union job."

"I know. I let my membership lapse down in Texas. Let me work for a week at half-pay, then after that pay me what you think I'm worth. If you think I'm worth union scale, I'll get my dues caught up again."

"You and I both know that it's not that simple. You're just lucky you showed up on the day I ran off my third union hod carrier for the month. I'm so damn disgusted, I'll try anything."

The foreman scribbled an address on a piece of paper and handed it to me.

"Show up at this address at eight tomorrow morning, and we'll see. We're doing the outside of a church there."

I limped through downtown Denver feeling as though I'd tricked the devil. The heavy clouds were lowering and the first sprinkles of rain were splattering down and I had to resist an impulse to break into a chorus of "Singing in the Rain," but the leg wasn't up to an imitation of Gene Kelly yet. I took shelter from the rain and the rising gusts of wind beneath a movie marquee just as a young woman had the same idea. She was beautiful and dressed for show, smiling conspiratorially at me as we both turned to watch the storm's little drama and the pedestrians scurrying for cover. She was queen of Denver, and I was king of the road—for a moment in time.

*** * ***

I left my pack at Denver's version of a resource center, another one of those places like the one in Albuquerque that had sprouted up during the sixties and seventies in almost every major city across the country to provide information and assistance to the thousands of young people who were on the road in America. Most of these travelers were living and traveling on a shoestring, maybe hitchhiking or in an old Volkswagen van. Flower children drifting from rock concerts to college campuses to anti-war demonstrations. Flower children tripping on acid, smoking dope, indulging in free love courtesy of the pill in the world before AIDS. Flower children running away from war, their parents, and adulthood for as long as they could.

The resource center had a message board, counseling referrals, and advice on where to go for inexpensive or free meals and lodging. One of the male volunteers had offered me the use of a sofa in his apartment if I needed shelter for the night, which I really, really did, what with being broke and the rain and all.

The day had been hard on the leg, so I slept restlessly on the sofa and had no problem waking up early enough to make the walk to the jobsite, which was way out on the eastern edge of town. I woke up all right. I woke up to the sound of rain cascading against the living room window. I got up from the sofa and looked out at a sky that seemed to have lowered itself to rooftop level. I couldn't imagine there being any stuccoing or plastering being done outside today, but I had to try. I didn't have any way of calling the foreman up to ask, and if, by chance, there was some work and I didn't show up, I would probably lose my chance at the job.

I walked in the rain, gimping along on the leg, for an hour or so. It was only a few minutes before eight when I got to the church building site, but there was no one there remotely resembling a construction worker. I went across the street to take shelter beneath the awning of a used-car lot, and waited without hope for a while, letting my mind wander up the street, which was also Highway 83 North. It did occur to me that if I walked out there and just stuck out my thumb, I could be eating Momma's pancakes in a day or two.

I looked at my watch and saw ten minutes after eight just before something drew my attention back to the church. There was a guy with a yellow hard hat sitting in a pickup in front of the building. I got over there in fairly quick time and knocked on the window, interrupting the daydreams of a middle-aged black man. He cracked his window open, and I told him my predicament while he grinned at me from beneath the brim of his yellow hard hat.

"Damn, I forgot they told us if it rains to come downtown to the library. I might have sat here all morning wool-gathering if you hadn't come along. Hop in and we'll go find us some work."

I spent most of my working time carrying buckets of plaster and hauling them by rope and pulley up the side of the scaffolding to where two Chicano plasterers were lathering the stuff onto the side of the building. I soon found that the only way I could keep up with them was to carry a bucket in each hand. That put a lot of stress on the bad leg which, in turn, put me in danger of taking a fall, which I really didn't want to do, especially because the leg seemed to have been healing pretty well up until then.

There was no paycheck for a couple of weeks, so I slept where I could, sometimes in a park and sometimes on someone's sofa, and found myself going hungry again. I suspected that the two Chicano plasterers were getting stoned on the job, but they were pleasant enough to work with and alert enough to notice that I wasn't eating lunch. Without anything being said about it, I soon found myself eating enough frijoles and tortillas at lunchtime to get me through the rest of the workday.

The problem was the leg. It didn't hurt me much at all anymore, but it didn't have its strength back yet, and every week spent carrying plaster around seemed to make it a little weaker. I knew that the leg needed some rest and that it couldn't stand up to the stress very much longer. However, I wasn't in any mood to go hungry again, either.

My first payday came, and to celebrate that night I went to a bar and had a couple of boilermakers that hit me pretty hard, probably as a consequence of eating so little and drinking even less alcohol during the previous weeks. I found myself talking to Frannie on the telephone at an hour which was late enough for Denver and must have been ungodly for her in Maine. She was sleepy and slow over the telephone and told me to call her back in a couple of days, to give her some time to think about it. It was the first time I'd talked to anyone about the accident, and it was embarrassing the next morning to remember waking her up to talk about my predicament. Somehow or another in the process of describing my situation, I had made her feel as though I were asking for help. The idea that she might take it that way hadn't occurred to me, though it should have.

I had promised myself from the beginning that if it came to a point where I needed to ask for help, I would have to get off the road. Easier said than done. I had betrayed that principle a few times already, but I was still struggling to honor it. This meant that I just had to accept being a little hungry, wet, or cold sometimes. It also meant that a broken leg couldn't keep me from taking care of business. It was always a question of just how much I was willing to pay, just how much I was willing to suffer for the outrageous degree of personal freedom I was insisting upon.

This also required secrecy on my part. The life choices I was making were worrisome ones for anyone who cared for me, anyway, and I had decided that sharing the consequences of those decisions with family and friends would just make them worry more and draw them into my difficulties, difficulties which I was willingly subjecting myself to and which I could remove myself from at any time. After all, my lifestyle seemed to evoke that response even in complete strangers at times. So I opted for silence. By sharing some of my life's rough edges with Frannie in a moment of weakness, I had broken my own rules and now she was feeling responsible for rescuing me. I have always regretted that phone call—especially considering what was to come to her later.

# CHAPTER 21

## *FALSE HARBOR*

Two weeks later, I was on Highway 80 hitchhiking east for Maine. With some trepidation, I'd called Frannie, as promised, but she had been all full of herself and good news. There was a part-time job waiting for me that would be easy on the leg, and her mother and her stepfather had agreed to let me stay in an extra room in their basement. I was more than a little surprised at all of this, remembering her taciturn, conservative lobsterman stepfather as not being overly impressed with a certain longhaired motorcycle outlaw bum/hippie, but I'd needed to override my doubts concerning her optimism, and so I had.

I burned my way across America and up to Maine in four days flat with my magic thumb, my only misadventure involving some liquid fertilizer being spilled all over my pack in the back of a truck as I'd passed through Indianapolis on the day of the Indianapolis 500. I called Frannie from a phone booth a few miles up the road from her house and found her at home.

"Hey, Frannie, it's me." A moment of silence.

"Where are you?"

"Just up the road. I'll be there in less than an hour. Is everything all right?"

"Oh, yes. I just didn't think that you'd be here this soon."

I said goodbye and hung up, taking note of the moment of silence and the subdued response. *Uh-oh.*

The road I was referring to was just a little two-lane paved highway that ran from the mainland across a bridge, along the crest of Orr's Island, across another bridge, then along Bailey's Island to Land's End. Her stepfather came from a long line of seamen who had apparently lived there for centuries, and the family house was a small white clapboard that looked like something from a picture postcard perched on its stone foundation high on the spine of Bailey's Island, with both front and rear views of the Atlantic Ocean.

The sky had been getting heavier and heavier for the past couple of hours, and I didn't have to be a seaman to be glad I was soon going to be in a dry, warm place as I turned off the road and began walking up the driveway to Frannie's house. A hot cup of coffee at a kitchen table across from a smiling face would be nice. It'd been a strenuous few months, and I could feel the fatigue pulling me down as I made my way to a resting place. The leg continued to send me its little messages of protest, too, though I figured that if it hadn't given out before this, it was probably going to be okay. Like me, it just needed a little rest.

Frannie met me at the door and threw herself into my arms. I held her very, very tightly for a while, then whispered in her ear, "All right, Frannie. Now tell me what's wrong." Still holding desperately on to me, her face buried in my shirt collar, she said, "After I talked to you in Denver, I found out that the job I promised you wasn't going to happen. They hired someone else."

"That's all right, I'll find something else to do. It'll be good just to be still for a few days."

Silence. *Uh-oh.*

"Ah—my stepfather put his foot down and said he wasn't going to have some hippie staying in his basement."

This was bad. It would be high tourist season on the islands, and every extra space would be rented out. Even if there were a vacancy, it would cost way more than I had to spend. Frannie sobbed once into my shirt, then pulled back to look me in the eyes.

"And I have a date picking me up in ten minutes—I'm sorry. I just never imagined you getting here this quickly, and I had no way of calling you."

My response well ran dry. There was nothing but rust and dust coming up the pipe.

Then she asked, "Do you still love me?"

I sort of wished that I didn't. I disengaged my arms and stepped back, turning to retrieve my backpack from the hallway floor and trying to smile reassuringly over my shoulder at her with lips that felt a little stiff and unresponsive.

"I'll have to think that one over for a while." I was out the door and walking down the driveway towards the road. A few tentative raindrops struck my hat brim. I just hoped that the boyfriend would hold off for a while and that the weather would hold off for a little while longer.

Well, this was one of those situations where no rose garden had been promised. Before I'd left on my motorcycle a year ago, we'd talked about the dating business and agreed not to have any expectations. We had both been clear on our love for one another, but we also knew that both of us had many miles to go and things to do before any promises could be made, much less kept. I couldn't seriously expect her to wait faithfully and chastely for me while I played out my crazy open-ended gypsy game. As for the rest of it, the job and the room and all, I really couldn't be angry with her. She was only twenty years old, for god's sake. She'd wanted so much to help me out that she had fallen prey to wishful thinking.

So had I, for that matter. I had let my guard down, allowing myself to build up expectations of emotional and physical refuge, expectations of her that were unfair and unrealistic, regardless of her desire to help. However, the timing was bad, and I was having to struggle a little bit with it. A little bit, hell. "I have a date picking me in ten minutes." *Jeez.*

Actually, I think that I was a little bit in shock from the emotional whiplash of recent events. The shock of disappointed expectations, along with the physical and emotional toll inflicted on me by everything that had happened since the motorcycle accident, including the marathon hitchhiking trip across America and its anticlimax, had left me exhausted—and more than a little stunned at the magnitude of my misjudgment. Years later, I would ask myself why it was easier for me to hitchhike over two thousand miles to place the burden of my situation on a twenty-year-old girl than it was to have simply hitchhiked the seven hundred miles home to the family ranch in Montana or tough it out with the job in Denver.

*** * ***

Regardless of the reason, I was in a spot and not tracking too well, at least not well enough to come up with any particularly creative or practical plan. For some reason, instead of heading back inland where

I'd have had a lot more realistic shot at finding housing and a job, I trudged down along the island towards Land's End, knocking on every door that showed any promise of employment or shelter. There weren't that many of them, and I had no real hope of finding what I was looking for, but I felt that I had to at least go through the motions. I had no luck, of course, in finding a room, and the rain was beginning to be a little serious as I arrived at the island's small bay with its little wharf and the cafe that sat at one end of it.

*** * ***

I was ready to take any shelter offered, and the warm lights of the humble little fisherman's cafe looked wonderful to me. I walked up the dock and entered, dropping my backpack to sit down on a red vinyl stool at the end of the counter, the same stool I'd sat on many times during the previous summer. I was the only customer in the place. I ordered a cup of coffee and waited until I got it before lighting up a cigarette. I took a sip and a drag and sighed deeply. It felt so good just to sit still and not think about whatever was going to happen next.

*** * ***

I watched as the rain settled in, gently dappling the water of the bay with a steadily increasing intensity. A fisherman dressed in bright yellow rain gear was working at something on the deck of his little lobster boat, ignoring the weather. A tingling wave of peaceful elation crept in from somewhere to flood through me, taking the edge off my fatigue. Sometimes the end of a rope can feel just like home.

# CHAPTER 22

*OIL FIELDS, SANTANA, AND FAGIN*

A month later I stood on the southern outskirts of Minton, Saskatchewan, a village south of Regina and just fifteen miles north of the border crossing into Montana. The shadows were lengthening across the almost deserted streets of the little town, and I'd just found out that the border crossing was going to be closed in a half hour. Four boys, all of them around eleven or twelve years old, had been riding their bikes up and down the town's main street, making a point of ignoring me whenever they were in my vicinity. On the third pass, I nodded and said hello. As though they'd been waiting for a signal, all of them pulled over and the five of us sat down on the rough grass by the still and darkening street and powwowed.

Mostly they were curious about me. Unlike the isolated rural community I'd grown up in, they were accustomed to seeing strangers driving through, but for them a hitchhiker was apparently almost as much of a phenomenon as it had been for me at their age. I didn't mind sharing a few stories, but I was concerned about how their parents might feel about them spending all this time with a gypsy stranger. They acknowledged after a little while that they needed to get home for dinner. An hour and a half later, they were all back, one of them with some warm cornbread wrapped in tinfoil, and another with a pork chop. Having decided that I looked as though I could use a good home-cooked meal, they had conspired to smuggle some food out of their homes for me, and the two that couldn't manage the petty larceny involved were obviously a little chagrined by their failure.

They seemed to get over it quickly enough and soon I was sitting with my back against my grounded pack, digesting the pork chop and cornbread and smoking a cigarette while the four boys nattered on comfortably. It soon was so dark that I couldn't tell who was talking to whom anymore. I must have fallen asleep because in the morning I woke to find the boys gone and myself lying under a blanket that one of them had evidently gone home and gotten for me, apparently concerned that I might need something more than just my sleeping bag to keep me warm. I rose and put on my pack, feeling as though my presence had probably triggered the biggest crime wave in the entire history of Minton, Saskatchewan. I left the blanket folded carefully beneath a nearby tree and walked south out of town towards the border crossing. Twelve hours later I was walking off the south end of the Snowden Bridge.

It has been more than forty years since my brief sojourn in Minton, and only as I write this does it occur to me that I might have had as great an impact on those boys as they had on me, that I might have been their hobo on Snowden Bridge. Did my passage cause them to dream, as that hobo caused me to dream? Even act on those dreams? That Snowden Bridge hobo probably died in a boxcar somewhere without any inkling of what he had given to me.

*** * ***

After visiting my parents for a few days, I spent the rest of the summer and part of the fall working on a jug crew with a seismograph outfit over in western North Dakota. The crew was young, harmlessly crazy, and tough as nails. We would walk beelines cross-country, climbing over or wading through most natural obstacles, spooling out light cable from reels suspended by padded hooks from our shoulders. One kid, who didn't weigh much more than a hundred pounds soaking wet, liked to take off running once in a while with that eighty-five-pound reel banging on his skinny little chest, cable flying out behind him.

I spent a few months trotting through coulees, wading creeks, and exploring in some detail the cattle country of western North Dakota. I wore a red bandanna tied over the top of my head, and the shoulder-length hair not covered by the bandana soon bleached out white. My days were passed roving between empty sun-etched horizons, and, with my injured leg strong and whole again, I would run at any excuse. The crew stayed mostly at cheap motels in small towns, paying by the week for rooms with kitchenettes which we seldom used except for storing beer, and moving on every week or two.

At the end of each workday, we would come rolling into town crowded into crew-cab pickups, laughing and calling to small-town teenage girls walking on small-town sidewalks, who'd grin back as though we were a visiting high school football team, which many of us were almost young enough to be. Our crew ate huge amounts of beef steaks and hamburgers, hash browns and eggs and bacon at local cafes, drank a lot of beer and wore out a lot of pool tables. We were a boisterous, reckless lot, but the hell we raised was mostly respectful and harmless, and the townspeople we encountered along the way seemed to be willing to indulge our behavior. We were unknowingly laying the groundwork for what would be the Bakken oil boom of the early twenty-first century.

Freeze-up was coming to western North Dakota. There were a few rain-out days towards the middle of September, the nights began to cool, and I began to dread the premonitions of frost on sleep-tender flesh in the mornings. The work became a little less like strenuous play, and all of us on the jug crew knew that every day was possibly the last of the work season. We began to yearn for that last day, even while being pushed by our boss to squeeze every bit of juice we could out of the remainder of the season, even as the work became more unpleasant. Finally, during the first week of October, sleet and rain settled in for the afternoon, and our Texan boss, who was sitting in his truck with a thermos of hot coffee, refused to let us shut down. I got on the crew-truck radio and told him that with or without his approval, we were going to piss on the campfire and take it to the house. And we did. What could he say? We fired ourselves.

\*\*\* \* \*\*\*

A few weeks later, just outside of Salt Lake City, fifteen or so other miners and I crowded into an elevator which was built like an oversized cattle squeeze chute, so they could get as many men on board as possible for the 1,000-foot stomach-lifting drop down to the next level. Then an amusement park-sized train carried us in open cars more gradually down to another level, where still another elevator awaited us. Finally, our crew arrived at the end of the line, to work at the deepest and most remote part of the mine. It had taken us over an hour to reach our destination.

The first day on the job, I was taken to a spot where they had removed some overhead supports to begin digging a vertical shaft. I was handed a spud bar, a heavy, six-foot-long piece of iron with a sharpened end, and told to pry rocks loose from the exposed ceiling. I found that in order to reach my target with my spud bar I had to stride from one side of the opening to the other, ramming my bar upwards as I went, to avoid the worst of the falling rocks. It occurs to me while writing this that that project was a little nuts and was probably a test or initiation of some sort—perhaps to see if I was crazy enough to work with them. I guess that I was.

I liked the place and the work. Sometimes, it was as though I were working at the bottom of the sea with the beam of my headlamp peering through black water everywhere I chose to look. At other times, it was like being on a distant dark planet, looking up from my work into a sunless and starless sky. We only saw our foreman two or three times throughout the day, and we could hear the machinery bringing him long before he arrived, so we had almost complete autonomy, as long as we got the work done.

We worked hard, even though we did take more break time than we were supposed to. I liked the element of danger, the pressure of the darkness and the endless rock and earth above lending a certain significance to the most mundane of tasks. I even liked the rattling whisper of the occasional little rockslide, sometimes distant and sometimes not so distant, that never ceased to make my heart do a little jump. If things fell in, perhaps one day my body would be oil in someone's Chevy.

Somehow, I had assumed that when I returned from Vietnam and was discharged, the war would be over—like high school graduation ends your high school experience. I had forgotten that my people, Vietnamese and American, would keep suffering and dying in-country without me, and that there would be constant reminders from the media of this. Down in the mine there were no television sets or radios. Just a few fellow moles and myself in the warm darkness, following restless beams of light. However, its increasing seductiveness and my awareness that I was being grossly underpaid made me decide to leave before I became really hooked and ended up spending the rest of my working life comforted by stone, earth, and darkness.

*** * ***

Through some Chicano roommates, I was introduced into the Chicano subculture of Salt Lake City. The town was controlled by the Mormon church, and the Mormon culture had a decidedly puritanical bent. Cigarette smoking was frowned upon, and it was impossible to buy a mixed drink there, except in the private clubs. The Mormons themselves seemed nice enough, if a little on the smug and self-righteous side at times, but the Chicanos were having none of the repressed lifestyle being urged upon them and were much more fun and interesting to be around, if a little dangerous at times. There were a number of bars and nightclubs frequented primarily by Chicanos in the greater Salt Lake area. With macho customers starting out on a Friday night with a fifth of expensive booze under their arms primed to throw themselves into loud Santana-flavored rock and roll with a lot of beautiful young Chicano girls, the Chicano nightlife often got pretty intense and was often punctuated with a fistfight or two. Knives were pulled often enough to lend an aura of real menace to the entire enterprise, though there didn't seem to be that much serious damage done.

I found myself living with a couple of Chicanos and relishing the undercurrent of potential violence and sex, the uninhibited lust for strenuous play, crazed rock and roll, and the chromed-up, shiny road machines rumbling by the entrances to these places. My housemates would go skiing on Saturdays, but only after having a bowl of a hangover-fighting, highly spiced tripe soup called *menudo* for breakfast with a warm beer for a chaser. I had a distaste for hangovers that was strong enough to keep my drinking in moderation most of the time, but I loved the *menudo* and enjoyed sitting around on Saturday mornings, watching the torments of my invariably hungover and just as invariably cheerful Chicano housemates. They seemed to enjoy paying for their sins almost as much as they enjoyed the sinning.

After quitting the mining job, I went down to the local union hall and managed to get signed on as a laborer working for an outfit building a huge magnesium-processing plant out on the salt flats sixty miles west of Salt Lake City, in the middle of nowhere. It was so remote that they had to build a ten-mile road that connected the construction site to the highway. I ended up commuting with a group of Chicanos in a 1958 GMC panel truck—one hour out, eight hours' work, and one hour back, five days a week. The money was good, however, and I decided to gut up and work there through the winter. It was an opportunity to put together a real traveling stake, for a change. I didn't mind going hungry once in a while, but the novelty of it had definitely worn off.

I settled into a working-class hero routine—of a sort—for a while. Living in a suburban home, commuting back and forth to work with my hard hat and a lunch bucket every day, I even bought myself a few extra clothes. My Chicano housemates were both slick dressers, so I got myself some slacks and shirts that enabled me to avoid embarrassing them too much. The truth is that I had more than my share of vanity anyway. It was just that traveling light and broke tended to cramp a dandy's style.

That winter I taught myself to ski. Wearing jeans and my fleece-lined denim work jacket, I'd hitchhike across town, pick up some cheap, battered rental skis and boots, and then hitchhike up to one of the ski resorts in the mountains above Salt Lake City, most often Brighton or Park City. Each ski trip cost me about six dollars, as I remember it.

On my first expedition, to Brighton, I ignored the beginner's slopes and took the lift to the very top of the mountain, where I immediately fell on my face as I got off the lift. I had no idea what I was doing, wasn't about to pay good money for someone to teach me to fall slowly down a hill, and consequently spent one of the longest afternoons of my life just trying to get down the mountain alive. Public humiliation, my worst nightmare, was the theme of the afternoon. I kept taking these endless falls, then having to climb back up the slope sans skis to retrieve the gear I'd littered the snow with during my fall. The most important lesson I learned that afternoon was to spend less time trying to get down the mountain and to spend more time watching the other skiers—all of whom seemed to have their act more together than I did.

*** * ***

Out on those salt flats, there was nothing to slow down the wind. Sand and salt blew during the dry season; sand, salt, and snow blew during the winter. Only the Great Salt Lake's waves, heavy and turgid with their dense salt burden, kept their heads down, reluctant to respond to the wind's coaxing touch. Massive concrete shapes were being built on a site near the lake to serve some exotic purpose which I never came to fully understand. The completed constructions had certain surrealistic, earthbound, and massively fragmented beauty that Picasso would possibly have appreciated. I imagined some space wanderer a thousand years in the future setting his ship down on the flats to contemplate those structures and wondering what kind of gods we must have worshipped.

It was a cost-plus project, which meant that the more money the contractors spent, the more money they made. Consequently, the contractors spent money like drunken sailors, purchasing as much material and hiring as many employees as they could possibly justify on paper—which meant, in turn, that sometimes there were more workers than work. Management addressed this problem by letting us know that there would be times on the job when some of us would have nothing to do, and if they caught us doing it, we would be fired.

All of which is why on this particular day I found myself wandering around through the snow for a couple of hours with the same three two-by-fours balanced on my shoulder. My wool-lined Levi's jacket, and the exercise of walking aimlessly around carrying a few boards, were inadequate to the task of keeping me warm, and I was thoroughly chilled and bored out of my mind. The wind was brisk enough to keep kicking up flurries of snow which maintained a running assault on the chain link and barb wire fencing that guarded the perimeter of the project. The place resembled a prison compound or even a small base camp in Vietnam. All that it needed was guard towers.

I decided that I'd walked long enough and that I was cold enough to have earned a little time in a warming hut. I ducked under the belly of one of the concrete monsters intending to take a shortcut to a warming hut I favored. Two middle-aged carpenters who always worked together, Karl and Joseph, were putting up some scaffolding there. When they saw me, they stopped working, took out a Book of Mormon, and began praying for me, two priests in Carhartts and orange hard hats. Karl, the taller and lankier of the two, read aloud as though in front of a congregation, while Joseph stood with his eyes squeezed shut and his hands folded, his nose red and dripping from the cold, swaying and repeating, "amen, amen," while snow swirled in around them, Mutt and Jeff at prayer.

Two days later, I was walking through the same area. Karl was up on top of a twelve-foot scaffolding, disassembling the structure and passing the pieces down, one by one, to Joseph who was standing on the ground. As I came upon them, I saw that their foreman was also there, saying something that was obviously making Karl very unhappy. Suddenly, Karl pulled his hammer out of its holster and leapt from the top of the scaffolding to go after the foreman with the hammer. His buddy, Joseph, was apparently expecting something like this and was able to grab Karl's arm before he could brain his boss. The intended victim wisely got the hell out of there without further comment. What was scariest to me was that Karl made no sound throughout the entire episode. However, Joseph was cool as a cucumber and seemed to know what to do to bring Karl down from his murderous intent.

The next day, I didn't see either of them around. I asked a carpenter I was working with about it.

"Oh, Karl and Joseph didn't show up this morning. They knew they were going to be sent down the road anyway, after that scuffle yesterday."

"But Joseph didn't do anything but help break it up."

The whistle sounded, and we began moving towards the break shack.

"Yeah, but he would never stay without Karl. They always work together. The story is that they grew up together, went into the army and survived the Bataan Death March together, and have been glued together ever since. They even live next door to one another."

The carpenter removed his hard hat and pulled a pack of cigarettes out from beneath the liner.

"I think that it's getting kind of hard for them to find work, though. Karl's temper keeps losing them jobs, and word gets around. He's pretty scary sometimes, although I've never heard of anyone getting seriously hurt. Joseph watches him pretty closely, I think."

*** * ***

Spring came to me in Salt Lake City like prison doors opening. I managed to put my head down and keep working until the middle of May for the sake of my traveling stake and good traveling weather. May finally did come, and I got ready to hit the road with some vague notion of ending up in California.

Our neighborhood was solidly middle-class and mostly white, with a lot of clean-cut, good Mormon teenaged children around. A little gang of five young boys, about twelve or thirteen years old, had somehow become attached to our household and dropped by now and then to hang out with us. I noticed that their visits were sometimes a little late in the evening for boys their age, but I didn't think too much of it until one Saturday morning when one of my housemates came in laughing from spending an overnighter with his girlfriend at her home in another part of town. He had been rousted out of bed in the middle of the night by these kids to be scolded for leaving his keys in his motorcycle. The little gang had been about to steal his motorcycle when they recognized it. It would seem that our clean-cut little Mormon boys had been spending a fair amount of late nighttime roaming different parts of the city stealing everything that wasn't nailed down.

I had mentioned to them at some point that I was planning on leaving town in a week or so, and they had insisted on coming over to say goodbye to me on my last night in town. I'd agreed, but with the understanding that it would have to be later in the evening, as I'd be out saying goodbye to the Chicano nightlife. I didn't really expect them to show up. I had underestimated their seriousness of purpose, however, and when I got home, I found bicycles and boys scattered around the lawn in front of the house. I invited them in to keep me company while I packed. They lounged around my bedroom, smoking cigarettes and drinking Pepsi and making generally unhelpful packing suggestions until around midnight, when I told them that I really needed to get some sleep. They said goodnight, but not before offering to come over and wake me up in the morning.

Whenever I was getting ready to hit the road, I always experienced a certain amount of stress, a mixture of fear and anticipation, I suppose, at the prospect of leaping off from some modicum of security into the unknown—again. I was accustomed to dealing with it alone and found the boys' intrusion into my usual solitary departure ritual to be both comforting and uncomfortable.

But what could I say? I'd had a long day, and I lay my head gratefully down on my pillow that night, only to find myself awakened at four-thirty in the morning by five junior hoods laden with stolen goods trooping unannounced into my bedroom. They apologized for being unable to rip off any bread and insisted on whipping up a slightly scorched version of bacon and eggs for me. Afterwards they presented me with some gifts that they thought might be appropriate for the occasion: a small flashlight, a carton of cigarettes, a cigarette lighter, and a compass. They told me that they'd made the rounds of a few quick stops during the previous evening before going home, then hit an all-night supermarket first thing this morning. The compass came from a big brother's camping gear. I didn't waste my time lecturing on the legal and moral issues involved, choosing instead to accept the gifts in the spirit with which they were intended. If they were headed for prison, nothing I could say was going to prevent it.

After breakfast, the boys cleaned up the kitchen while I smoked a cigarette and supervised from a kitchen chair. That finished, I gave the interior of the house the usual once-over for any overlooked detail before picking up my waiting pack. Living out of a backpack and traveling with very few resources had made me extremely wary of leaving anything important behind. Forwarding addresses were not part of my game.

We all trooped outside to say our goodbyes—at least, that's what I had in mind. However, my crew decided that they wanted to walk with me out to the interstate. Again, what could I say? So off I went with my five undersized Mormon mercenaries following along behind, taking their turns carrying my backpack.

They obviously thought that trudging along a busy street, carrying a sixty-pound backpack behind a long-haired gypsy was a great way to start a day. It was a half-hour's walk to the on-ramp I had in mind that would get me and my stolen goods onto Interstate 80 west across the desert towards Wendover, Winnemucca, and San Francisco. As we walked, I thought of those boys who'd stolen for me back in Minton, Saskatchewan, and wondered if I wasn't becoming some sort of latter-day Fagin.

We had come into some fairly solid daylight by the time we reached the spot I had in mind and my native bearers grounded my pack, lining up to shake my hand before trooping off back down the highway, back towards their loving mothers, suburban homes, and criminal careers. The presence of the boys had eased the tension in my stomach, but their departure brought the feeling back. That was all right. I had gone through this often enough to know that after I had stood in the waning shadow of the Wasatch Mountains for a while and after a few cars had passed me by, I would be myself again.

# CHAPTER 23

## *CALIFORNIA DREAMS*

A family traveling in a huge, green Mercury station wagon carried me west into Reno, Nevada, where they invited me to sleep in the back of their car. They went off to eat and I wandered over to the motel pool to catch the last rays of the setting sun. I had the fenced-in pool area to myself and took off my shirt before dropping into a lawn chair and drifting into a semiconscious state. After a while, some movement nearby spooked me awake. A young woman was tidying the pool area, picking up abandoned soggy towels and putting some order to the lawn furniture.

Her name was Kelly, Reno was her hometown, she had just graduated from high school, and she was getting ready to go out into the world with college as a first stop. After we chatted for a while, I asked her what I could do to entertain myself in Reno for the rest of the evening on a five-dollar budget. "You wait an hour for me to get off work and follow my lead, and you'll get by on six."

I knew enough to obey a beautiful woman's instructions and waited in the cooling evening, half dozing in the lawn chair on its little island of wet concrete surrounded by parking lot while she did her Irish maid routine. When I opened my eyes, she was standing in front of me in some yellow, one-piece summer thing. She was making absolutely no effort to charm me. She had simply decided to take me in hand.

The Nitty Gritty Dirt Band was on its way up and Donovan was on his way down, and they were both appearing in Reno on that night in the spring of 1971. Kelly led me by the hand into the club where Donovan was performing, the hand-holding less a gesture of affection than one of control, as a busy mother might tow a child into a crowded store. There was no cover charge, but she told me that I'd be expected to buy a couple of drinks. A buck and a half for each of our drinks, one-half of my budget for the evening.

Donovan came on and did his somewhat desperately sincere routine. I liked to listen to him, but it seemed to me that the singer was refusing to leave his flower childhood, still holding on to an innocence which left him peering through a chain-link fence into a roughhouse playground ruled by Dylan and the Rolling Stones—an innocence which seemed even more of an anachronism in a gambling casino in Reno, Nevada.

Afterwards, the two of us strolled down the main drag of Reno to the casino where the Nitty Gritty Dirt Band was appearing. Four years ago, as a young second lieutenant, I had escorted a young woman into a debutante's ball in Baltimore, Maryland, to be struck dumb by Duke Ellington and his band. Wearing my dress blues with highly shined low-quarters, I had been walking in high cotton, a long way from chasing cows in a river bottom in eastern Montana, but, of course, not as far away as I thought I was and not nearly as far away as I was going to be.

Having gotten our money's worth out of the Nitty Gritty Dirt band, Kelly walked me back to the motel, which was on her way home. I kissed her freckled Irish forehead and thanked her for the evening before crawling into the back of the station wagon and falling asleep. The next morning, I was back on the road for San Francisco.

*** * ***

I didn't quite make it there, the nature of hitchhiking being what it is and the vagueness of my plans being what it was. I wound up coming into San Mateo early on a Sunday afternoon and being directed by a longhair on the street to the local hippie park and spending most of the rest of the day there resting on damp grass, talking comfortably to people who felt like sharing some shade with me and catching an occasional whiff of marijuana.

It was as though during the sixties, our young people had somehow spontaneously created freewheeling, gypsy, nurturing, carnival/communities, and they chose to celebrate those communities on Sunday afternoons in every major city across the country. There was something wonderfully life-enhancing about them, something that pushed the limits of human generosity and freedom further than society, and perhaps human nature, could tolerate. So, inevitably, it all began to go to hell almost as soon as it came into being, as most revolutions do.

I did not really belong to the hippie movement, being a loner who enjoyed hard physical labor and lacked much of an interest in politics, drugs, and free love, but these weekend park gatherings always felt like safe places to me, places where I could let my guard down and relax, invisible in a crowd. I let myself enjoy the ambience of the San Mateo Park and casually let people know what I was looking for— which was a place to stay for a few days. About the time that the day and I were beginning to fade a little, a redheaded hippie about my age invited me to roll out my sleeping bag in his unused garage.

The garage wasn't much, but it did have a half-bathroom in it and a piece of shag carpet to unroll my sleeping bag on. Not bad for ten dollars a week. San Mateo, with its beaches, seemed a nice place to laze around in for a while and, after the long winter I'd just spent out on the salt flats, I was in the mood for some lazy time before I moved along down the coast to do some backpacking in the Big Sur area.

Most mornings, I would hitchhike the ten miles out to Half Moon Bay to spend a few hours on the beach. The only water I trusted was still either water I could drink or water I could take a bath in, but there was something about the ocean that I found to be emotionally reminiscent of the badlands and hills of home—as long as I could reassure myself occasionally by touching my feet to the bottom.

The early morning was the best time to go to the beach. Hitchhiking was easier then, with the lighter and less frenetic traffic, and the beach itself was usually almost empty. I would sit and watch the shades of gray brighten slowly into different shades of blue. The ocean was flattened and almost waveless on this particular morning, so the surfers were somewhere else being whatever they were when they weren't being surfers.

A young woman with a luxuriant, dark-brown braid swaying down her back cantered a joyful little black Arabian horse down the beach from the north, as she did almost every morning. She had the horse under what seemed to be perfect control even while allowing it to meander along the waterline flirting with the surf, finally turning out into deeper water directly in front of where I sat. She smiled back over her shoulder as the water climbed up the horse's sides and submerged her jeans-clad legs from the knees down, the Arabian having to swim a little in the swells, and I chose to believe for the rest of my life that the horsewoman had been smiling at me.

My landlord was mellow, and his name was Ned. Ned was mellow because he smoked dope almost constantly—and because he had absolutely no responsibilities or ambitions as far as I was able to determine. One day, sitting on the huge waterbed that pretty much filled his living room and stoking up a bong, he told me his war story. The waterbed was the only place to sit down in the room except for the floor, so I joined him at first, but I found it somewhat disconcerting to lounge around on a bed with another man who was bobbing up and down and sucking on a bong at the same time.

Two years earlier, he had become eligible for the draft and went to one of those draft counseling centers that sprouted up in the sixties and early seventies. Ned was presented with a short list of professional therapists who, he was told, would falsify a personality disorder diagnosis for a prospective draftee which would disqualify him from the draft. Ned's diagnosis of choice was multipersonality disorder, and in the spring of 1968, he became officially crazy. That got him out of the draft, and then the shrink suggested that he would support Ned if he wanted to apply for disability compensation.

Ned continued to bob up and down, a sailor lost at sea in his own living room, while smoke from the bong drifted around the room and out the open windows. I wasn't quite sure whether I was experiencing the beginnings of seasickness or a contact high.

They had been successful in scamming a one hundred percent disability for Ned, and at the age of nineteen, he retired with enough income to buy a surfboard, make payments on a house, pay the bills, and keep himself mildly stoned pretty much around the clock—the American dream.

I often wonder how all of that worked out for mellow Ned in the long run.

*** * ***

A week later, I awoke in a raft suspended motionless in the midst of a turbulent dark sea, with seagulls crying and waves pounding all around me. There was a moment of confusion before I remembered where I was. The evening before, I had hitchhiked in from San

Francisco with the intention of hiking into the mountains in the morning. Near the trailhead, two young men and a girl struck up a conversation with me and suggested that I camp out with them on one of the huge rocks that lay on the beach abandoned by low tide.

They were good company at first and the tide was coming in before I realized that I had become an unwilling witness to some kind of competition between the two men for the attentions of the girl. All I could do was wait for the tide and the passions to subside, whichever came first. I pulled out of camp before daybreak to avoid waking up in the middle of the next episode of someone else's soap opera. The tide was out, and I made my way easily across the sandspit leading back to the beach. I found the trailhead I was looking for and headed up the trail a short distance before nestling down in a secluded spot to take a nap.

Around noon, I was up and back on the trail. I didn't intend to go very far up into the hills, so I hadn't bothered to get a map and was just sort of feeling my way. I didn't get much more than a quarter mile up the trail before I found myself facing a grotto where a good-sized stream cascaded down over a steep granite face, forming an impressive little waterfall into a deep pool before continuing on its way down to the sea. Naked hippies were leaping down the waterfall. The rock formation was spectacular, and a dozen or so tourists had made their way up from the highway. Some were taking pictures and others were outraged and some seemed to be doing both.

Someone told me that there was a beautiful meadow up behind the waterfall where people were picnicking and sunbathing in the nude. You could get in there by hiking way back into the mountains and coming back down, but supposedly the only direct way in there was to swim across the pool and make the easy climb up the rocks alongside the waterfall. Consequently, the park service rangers left them pretty much alone up in there.

I figured what the hell. I rigged a float for my backpack with my poncho, stripped down and climbed into the pool, adding to the confusion and outrage of the tourists. I swam across the grotto, made the climb up the rocks, and found myself looking up a little green valley sloping gently down from both sides to the fast-moving stream I'd just climbed out of. Naked bodies were sprinkled like flesh-colored flowers here and there all across the meadow, open to the sun and sky. I made like Ramblin' Jack Elliot in "912 Greens" and followed suit.

Three days later, it was late morning when I woke from a catnap on a hilltop some miles farther up from the sea into the Big Sur. I took a drink of water from my canteen, lit up a cigarette, and gazed out towards the distant blue haze hanging over the Pacific in the distance. Unzipping a pouch on the side of my pack and pulling out a plastic baggie, I opened it up and removed the passport that I'd applied for while I was in the army. I'd known that I'd want to leave the country sooner or later. I looked again out over the hills towards the Pacific and decided that the time had come.

# CHAPTER 24

## *AN INNOCENT GOES ABROAD*

A Volkswagen van with four girls in it stopped for me on the coastal highway near where I had come down from the mountains. They were all college students headed up from LA to San Francisco. It was already early evening when they picked me up, and we camped out that night, planning to go on to the Bay Area the next day. When I woke the next morning, there were five sleeping bags fanned out around a dead campfire, with one of them cuddled up extremely close to me—close but no cigar.

It might have been better if I had taken a vow of sexual abstinence before I went out on the road. Drugs and alcohol were never a problem for me, but my relationships with women between 1969 and 1979 left too much confusion and pain along my back trail. The pill, free love, and women's lib were upon us and made me a bit of a danger to both the opposite sex and me. I wanted and needed the comfort that women offered me, but I had nothing to offer in return, not even an explanation. I just kept going away.

I wound up escorting my feminine companions to a Greek wedding in a flower garden behind a house in Mill Valley, complete with a group of older men in ill-fitting black suits who looked as though they might have come over on the boat from Messini in 1919 and who were watching the mostly longhaired crowd with slit-eyed suspicion. The paranoid bodyguards turned out to be musicians who began to play Zorba the Greek music as dusk settled in, and everybody started dancing in erratic circles and making yipping noises. I had never seen anything like it in my life.

I was awakened in the morning by four cheerful teammates who seemed determined to help me get a good, early, and well-fed start on my way east. They fixed a huge breakfast and, as a bonus, had made four extravagant sandwiches for me to take along for the road before trundling me off to an Interstate 80 on-ramp. Four full-body hugs, another kiss, and I was on my own with my backpack, four sandwiches, and a part of my anatomy that seemed determined to precede me all the way back to Mormon country.

There were three other hitchhikers ahead of me scattered along the on-ramp, trying to get rides east. I strode along the ramp to take my place at the end of the line, giving all but one of my oversized sandwiches away to the other hikers. My billfold was empty, but my emergency cash stash, a twenty-dollar bill, was taped to the inside of my boot. I usually carried all my money with me, but this time, for some reason, I'd left most of my savings in a Salt Lake City bank.

I knew that twenty dollars and that big half-sandwich would be more than enough to get me the eight hundred miles to Salt Lake City, so I'd played sandwich Santa Claus to the hungry-looking hippies waiting with me on the ramp. I was feeling a little smug about the whole thing, handing out largesse to the world's hungry. Of course, the first car to stop skipped the first three hikers and pulled over to offer me a ride. The King of the Road accepted the gift as if it were his due and slid graciously into the shotgun seat after stuffing his pack into the back seat.

Four hours later, I was dropped off outside of Truckee, California. As usual, I felt relieved to have gotten clear of the big city. It's not that I minded being in cities that much. It's just that they were expensive and usually a pain in the butt to get out of. Too much traffic moving too fast made catching a ride difficult and sometimes dangerous. Too many boogers with knives and guns looking for easy prey. If the outlaws didn't hassle you, the law was likely to. Plus, the view from the on-ramps usually sucked.

My next ride was a pretty lady in her middle thirties driving a big boat of a 1969 Plymouth, similar to the one I'd rented when I first got back from Vietnam. It was getting on to two in the afternoon and I was getting a mite peckish, so I pulled that last half-sandwich out of a side pocket before putting the pack in the trunk.

After she got that big machine wallowing like a hyperactive whale east down the freeway, I asked the driver if she'd like part of the sandwich, pointing out that there was plenty for two. The sandwich was a little squashed but still looking pretty good, with a thick layer of turkey in it, and another layer of crisp bacon, topped off with garden fresh lettuce slathered with a mixture of mayo and hot mustard. Homemade bread, too. She declined but indicated a willingness to watch me eat it.

Women didn't often pick me up, and I didn't expect them to. Inviting a male stranger to share the front seat of a speeding car seemed to me to be a scary proposition for a woman, and I had no interest in scaring anyone or being in a car with someone who was afraid of me. This lady seemed to be extremely comfortable in her own skin and unafraid. In fact, she seemed not to be taking me very seriously as I gave her the short version of the Greek wedding and the sandwich story, including my gig as sandwich Santa Claus back at the San Pablo on-ramp.

"That *was* sweet of you."

"No, you don't understand. I was being a jerk. I was letting them think that I was a lot more generous than I really was." Then I told her about the money waiting for me in Salt Lake City, and the twenty-dollar bill in my boot. She smiled. "You really keep a twenty-dollar bill in your boot?"

"Yeah, taped to the side above my ankle." I slipped my boot off to show her, figuring that with my shower and change of clothing that morning, my foot shouldn't be too rank. I was right in believing that my socked foot would be reasonably clean. However, I was wrong in believing that I had a twenty-dollar bill taped to the inside of my boot.

I was silent for a moment, then I had to laugh. My more-or-less perpetual state of arousal during the past two days, the hilarity of the four women at my expense, the generationally gapped Greek wedding, my falsely generous Santa Claus routine with the sandwiches, and now a cashless boot.

The lady behind the wheel asked me why I was laughing, and I showed her the empty boot. "Why, that's terrible."

"No, it serves me right. No rest for the wicked."

The lady was driving home to her family ranch outside of Winnemucca, Nevada, and it was a three-hour trip. The company was charming, the scenery was beautiful, and the desert was still in the gentle hands of its spring season. The big Plymouth thundered down the highway without faltering while the Winnemucca lady and I told lies to one another and laughed. I liked watching her drive. She kept her eyes on the road, with only a brief and occasional glance at me or the scenery, two hands firmly on the wheel at all times, and her dress hiked somewhat immodestly up solely for purposes of ventilation and driving ease. She seemed supremely confident and relaxed—and in control. She also seemed to trust me, which I found immensely flattering.

When we got to the Winnemucca turnoff, the lady drove down the off-ramp and stopped her rig to let me out. No traffic in sight and a sudden and complete stillness. She stepped out to stretch while I went back, got my pack out of the trunk, and walked around to the driver's door carrying my pack by one strap. She rolled down the window, and I leaned down to her eye level and let the air conditioner's cold breath dry the sweat off my face while I apologized for holding her up. She laughed and reached up to give one of my sideburns a little tug. Still smiling up at me, she told me to check my shirt pocket and then poured the coals to that shiny monster Plymouth, leaving me standing there gaping into her dust with a carefully folded ten-dollar bill in my hand.

*** * ***

I stood cooking in the sun on the Winnemucca on-ramp with my thumb out for three hours, with no takers. By eight in the evening, there were five other hitchhikers standing out on the freeway with me. They were a pretty downtrodden looking bunch of pilgrims, and I knew that their presence and demeanor wasn't helping me one bit. I finally decided to stop whipping a dead horse and walked off towards town, figuring to buy something cold to drink before bedding down out in the desert for the evening. That sandwich I had eaten earlier in the day was just a memory, but I figured I could get a good breakfast in the morning. Right then, I just wanted some shade, something cold to drink, and some solitude.

The other hikers followed my example, however, and trooped off towards town after me like five of the seven little dwarfs. I was developing a bit of a bad feeling about the situation. I was out in the middle of nowhere surrounded by desert, rednecks, and five lost souls with greasy, long hair and defeated body language. Henry Plummer had learned the hard way that you could get hanged for the company you keep. I stepped into a gas station on the edge of town, and the five followed me in as though I had a sign on the back of my head that said "lonely."

The front room was empty, with country music and mechanical sounds coming from the back. There was a pop machine and the ubiquitous slot machine. I played it safe and put some change in the pop machine. As I turned around with my payoff in my hand, two of my fellow travelers had somehow ripped the slot machine off its moorings and were making for the front door with it. I let out a yelp and knocked both of them sprawling on my way out. I could hear them floundering and cursing on the floor behind me as I pounded flat-out for the highway, desperately trying to sprint with sixty pounds of backpack jouncing against my spine.

Once I hit the brush across the road from the gas station, I found a spot that seemed secluded enough and collapsed to the ground. I hoped the locals would catch those two clueless jerks and get their evening's entertainment by stringing them up for general stupidity. I was soaked with sweat from a combination of stress, heat, and exertion, and I thanked god that I'd been able to save the can of Pepsi. It was still relatively cold, and, with a cigarette as a chaser, tasted like heaven. When first light came, it was going to find me moving east down that highway, ride or no ride.

I was pocketing $1,500 from my Salt Lake City bank by four the next afternoon. I'd left my camp outside Winnemucca at two in the morning and had tramped the fifteen miles to the next exit in five hours without even trying to get a ride. Once I began hitchhiking, it'd taken me another hour to catch a ride, but that ride took me all the way to Mormon town, with one stop in Elko, where I blew a good chunk of that ten dollars on one helluva late breakfast spread for my driver and me. The lady in the Plymouth would have approved.

# CHAPTER 25

## *THE GRAND TOUR*

It took me four days of hard traveling to hitchhike to New York City. I purchased my airline tickets at Rockefeller Center around noon, and by eight that evening, I was flying away from the sunset across the Atlantic Ocean. As I remember it, it cost me thirty dollars to cross North America in five days, and sixty-five more bought me a round-trip plane ticket to Luxembourg. I went six thousand miles in six days for a little less than a hundred dollars.

Next day, I stood with the Kelty leaning against my leg in front of Luxembourg's one and only air terminal, feeling intimidated. Other than my military time in Panama and Vietnam and my one trip across Canada, this was the first foreign country I had ever been in. I didn't know much about European culture, and my foreign language repertoire consisted of about twelve French words, about all I had to show for my high school and college French courses.

When I had been up in Maine, Frannie had talked a lot about her father, her mother's first husband, who was a successful Belgian restaurateur. She often spent at least part of her summers there with her father at his hotel-restaurant, near Dinant, Belgium, and had given me his address and telephone number in case I got that far in my wanderings. I decided that a good way to begin my travels in Europe was to swing by on the chance that she might be visiting her father.

The rides were few and short, and I ended up walking most of the day that it took to get from Luxembourg to Dinant—a long, hard, hot day, made harder by simple false pride that made it difficult for me to ask for directions, or even a glass of water. I chose to suffer instead and walked for hours in the sweltering heat, looking for a water fountain or stream or anything. Finally, I realized that I was feeling a little nauseated and lightheaded and began to suspect that I might actually be on the verge of heatstroke, intensified by a combination of jet lag, fatigue, stress, and terminal self-consciousness.

Besides all of that, my feet were sore. I didn't get into Dinant until dusk, and by that time I had turned pretty much into a little robot, not thinking anymore, just putting one foot in front of the other, determined not to stop until I got somewhere. I remembered Frannie telling me that her father's place was a couple of miles upriver from the town, so I went straight on through Dinant, crossing over an old stone bridge, and began following a secondary road down the north side of the Meuse River. I walked a mile or so into growing darkness without sighting anything that resembled a restaurant, before finally caving in and asking directions from a man walking his dog. When I said the restaurant's name in French (thank god I at least had that written down in my address book) the old man turned and pointed almost directly across the river at a small cluster of lights that seemed to be right down next to the water. I could just about have thrown a rock and hit them. Then my guide took me by the shoulder and faced me back where I had just come from and made a broad, sweeping motion with his hand, indicating quite clearly to me that I had to walk all the way back into town, recross the bridge, then return on the far side to that cluster of lights.

As stubborn as I was, I had had enough. I made the universal sign for telephone and my rescuer, who seemed to understand my predicament and state of mind, motioned me to follow him and his dog back towards town. A few minutes' walk, and we turned into the yard of a small cottage. A few more minutes and I had dialed the telephone number I had listed for Francine's father, whose name was Paul Leyman.

The phone rang and a man who identified himself as Paul Leyman answered. When I asked for Frannie, Paul excused himself to fetch her. I breathed a sigh of relief. I'd accepted the possibility that Frannie might not even be there, but I wasn't really in the mood to sleep on the ground that night. I didn't care if she had six dates lined up for the evening; I was in a mood to fight all of them for a chance at a hot shower, hot food, and a soft bed. When she answered the phone, I recognized her voice and identified myself. There was a moment of silence.

"Where are you?"

"Standing in this guy's living room right across the river from you, looking at your lights."

I heard the cold click of an emphatically broken connection. I stood there for a few seconds staring at the telephone in my hand before I turned to the old man to thank him for his hospitality and made my way out of the cottage back onto the road to begin the trudge back towards the bridge and the town. With a little luck, I'd find a hotel room for the night.

I was on automatic pilot. In the army, I'd learned that as long as I had good boots on, I could walk almost forever. So, I was just numbly walking it out down the empty dark road when oncoming headlights caught me from in front and a car pulled up next to me. The opening car door almost knocked me down, and then Frannie leapt out of the car, grabbing me so hard that the combined weight of the woman and the pack buckled my tired knees and almost put me down on my back like a flipped-over turtle. I did not complain as I stood there on the dark road watching stars, my nose buried in Frannie's blond hair and the good feel of her body pressing into mine.

*** * ***

A week later, while crossing the border from Belgium into France, the French customs officer asked for my passport, then told me that I'd have to wait while they checked with the American military.

"Check with the American military for what?"

"They look for deserters, *monsieur*, and the draft dodgers."

I sat on a bench in the little booth with big windows, smoking and contemplating the fragile nature of my freedom, which I wouldn't mind so much except that they seemed to enjoy yanking on my leash occasionally, just to remind me that they could have me anytime they wanted me. I was acutely aware that, with the war dragging on, I could be pulled back into the military at any time for the next two years or so until my reserve status was up. Going back into the army, much less going back to Vietnam, was something I didn't want to do, even in my imagination. Twenty minutes later the phone rang, and the customs officer apologized and told me I could go.

My first ride once I got over the border was with a Finn who was headed down into southern France. He spoke excellent English and explained that he was on an urgent business trip and would be driving straight through. We rode in relative silence for a while before stopping for lunch, when the driver offered to pay for my meals if I'd stay with him while he drove across France, just to keep him company and help keep him awake. I was in the mood to keep moving and, to be honest, willing to postpone being alone again in a strange culture with a strange language, so I wimped out and agreed.

Consequently, my first experience of France consisted of blazing all the way north to south across the country with a red-eyed speed-dropping Finn who gave me a thirty-second history of the cathedral at Rheims and other tourist attractions as they receded in the rearview mirror.

It was late afternoon when I walked into Lourdes, and it seemed to me that everything there was black or gray. A long, long line of people dressed in black waited to get into the grotto beneath a darkening sky, some of them alone, most of them accompanied by others, many in wheelchairs pushed by others, some of them even on wheeled stretchers. Most of the wheelchairs were old-fashioned ones built of hardwood, worn and darkened by decades of use. I imagined small villages with one or two community-owned wheelchairs, passed on from generation to generation for the damaged ones, the chairs taking on a character of their own over the decades, as familiar to the villagers as the old local taxi.

The damaged ones and their caretakers ran a gauntlet of vendors with their carts hawking plastic statuettes of Jesus and Mary, crucifixes, and miniature bibles. There were no tourists here, just peddlers, priests, the handicapped and the ill with their caretakers, and me. I walked along the line of slow-moving supplicants to the grotto itself, which was a kind of deeply overhanging cliff face, dotted here and there with abandoned crutches or canes attached to the stone, apparently as testimonials to the grotto's healing powers. There were numerous places on the stone face of the grotto that appeared to be smoke-blackened, as though at some time there might have been torches burning there, although some of the blackened areas were so high up the face it was difficult to imagine how that might have been possible.

I stayed out on the periphery of all of this, my longhaired gypsy/spaghetti-western cowboy persona looking wildly out of place, I'm sure. In a gathering of caretakers and their physically maimed and twisted charges, I was alone, young, and whole—and taller than almost everyone there. Thoughtlessly I lit up a cigarette while I stood watching the somber rituals of suffering and prayer.

An old woman, one of the caretakers, separated herself from the column of supplicants to come over to me, smiling but pointing at my cigarette and hat in turn and shaking her head. I apologized, belatedly realizing that I was, in fact, standing in an outdoor church. Complying with her instruction, I obediently sat down, smokeless and hatless, in one of the metal chairs that were arranged in rows for onlookers. The anxieties and self-consciousness that had been with me ever since I got off the plane had been gradually lifting ever since I arrived at Francine's home back in Belgium, and now I sat alone in the darkening grotto, comfortable and confident in my own skin again. A miracle.

*** * ***

Much later, I walked out of town and headed west until I came to a place where a meadow sloped down from the road to a river, and I struck off through the thick, high clover until I found a good spot to spread out my sleeping roll. I ate some cheese and bread, washed it down with some red I'd bought in town, smoked a couple of cigarettes, and watched the stars arrive in a now cloudless sky. Then I slept.

When I opened my eyes in the morning, everything was dew-soaked, and wisps of fog were floating like shape-changing feathers along the surface of the river. Luckily, I had thrown my little plastic tarp over my sleeping bag the night before, so it was relatively dry. I hurried to break camp, rolling up the bag first to keep it from absorbing any more moisture than necessary, then headed out for the highway quickly to keep the wet chill air from getting too strong a grip on flesh that wasn't quite ready to face cold reality.

As I swung across the ditch onto the road, I heard a strange yet familiar rhythmic ringing buzz coming from the trees on the other side. When I investigated, I found a farmer alone in a little meadow just finishing up milking a cow. I waited until the farmer had released his animal, then walked over to him and offered to buy a cup of milk, but he just smiled and poured carefully from the bucket into my canteen cup until a bit of foam slipped over its side. He casually waved off my offer of payment before wandering back up the road towards

Lourdes with his bucket rubbing against his leg. I stood sipping sweet, white warmth as the farmer disappeared into the mist, and thought of milking cows back home, of kittens standing on their hind legs to catch with gaping mouths the milk that I sprayed at them from the cow's teat.

*** * ***

Two days later, I was sitting at a kitchen table on a small farm near Coutance with a half-empty bottle of Calvados and two glasses sitting between me and an old man in farmer's clothes grinning at me with teeth blackened by a lifelong diet of Calvados in a region where mothers still gave their babies the local booze strained through a lump of sugar as a soporific.

The man's son had picked me up on the road and brought me home with him, complaining all the while about his father who had been staying out too late at night drinking with his friends and who had hired a housekeeper and begun sleeping with her just months after having become a widower. The boy was home from a school year of being a dope-smoking hippie/student in Caen and seemed to be oblivious to the fact that his father was simply practicing what he and his counterculture friends preached.

My French was awkward at best, and the Norman dialect was completely incomprehensible to me. Regardless, it seemed to me that I understood the old man better than I did the son, who spoke good English and who became thoroughly disgusted when he realized that I was going over to the enemy camp. After the first day, the boy pretty much stayed away from home, spending his time with local friends, leaving the old man and me to babble uncomprehendingly at one another to our heart's content. The Calvados helped, and the housekeeper, who was about half the old man's age and obviously worshipped him, kept the booze and the food coming.

The farmer had been a soldier stationed on the Maginot Line when WWII broke out, and he had immediately been taken prisoner by the Germans, who had shipped him back to Germany to work on a farm for the duration of the war.

"Best thing that ever happened to me, except for my wife dying. I got to learn how to use all the latest farm machinery and techniques, and after the war I came back here and was able to make something of the home place."

Sometimes the old man would say something, and I would understand his words spontaneously, as though he were speaking English rather than some obscure Norman dialect. Then somewhere in there I would realize that I shouldn't be able to understand—and then I wouldn't. I had noticed this phenomenon a few other times while traveling in Europe. I might be sitting half-asleep on a train or a bus and then be startled awake by the recognition that I was understanding everything that was being said around me in a language about which I had little or no knowledge. Of course, once I became conscious of the phenomenon, it would dissipate.

On the third day, the two of us went to visit one of the old man's friends, a man he'd known since childhood who had been with him on the Maginot Line and had also gone to Germany with him as a POW. If I understood correctly, we were going to help the friend build a ladder. We walked through a little unpainted, failing gate down a dirt path through a yard that looked as though it had never known anything but a hand scythe. An old man was just coming out from the door wearing a pair of high rubber boots that most European farmers seemed to favor. Those boots seemed such a practical thing to wear around the farmyard, but I'd never seen anyone back home wearing anything like them.

The man shook hands with us and told us that he had to feed his rabbits before he could begin work with us on the ladder. We followed him around the house to where he had a whole bank of little rabbit hutches, perhaps thirty or so. Each of the cages had one big, fat, cuddly bunny rabbit in it. I was a little shocked when I realized that these fuzzy little things were being raised for butchering just as we raised sheep and cattle for butchering back on the ranch.

As I watched the old man doing his chores with the rabbits, I realized why he needed help to build a ladder. The old farmer's fingers were all grotesquely gnarled and swollen, probably from arthritis, and didn't look remotely capable of handling a saw or a hammer. After the rabbits had been watered and fed their little piles of grass, we abandoned them to their fate and moved on to a small shed across the yard from the rabbit hutches. It had a small workbench in it with hand tools neatly arranged on the wall behind it that looked like they were all manufactured before the Great Depression. There was no sign of electricity. There was also a waist-high stack of what looked like firewood against the opposite wall from the bench. Our host excused himself, apparently suddenly remembering some chore that needed attending to.

My partner in crime picked up an axe in one hand and, holding a quarter round of wood about eighteen inches long with one end braced against a chopping block, used the axe to trim the wood into a roughly round shape with tapering ends. The old man then braced the stick between his belly and a notch in the workbench, and he used a drawknife to finish shaping the wood into what I finally recognized as a ladder rung. Just then our perpetually smiling host walked back in the door holding a tray in his clublike hands that contained a full bottle of Calvados and three glasses. I got the picture. One old man was going to pour the booze, the other old man was going to do all the work, and I was going to be the audience.

I have only one memory from the remainder of that workday, and that is of the three of us standing in the evening light in the shed grinning drunkenly at one another, standing next to the pile of finished ladder rungs, and looking at the bloody holes in the palms of my hands that had been gouged out by the day's work. Somehow, the sight of my maimed hands struck all of us as hysterical. I was too drunk to feel much pain until our host opened up a third bottle of Calvados and poured a liberal dose over each of my Christ wounds. My yelp of pain from that treatment brought on even more merriment. Our host suggested with appropriate sign language that my masturbating days might be over for a while. More merriment.

Somehow, the two of us made it back home that night and the next morning we slept late. When I finally wavered into the kitchen around ten o'clock, the old man was cheerfully pouring Calvados into two cups of steaming coffee. He had our day planned out already, and it seemed to involve the two of us driving somewhere and, I assumed, drinking more Calvados.

The old farmer had one of those old Renaults with canvas seats and a unique suspension system that caused the car's progress down the highway to resemble that of a bounding kangaroo. I had never ridden in one before, and I had never wanted to. Just watching one of them going down the road was scary. On the previous day, our little journey to the ladder-building site had been short and slow, so I hadn't had an opportunity to experience the unique handling characteristics of the Renault, but today's journey put us on the highway for fifteen minutes or so, and during that fifteen minutes I concluded that I'd much rather be doing eighty miles an hour on a motorcycle than traveling fifty miles an hour in that Renault.

We finally bounded off the highway onto a narrow unpaved lane that wound through some gentle grass-covered hills into an isolated valley where we found what appeared at first to be some kind of gypsy gathering with a lot of tents and fifty or sixty trucks and cars parked haphazardly on the outskirts. We parked the Renault among them, and as we walked towards the tents, we encountered an assortment of farm animals, mostly cows, calves, bulls, sheep, goats, and pigs staked out in the grass, each with a bucket or pan of water. There were even a few rabbit and chicken hutches. There were, however, very few owners in sight.

It was a country fair. There were a few humble commercial exhibits selling such utilitarian items as gloves, boots, and hand tools with one carnival ride provided for children, none of whom seemed to be in attendance. There were also a few food concessions, but most of the tents provided shelter for makeshift bars in which it seemed that farm couples from miles around were having one hell of a party.

Once in a while, some of them would get into a discussion or argument about bragging rights on their prize livestock and wander off to look at a pig or a cow out in the parking area, but most of their attention seemed to be focused on bellowing at one another, telling dirty jokes—and drinking Calvados. My old farmer friend also seemed to be intent on getting drunk, along with showing my wounded palms to every fellow drinker we encountered as we worked our way from one tent to the other and repeating his joke about my abbreviated masturbation career. I at least knew enough not to try keeping up with the drinking pace of these red-faced, black-toothed, calloused, and weather-beaten people, but all of them seemed to forgive me for my lack of staying power and were terribly good company in that place among green hills.

For years I carried a photograph taken by that farmer (it might have been taken by his son, come to think of it) of me as I was preparing to leave. I was out in the driveway, all decked out in my traveling gear—slouch hat, red neck scarf, fancy boots, backpack, and all—and was down on one knee petting the old man's dog, with the late morning sun just above my head, so that my features were mostly concealed by the dark shadow cast by my hat brim. I lost the photograph eventually, like I lost a lot of things, but it's the only photograph of myself that I've ever really had any use for.

*** * ***

A week later, I was walking up a long gradual slope towards the English Channel and the setting sun. It seemed a little strange to be walking *up* to the sea, but it was a beautiful afternoon, and a crew of men were just finishing up their day's work in a hayfield next to the road as I walked by. One team of four was on the ground, picking up bales and passing them up to another team who were stacking the bales in a tractor-drawn wagon. I walked a short distance past the farmworkers to where the road teed off and, instead of turning left or right, I continued straight ahead through the intersection, crossing a ditch into another field just beyond where the hay bales were still lying scattered about in irregular rows.

I constructed a little house out of a few bales then sat down to lean against it, facing back away from the sun and the headlands to watch the haying crew finish their day and to eat my dinner of bread, sausage, cheese, and wine. By this time, I was in the shadow cast by the setting sun from the top of the headland, a shadow which was slowly creeping towards the east to engulf the hayfields I had just passed through. The hay crew all piled into the half-filled wagon and the tractor towed them off towards the east, moving just ahead of the shadow, bathed in the last of the bright day's light. The workers laughed and passed a bottle of wine around, the sound of the laughter and the clink of glass ringing across the field to where I sat in my shadowy little den.

I woke to a cold, wet morning, swirls of heavy fog moving here and there on a light breeze about the headland. I was glad that I'd had the hay shelter to sleep in, but the damp cold began to seep through my clothes into my flesh the minute I got out of my sleeping bag. I hurried to break camp and get moving down the road.

It was only a quarter of a mile or so to where the headlands crested and dropped down to the English Channel below, and I blessed my luck to find a cafe out in the middle of nowhere that was open for business at this ungodly hour. It had an outdoor deck and was perched near the edge of the cliff overlooking the ocean. There were tables and chairs out on the deck, and I found myself drawn towards them, unable to bring myself to enter the building despite the yearning of my chilled body for the light and warmth glowing through the cafe's windows.

The heavy cloud cover and the fog had slowed the dawn, and it was still almost completely dark when I seated myself at a table on the outside edge of the deck, where I could look directly down over the hand railing to the channel waters roiling into the base of the cliffs below. The air was so wet that it was almost like sitting in the rain. I lit up a cigarette and found myself at peace with the chill and hunger that I had been experiencing as adversaries just moments before. Down below, wisps of fog drifted in with the tide like ethereal sailboats foundering in the shallow surf or colliding with the old WWII concrete and steel breakwaters still lying in the water. I could see where a couple of old gun emplacements and bunkers were still embedded relatively intact in their recesses in the cliff's face.

Somewhere around the middle of my second cigarette, a waiter finally came out of the cafe and crossed the deck to my table, obviously not enjoying the cold and wet and obviously not convinced of his new customer's mental stability. I ordered cafe au lait and a croissant but have no memory of eating the food or of the next few hours.

*** * ***

When I became aware of my surroundings again, the tide was coming in and the fog and most of the clouds had mostly been driven away by sunshine. I was alone, stumbling across the sand with my hunting knife in my hand. There were vaguely human projectiles restlessly careening about in the air above me like stray bullets with contorted faces on them, as though they were fleeing the pain and terror that had become their existence, like dogs trying to get away from tin cans tied to their tails. Long disconnected from the events that had created them, they seemed unaware of one another and my presence.

I screamed words I don't remember at them, feeling compelled to break into their horrific isolation, even offering to shed my own blood there, but they were silent in their turbulent trajectories and oblivious to my offer of companionship. There was nothing in response but the cry of a few seagulls and the whispering of tiny waves racing across the sand as I began to come back to myself.

I had no place to put this experience, or vision, or whatever the hell it was—any more than I'd known what to do with my Gettysburg experience. So, I did the same thing with this one that I'd done with the other—I put it in a little box and didn't deal with it. Decades later, I took it out of its box and faced the fact that (a) I was not schizophrenic, (b) I was a relatively healthy person psychologically who was prone to having unusual, inexplicable experiences, (c) these inexplicable experiences had had a powerful impact on my life, and (d) it would have helped tremendously if I'd had a guide or mentor to help me deal with the phenomena that I had experienced.

*** * ***

I drifted aimlessly east into Paris, coming to the city late at night, tired and a bit scorched around the edges, in no mood to shop around for a place to stay. I took the first hotel room I could find, even though it seemed outrageously expensive. The man at the desk looked at me a little oddly, but I was too worn out to speculate much about it. I just wanted a bed.

The next morning, the deskman stopped me on my way out and started babbling at me in a manner that I could only interpret as apologetic. He insisted on refunding part of my money, and I finally got it into my thick skull that I'd rented a room in a whorehouse where they rented rooms at exorbitant rates to whores and their johns, the whores getting a little kickback every time they used a room. My lack of a female companion had really confused the poor guy.

I spent a couple of weeks in Paris. A doctor and his wife had given me a ride in southern France a couple of weeks previously and had invited me to call them if I ever got to Paris. The doctor was the administrator for one of the city's largest hospitals. One of their sons was out of town for the summer, and they moved me into his empty apartment and gave me the use of his motorbike, one of those things that you have to pedal in order to start. There was a good stereo in the apartment and a collection of records that included a lot of American artists. Simon and Garfunkel sang "The Boxer" while I looked out over the streets of Paris.

Wandering about the city, I found myself in a subdued mood and disinclined to see the tourist sights. Mostly I buzzed about on that little motorbike, pursuing my quest for the perfect sidewalk cafe. There were a lot of perfect sidewalk cafes in Paris, and I would sit for hours drinking coffee or brandy, reading and writing, and eavesdropping on imperfectly understood conversations. I played around with the idea of attending the University of Vincennes on the GI bill, but the idea died a natural death, and I left Paris eventually to find my way back to Belgium and Frannie.

*** * ***

A couple weeks later on a hot clear day on a rather desolate plateau somewhere in northern Spain, Frannie and I were in the mood for something cold to drink and were quite happy to come upon a Spanish version of a convenience store out in the middle of nowhere. A short distance behind the store was a flock of at least a few hundred sheep being watched by a solitary shepherd and his dog. There were two picnic tables outside the place, and one of them was occupied by four men whom I guessed to be herders taking a break from their duties with the sheep. We purchased our cold drinks and went back outside to take up residence at the unoccupied table.

The sheepherders were having quite a time, eating their lunch and drinking from their leather wineskins, or *botas*, and talking and laughing uproariously in the sunshine with Frannie and me an appreciative audience as we rested, sharing the same friendly light. There was one young herder in particular who was extremely animated, obviously the favorite of the other older men as he joked and flashed his white teeth, handsome devil that he was. As we passed by the group on our way back to the highway, he held his *bota* high against the sun and squirted a long ruby stream of wine into his mouth.

Unable to resist, Frannie stepped away from me to reach out and slap the *bota* between her open hands, causing wine to spurt all over the young Spaniard's laughing, sun-dark face, and washing away some of the clean dust and sweat of his young life. It dripped off his chin as his eyes met hers for a moment before she wheeled away to return to my side, inordinately pleased with herself at first, and then, on second thought, a little abashed at her own audacity. We walked down the shoulder of the road in silence for a bit before Frannie said, "I hope you don't think that I was flirting with him."

"Frannie, I'm glad you felt easy enough with me to do what you did back there, but don't try and tell me you weren't flirting." It was a good moment.

*** * ***

The next day, we were picked up by a German man who had driven his big Mercedes straight through from Berlin, hell-bent for Malaga on some urgent business that he didn't seem interested in talking about. He was an obese man with a little black goatee that made him resemble photographs I remember seeing of King Farouk of Egypt. Soon after we got going, he asked me if I could drive. I told him that I didn't have a European driver's license. He said, "I did not ask if you had a driver's license. I asked you if you could drive. I have been getting tired." I allowed as how I could.

Shortly afterwards, he stopped to fuel up and let me take the wheel. He was nice enough to purchase cold drinks for the three of us, but when we thanked him, he said with a cold little smile, "Is nothink, is nothink. If it were somethink I would not have done."

I cruised along sedately at first, familiarizing myself with the controls and the feel of the car. I was being cautious with the whole proposition, especially considering I was driving an exotic, unfamiliar car on completely unfamiliar, fairly crude two-lane roads. The German was in the shotgun seat beside me feigning sleep, watching me through slitted eyelids. I doubt that that guy ever took anything for granted. After a short while, I brought the car up to speed and began enjoying myself. When I glanced over at him again, King Farouk had relaxed into genuine slumber.

As we got into rougher country and the road began to shape itself to the hills which soon became mountains, there were a growing number of sharp blind curves which I took a great deal of satisfaction from negotiating at maximum speed, pulling the rear tires out of their skid out of every curve and accelerating into the straightaways.

Soon I was doing things with that car that nothing in my experience had taught me to do, that no one should be able to do, and performing them with absolute deadeyed confidence and competence. Call it delusional, call it lies, make of it what you will, but I was having a transcendent driving experience.

At one point, a little while after it had begun to rain, I visualized the rear end of a hay wagon waiting for me just around the next blind curve. Instead of slowing down, I hit that turn as hard as I could, knowing that I would have a foot or two to spare. Sure enough, the tractor-pulled hay wagon was waiting for me, but I was already reacting, and I tucked the car tightly in just behind the wagon without breaking traction. There was a moment of silence as the three of us sat there ensconced in our air-conditioned German leather and steel while two oncoming cars whizzed by.

Frannie began yelling at me from the back seat. I thought that her concerns and anger were reasonable enough, but what could I say? That I was experiencing some kind of road dog ecstasy? That I was talking to god through an overpowered Mercedes-Benz with a leather-covered steering wheel? That I couldn't/wouldn't stop? King Farouk, completely awake now, with a two-fisted, white-knuckled grip on both sides of his bucket seat and his wide eyes fixed on the rear end of that hay wagon, said, "No, no, is very gute, every time he almost leaves the road but not quite, is very gute."

Frannie should have seen a big red flag in that moment and caught the first available bus back to Belgium and her family. She should have seen during our little mountain ride that there was a part of me that was too wild and unpredictable to be constrained by concerns for other people's fears and feelings. She should have run from me like a pony with its mane on fire. But she didn't run, and we never talked about it. Like we never talked about so many things.

*** * ***

I was standing just inside the entrance to the Madrid train station a couple weeks later, having a cigarette just after saying goodbye to Frannie and putting her on a train to Paris. I would rejoin her in Belgium in a month or so. A man came up to me and asked if I had a cigarette to spare. I allowed as how I did. He was a somewhat worn-looking specimen about my age, wearing a little too much gold with expensive-looking clothes and boots with a kind of seventies mod look to him. His long hair looked like it might have been professionally shaped and cut. The image was disturbed a little by a serious-looking scar that ran from his forehead down across his left eye and cheek almost to his jawbone. He called himself Liberty, though I suspect that was an ironic pseudonym.

We talked for a while, and it came out that both of us had served in Vietnam. Eventually, we wandered off to have a few drinks together. There was something a little hyper and edgy about him, but despite a few warning bells, he seemed reliable enough to me. I had planned on hitchhiking out of Madrid the next day, but somehow or another I kept putting off my departure, and the two of us spent too much of the next few days together drinking.

Liberty seemed to me to be a bit of a hard man and, as it turned out, had led a fairly desperate life. He had an air of extreme self-sufficiency about him with a strong touch or two of survivor's paranoia, yet it was apparent to me that on this particular occasion he wanted company and had decided during that first meeting at the railroad station that I was it. The truth was that I tended to gravitate towards the company of hard men, but that tendency sometimes put me in situations that were just a little more interesting than I could stand.

We spent our time and mostly Liberty's money drinking in Madrid's upscale bars. My share of the bar bills was usually almost unnoticeable but, although Liberty was a big spender and a serious drinker, he didn't seem to hold my relative sobriety against me. In fact, it seemed as though he might have preferred it that way.

I didn't understand Liberty's erratic behavior at first. A man didn't survive the life he had supposedly lived by being an out-of-control drunk, yet that was what I was seeing. Something was going wrong, some relatively new development that caused him to behave in a way that was dangerous to him and to anyone around him. It was another reason to keep myself alert and somewhat sober while we made the rounds in Madrid and Liberty indulged himself in drinking bouts that often ended in smashed glass, yelling, and threats.

I got the impression that Liberty had had at least his share of war in Vietnam, but that was not the story that he had to tell. He, like many other GIs, had gotten addicted to heroin while in-country. Heroin was used as a kind of currency by many of the power players over there, and our own government was known to turn a blind eye to its trafficking. Consequently, large quantities of pure, cheap heroin were made available to American soldiers, making it very easy to develop a serious habit. The problems tended to arise when the addict in uniform returned to the Land of The Big PX only to find that his habit was impossible to support in Montpelier, Idaho, without robbing a bank.

Back in the States, Liberty solved his drug supply problem by riding with the Hell's Angels, playing with the devil for a couple of years until one day federal officers caught him off by himself and had a little one-sided conversation with him in which they described the case against him and gave him a choice. Either work for them as a narcotics agent or spend a good chunk of his remaining adult life in prison.

Liberty had ended up cutting a deal with the feds. He'd narc for them, but only if they shipped him out of the country to do it. That's how he ended up in Europe, going from city to city, using his Hell's Angel bona fides and persona to infiltrate the local drug scene, collecting names and evidence until the situation reached critical mass, at which time his supervisors would pull him out and ship him elsewhere. At least that was the plan.

However, the feds had required him to successively negotiate an intensive drug rehab program, and once he'd successfully navigated that program, a clearer and calmer Liberty realized a couple of things. Number one was that no one had mentioned just how long he'd be required to continue his undercover work. Number two was that the feds didn't seem to be as concerned for his survival as he would have liked them to be. That was how he got the scar on his face. They'd kept him in Berlin for weeks after he'd told them that it was time for him to leave, that the situation was going to hell on him. He'd been lucky to get out of there with just a scar to show for it.

By the time Liberty got to Madrid he knew that he was one doomed cowboy, that the feds intended to use him until he was used up. They weren't trying to get him killed. It was just that the game they were playing did not require his survival. There would always be someone to take his place. There was nothing he could do with this recognition of his own expendability. He couldn't even cross a border without their permission.

Spain needed tourist dollars badly, so the police tended to avert their deadeyed gaze from unseemly behavior on the part of American tourists wearing Bermuda shorts and heavy wallets, behavior that would have landed a Spanish citizen in jail. But there were limits to even their patience, and I wasn't sure just how far Liberty would go, or what they would do to him if they lost patience with him. Even if his employers decided to rescue him, why would they help me? Again, that old expression, "You are the company you keep," came to mind, especially when it came to law enforcement.

That is the story that I pieced together, anyway, from the fragments that Liberty shared with me during the long drinking hours that we spent together. Somewhere in there, the doomed cowboy had decided to embrace his doom, hence his violently aggressive behavior in upscale watering holes—and he had apparently chosen me to be his witness.

Liberty and I had agreed to meet for late breakfast on the eighth morning of our friendship. Instead, I rose early, packed my Kelty and walked out of Madrid. The smoke from the gypsy camps on the edge of town reached up to the sky like dirty fingers stretching out to stroke the soft gold of early dawn.

# CHAPTER 26

## *A FOOL'S PARADISE*

The Leyman family restaurant was just north of Dinant, standing alone by a two-lane highway which wandered along the Meuse River on its way to Namur. An ancient, unused brick towpath still followed close by the river where barges were now powered by diesel engines, but the barges bore little resemblance to the giants I had seen on the Mississippi. These were much smaller affairs, often with a family serving as a crew and living in brightly painted wooden superstructures with flowers in window boxes and usually a little sedan or truck parked on the stern.

The restaurant itself was a stone, three-floor structure built up against the side of the valley with a small, detached guesthouse. The first floor had the restaurant on one end, with a family dining room separating it from the large kitchen. The second floor had five spacious hotel rooms, with a master suite in which Francine's father, Paul, and his mistress, Michelle, slept. The third floor was for the live-in kitchen help, Michelle's three children, and me. Frannie stayed in the guesthouse.

On most mornings, I would rise before the rest of the household and take my host's hunting dogs running along the towpath on the river, sometimes paced by barges burbling their way from lock to lock. I ran along the shadowed valley floor with steep hills rising on both sides, hills so steep and high that the valley was almost a canyon, a barrier that had served to interfere with almost every European marching army since Caesar's. The summer was aging and beginning to fade into a fall with frequent heavy fogs, which seemed to evoke a kind of mad ecstasy in both the dogs and me. We would careen dangerously down the worn-smooth and fog-slickened brick pathway, the dogs young, brimming with life, and wild with being off the leash. I had been told to keep them leashed, but I couldn't stand it and would disobey my host every morning, releasing the dogs the minute we were out of sight of the house. The dogs loved me for the illicit freedom of those early morning runs but would turn willingly to me when we returned, standing like humbled outlaws to be put back on the leash.

Frannie's father had eight employees under the age of eighteen, and they all lived in the hotel. Belgium had some sort of law that required Paul to take full legal and moral responsibility for them, almost as though he were their father. I didn't quite understand the system, but it seemed to work rather well for everyone involved, at least in this particular situation. It was like living in one large, rather uproarious extended family who, nonetheless, were very good at what they did.

Every morning, all fifteen or so residents of the house would descend on the kitchen to sit around the huge, scarred-up wooden table to drink coffee and eat fresh croissants and jam. Usually the maître d', an older man who lived away from the hotel in his own home, was there to breakfast with them and talk business with Paul. The workday began around eight and often lasted until ten or so in the evening. This might have made for a very long day, but there was such an informality and a good humor about the way Paul ran things that all concerned seemed to thrive on it, and the result was a very fine restaurant that always seemed to have more than its share of Jaguars, Bentleys, and BMWs parked out front.

In the evenings, Paul, Michelle, her three young children by a previous marriage, and Frannie and I would gather for dinner in the family dining room. This was the one downstairs room that was reserved for family use, and, except for on special occasions, the one room that the restaurant employees never entered except to serve meals. The table was huge, almost filling the room, and often the evening meal would go on for hours, often followed by entertainment provided by members of the family. The children would sing, and stories and jokes would be told.

One night, as part of the entertainment, each person was required to sing a song to the rest of the company, and the only song I could come up with was "Nine Pound Hammer," a song by Tennessee Ernie Ford that I remembered from childhood. I was probably the only person in the world, besides Tennessee Ernie, who had memorized that song. The family group sitting around that little Old World dining room beside the Meuse River had never heard anything like it in their lives. I was a hit.

One evening, we sat at the long table, Michelle on one side with her hand resting on my shoulder, Frannie on the other side holding my hand against her thigh, all three of us watching Michelle's three children singing like angels for their supper. Someone took a picture of this that I still have with me, though it hurts me to look at it, even after all these years.

*** * ***

On a late afternoon in early November, I was prowling the hotel, trying not to give in to my curiosity and peek out a window. Frannie and Tom, the classmate that she had been dating back in the States, the same man that she had had a date with when I had arrived from Denver with my broken leg, were out taking a walk along the river. When Frannie had written to tell him that she was marrying me, Tom had immediately gotten on an airplane to come and plead his own cause.

I wasn't concerned about the outcome of their conversation, but it felt unnatural, somehow, to be in the catbird seat. I was much more suited than this college kid to be on the outside looking in, to be the one who had to walk away alone. In a secret, carefully unexamined place in my heart, I knew that I was the expendable one. It would have saved everyone a lot of trouble if I'd been able to face that truth at the time.

In late November of 1971, Frannie and I sat on velvet-covered stools in front of the mayor of Dinant and his assistant and took our wedding vows. Paul, Michelle, and the three children were a tiny audience sitting on wooden benches in the front row in the ancient meeting house. No one stopped smiling throughout the entire ceremony, brief as it was.

Afterward, we drove into Namur, where Paul treated us to dinner in a very exclusive restaurant. We stayed another two weeks before heading back for the States, and during all that time, the sun did not shine. In fact, there were thirty straight days of overcast skies and dense, heavy fog, broken only by the few hours of sunshine allowed us for our wedding.

I didn't mind, however. I had my awakenings to legally sanctioned, entwined nude bodies and bedsheets, my runs with the outlaw dogs alongside the invisible river, the muted diesel heartthrob of the barges groping their way through the fog, and the long evening meals with their aftermath of jokes, stories, and the three children proudly singing their songs for us.

# CHAPTER 27

*FOOL'S PARADISE LOST*

I sat in the window seat of the Icelandic Airlines flight pointed west across water towards America, Frannie's sleeping blond head on my shoulder, tendrils of her hair fanning out down and across the front of my shirt. I stared out at the flowing surface of the clouds below, gleaming white-gray in the moonlight, imagining myself outside of the airplane walking alone on those clouds, breathing scant oxygen that hurt my lungs, and watching the plane floating by, perhaps catching a glimpse of a woman's hair flowing gold across a man's shoulder. I looked down at Frannie's sleeping face with love but did not find it strange that I had no dreams of a future with her. There was nothing but the moment, a moment to which I was incapable of saying no.

We caught a twin-engine commuter flight from New York to Portland. Frannie's mother was at the airport to drive us up the coast to their home out on Orr's Island. The next morning, both of us woke early. Still tired but unable to sleep, we dressed for winter and sneaked out of the house to take the family's golden Lab for a walk along the beach. It was still almost completely dark and extremely cold, but the dog was insane and ecstatically romped in and out of the water, smashing the filigreed patterns of ice that the ocean had woven along the shoreline.

We bought a 1964 Volkswagen van and made the trek across the continent to Montana, driving up through Vermont into Canada, then six hundred miles west to drop back down into the US through Sault Ste. Marie. The heater didn't work, and the tiny engine wouldn't push the car any faster than forty-five miles per hour. Every little incline or hill seemed to threaten to reverse our direction. It was like driving across North America in a German-built refrigerator. It wasn't so bad during the day when the sun was shining through the windows and providing us with at least the illusion of some warmth, but most of the time we drove beneath overcast skies or in darkness.

Because of our inability to make any speed, we stayed on secondary roads as much as possible, and the countryside and its inhabitants moved slowly by in great detail, like a slow-motion movie. West of Sudbury, Ontario, a farmer walked out towards a barn through sleet squalls, the collar of his red and yellow flannel shirt sticking up out of brown insulated coveralls. Through a picture window in Sault Ste. Marie, a group of old men and women sat in their recliners watching soap operas flicker across a television screen. On the outskirts of Marquette, Wisconsin, a woman wearing battered sweats stood by a mailbox with an open letter in her hand, staring off across a dead apple orchard.

North Dakota, contrary to rumor, is not flat. Rather, it slopes gradually upwards from east to west—all the way to Montana. This long, slow climb, along with a brisk headwind, made driving the little Volkswagen seem like trying to fly a goose into a gale. The weather was overcast and chilly, down to about ten degrees below, and the interior of the bus was as cold as anything we'd experienced so far. What made things even more interesting was that many of the towns along the way were completely closed down for the holiday, so that there was no way of predicting where we'd find an open gas station, and it was necessary to stop at almost every town and look for gas, whether we needed it or not.

*** * ***

We arrived home to a deep winter come early along the Missouri River. It wasn't uncommon for the heavy snows to hold off until January, but not this year. Cars and trucks purred like ancient cats as they lumbered along, the sound of their engines muffled by high banks of snow. People were already paying close attention to the status of the coal piles in their cellars.

It had been a long day and a longer journey for Frannie and me. After driving four hundred miles of winter roads straight through, after all the hellos had been said, the Christmas turkey eaten, and the presents opened, lying down between fresh sheets with my golden wife felt a little like dying at the end of a long, hard life. Frannie returned from her trip to the bathroom smiling to herself and told me that she had heard my parents making love. The two of us found ourselves inspired and followed suit. The old house, accustomed to the love of compressed lips and gritted teeth, was amazed at Frannie's song. So too, I suspected, were my parents.

On the fourth night of our stay, a parade of neighbors found their way behind cautious headlights down the ice-rutted hill to my parents' house, a carefully planned surprise party to celebrate the return of the prodigal son with his new bride. Most of them were under the impression that I had been living the life of a dope-smoking hippie/bum, so they arrived with extremely low expectations of any woman who would be fool enough to marry me and were more than a little relieved to find Frannie to be more than just a few cuts above gutter trash.

I had grown up with the winter ritual of community ice-skating parties on the river, so a few days after we arrived, I made a few phone calls, and that night we had a skating party with a few young people who had grown up in the neighborhood with me. We threw a couple of old tires on the fire after we got it going good. It was cloudy with no stars, but the snow along both sides of the narrow strip of ice was fresh enough to be almost fluorescent in its whiteness, and it provided all the light we needed, with the tire fire out on the sandbar serving both as a constant beacon and a refuge from the cold where we would retreat for occasional rest and warmth.

At some point, we decided to play ice tag, which I had always loved as a child. I soon found myself the quarry of a persistent and swift pursuer, skating flat-out and almost effortlessly over the dark and perfect ice, down a dully gleaming path which went on and on into the night. Glancing over my shoulder occasionally to keep track of my pursuer, I began to lose perspective. For a few moments, the shadow darting across the ice behind me became something vaguely malevolent and sinister.

*** * ***

Somewhere in all of this homecoming, Frannie and I decided to make our first home in Salt Lake City, for no particular reason except that I was familiar with the town, and it was relatively close. Frannie was up for settling down in a strange city. Actually, she seemed to be up for just about anything. To me, she seemed almost fearless while I, on the other hand, was already beginning to feel some of the trepidation about my fitness for marriage that I should have been feeling before proposing to her. However, I avoided confronting those doubts and certainly never considered sharing them with my wife or anyone else.

We were in Salt Lake City by the third week of January and moved into a small efficiency apartment on the north side, on a side hill looking out over the town. I got a construction job as a laborer, and Frannie went to work as a waitress in an upscale restaurant. Her idea was to work hard and save money until fall, then cut back to part-time and resume her college education. She talked now and then of having a child but wanted to wait a few years for that. As for me, fatherhood was another item I hadn't allowed myself to think about too much.

It came as somewhat of a surprise to me that Frannie actually had plans for her life. The two of us had never really discussed our future together, never checked to see whether we had any goals in common, beyond that of staying together. She, understandably, seemed to take it for granted that getting married meant settling down to careers and a family. However, this had never occurred to me. I had no plans, no career in mind, and no particular desire to be a father. I had really only thought about wanting to be with Frannie and her family. It was beginning to sink in that this might not be enough.

Over time, I got into the habit of getting out of bed an hour before I had to in the mornings and, after getting ready for work, I would sit down at the kitchen table to write poetry, daydream, and think a growing number of dark thoughts. The apartment was really one large room with a bath, so from where I sat, I was able to see Frannie's hair flowing over the pillow like golden water as she slept and the slightest hint of a smile that always seemed to be on her sleeping face.

Once I asked her if she minded my early risings and writings. She said that she'd asked her father about it, and he'd said that she should let me be with my poetry, that it was just a youthful phase that I would grow out of after we'd been married for a while, especially after the children began to arrive. I took little comfort in this response.

This might have been a good moment for me to open my mouth, to talk about my doubts and fears, to tell her that I was struggling with the loss of my freedom and that the only thing I was sure of was my love for her and for my writing. However, I had never confided in anyone in my life, and I had no idea how to begin. I didn't know that people actually talked about such things. So I just continued to love her, act as though the doubts and questions did not exist—and keep my early morning vigils.

We weren't making much money, especially considering that we were trying to save, but Frannie had inherited her father's cooking skills and kept us well fed on the cheap. Beef kidneys, hearts, and tongue were sold as dog food locally, and I managed to hide my distaste for the kidneys in the interests of our budget. We were able to go skiing once in a while and even attend an occasional concert, although John Denver and Neil Diamond were about as wild as things got for the white folks of Salt Lake City. It never occurred to me to introduce Frannie to the Chicano nightlife.

The construction business kept me busy, but sometimes, when I was between jobs or a job was rained out, I would have some time on my hands. Of all things, I began hanging out in a strip joint, a place called The Blue Bottom. Businessmen would come in to sit in the booths, drink liquid lunch, and talk capitalism while the girls ground away.

The kids who performed in the Blue Bottom during the day ran towards baby fat and danced as though they were doing a chore. It was about as erotic as watching sumo wrestling. I got the impression that they were mostly farm kids, fresh out of high school perhaps, the ones who hadn't made the cheerleader squad. It was the most depressing bar I'd ever seen in my life. I felt right at home.

One Friday in early June, I left the job at noon and went to our bank where I drew out what I figured was my fair share of the account. Then I went home where I packed the essentials into my backpack, which I then returned to its usual spot in the back of our closet. I doubted that she'd notice anything. I then showered and put on clean clothes before heading for the strip joint where I sipped a couple of drinks, smoked, and watched the strippers sweat at their labor for oblivious customers, leaving only when I was certain that Frannie was home from work.

I watched her face as I told her that I was leaving on the midnight bus. I watched as the corners of her mouth drew down in shock and she burst into tears. She cried for a long time. I held her, and after a while, she fell asleep for a few minutes. She woke to cry some more, only to fall asleep again. Finally, after this had gone on for a couple of hours, I fell asleep after setting the alarm so I wouldn't miss my bus. When I awoke, she was sitting on a chair next to the bed, watching my face. I glanced at the clock. I had missed my bus.

"Are you angry with me?" Frannie was still sitting there with her hands in her lap, looking at me.

"For what?"

"For turning your alarm off and making you miss your bus."

I smiled up at her, and pulled her back down into bed with me, and the two of us slept quietly through the remainder of the night in one another's arms.

The next morning was Saturday, and we decided to go up into the mountains and take a hike. We spent the day walking in one of the many canyons above the city, stopping in early afternoon to eat the lunch we'd packed and ending up making love afterwards. We walked home in long shadows stretching out from the mountains. There was an easy silence between us that was replaced with a growing tension as we got closer to home.

"You're going to leave anyway, aren't you?"

"As soon as we get back to the apartment."

The truth was that I was already gone. She had nothing more to say.

*** * ***

I carried my sin buried deep in a cold place in my belly as I made my way across America towards New York City. Not the sin of leaving my wife, but the sin of having married her in the first place, the sin of taking something fragile and beautiful in a hand that was clumsy and directed by a blind eye. I didn't have the heart for hitchhiking, so I rode in Greyhound's working-class, air-conditioned comfort, smoked cigarettes, and watched the movie of Colorado, Kansas, Illinois, etc., flicker by my sealed window.

Killing kittens.

# CHAPTER 28

## *ON THE RUN*

A few weeks later, I sat at a small table on a hotel room's balcony, watching the sun rise over the Atlas Mountains, its fire reddened by the smoky haze from the cooking fires of the village in the valley below. I had already eaten breakfast in the little hotel restaurant and was drinking a cup of coffee salvaged from that breakfast while I alternated between scribbling and watching the view.

The bloom was coming off the rose. The road felt less like home. Frannie had paid too high a price for my freedom. Traveling in Morocco, I felt vulnerable and off balance. There were times when I had caught glances from the men that were almost contemptuous, especially in the cafes or bathhouses, and that made me uneasy. It was as though I were a transparently gay guy attempting to blend into a Saturday night in some redneck bar in rural East Texas. Someone finally told me that in Morocco a man without a large knife displayed prominently on his person was considered fair game. I went out and bought a large ivory-handled knife and began wearing it on my belt. This helped, but it did not restore my fall from grace.

I fell into the habit of walking up into the mountains around eleven every morning through a little valley that was kept green by a brook that wound through it on its way down from the mountains. Women came up from town and did their laundry on the large flat stones that were scattered along the streambed. They would heat up kettles of soapy water on small campfires in which they soaked and scrubbed their clothes before rinsing them out on the stones with fresh water from the creek, after which they spread the wet clothes out on bushes to dry. The women wore beautiful long dresses and robes of fabulous colors, and when I came down from the mountains in the afternoons, the dresses would be spread out on the bushes in the narrow meadow below me like giant flowers scattered about.

After a week or so in the mountains, I caught a bus to Meknes, where I got on a train headed north towards Tangier. The trains in Morocco were like something out of the old American West. The cars were gas-lit and wooden, with the passengers seated facing one another on wooden seats. I was supposed to get off, I think it was in Sidi Kacem, to make my connection to Tangier, but I dozed off and managed to sleep through the stop, not realizing what I'd done until the conductor woke me up to check my ticket. The only choice I had was to get off the train as soon as possible and wait for a train going back to Sidi Kacem.

There was nothing where I got off except an old, abandoned adobe depot. It had obviously been there a long time and was slowly collapsing into itself. There was no other sign that a town had ever even been there, just a beaten track that branched out into a network of smaller trails just a hundred yards or so away from the railroad depot, trails that seemed to wander aimlessly out into the desert. It was going to be a long wait, so I placed the Kelty in the scanty shade of a crumbling depot wall and sat down with my back against the familiar cushioned bulk of the pack. I was still tired but willed myself to stay awake for fear of missing my connection—again.

The sun ran things here. There was nothing to challenge it, nothing to stand against it, no trees and no hills except for some buttes off in the distance and some scanty bushes and brush scattered across the desert. My eyes filled with white sandy light and in spite of myself, my eyelids began to droop, and I drifted in and out of sleep, keeping faltering vigil over steel rails and the indifferent landscape.

I felt something brush against my cheek and woke screaming into failing light to see a woman's hand pulling abruptly back from my head. Then my vision was filled for a moment with astonishingly green eyes in a young woman's beautiful desert-darkened face, eyes wide with fear and shock. She whirled away from me and ran, even as I opened my eyes. I sat helplessly in the dirt of the depot and watched her fly down the track into the bush, her robe ballooning against the still desert air. I fought back an impulse to pursue the woman and attempt to reassure her, but I knew that pursuit would probably just frighten her more and that she might have armed friends or relatives out there who could also misunderstand my intentions. Eventually I dozed off again to dream of mist rising from a waterfall so monstrous, I knew it was cascading off the edge of the world.

It was early dark when the train I was waiting for pulled in beside the dark remnants of the depot, headed back in the direction I had come from earlier in the day. Except for the engine's headlight probing the railroad track into the desert, the only lights in sight were the dim and sparse gas lights in the interior of the train. I had been roused from my reverie by the sound of the train whistle echoing across the desert, and I walked towards the train as it pulled to a final stop. It surprised me by immediately disgorging a small crowd of passengers with battered sacks and boxes as their only luggage. Without hesitation they all moved on down the moonlit trail out into the desert, while I boarded the train, leaving the depot to its ghosts.

I was lucky. I only had to wait an hour in Fez before resuming my train journey north. The passenger cars were the same Old West style I had been riding on, with the comfortless wooden benches and the sparse gas lights. It was crowded, but I found an empty seat and lay claim to it by placing my pack so that it filled up the entire remainder of the two-person bench. I was in no mood for any transcultural interactions tonight. Two young women who looked as though they were either American or English were sitting together across the aisle, with two young Moroccan men on the bench facing them, but I was never eager to make contact with tourists and made no effort to start a conversation. Instead, I put my back to the wall, pulled my hat down over my eyes, crossed my arms, and proceeded to doze off.

Something woke me—some quick movement, a change in the air. I scanned the dark-shadowed passenger car from beneath the lowered brim of my hat without moving my head. Nothing was moving. After a while, I slipped back towards sleep again, only to be awakened once more. The two girl tourists across the aisle were sitting rigidly upright and staring at the two men seated across from them, who were staring defiantly right back.

This time I remained awake, watching the drama across the aisle through slitted eyes. Eventually the girls, who were obviously exhausted, relaxed and fell asleep, only to have one of the young men reach across and put his hand on the inner thigh of the woman seated across from him, who promptly startled wide awake and roughly brushed his hand away. The groper just sat there staring at her, making it clear that he was just waiting for her to fall asleep again. The woman was obviously terrified, with no idea what to do—terrified of what was happening to her, but also terrified that anything she said or did might make things worse.

A white man, easily the biggest man in the railroad car, wearing a slouch hat over long blond hair, a red neck scarf, a Levi vest, and leather riding boots, was suddenly standing in the aisle with one hand resting on the butt of an ivory-handled knife, snarling at the two Moroccan men. It was me doing my best John Wayne.

Everyone in the car was definitely awake now, the whites of their eyes gleaming like little, black-centered moons in the shadows. I had no idea what they were thinking, but I wouldn't have been surprised if they had jumped on me with flashing blades and torn me apart, leaving chunks of my flesh scattered along the tracks to provide a feast for feral dogs. But I was way beyond caring, and it probably wasn't a pretty sight as I told the two molesters in a horrible mixture of broken Arabic and French that if they didn't leave their seats immediately, I was going to cut their throats and throw their dead bodies off the train.

I had frightened the two girls perhaps more than I had their molesters, and they sat frozen in their seats, staring straight ahead as though willing all three of us out of their existence. The two creeps finally got up and left. I remained standing in the aisle for a moment, trying to think of some way to reassure the young women, then gave it up as a bad job and returned silently to my seat. It did occur to me that I might have overreacted, that it might have been handled better without all the drama, but who knew? It was the best that I could do at the time. Besides, it makes for a good story.

# CHAPTER 29

## *NOTHING LEFT TO LOSE*

At some point, as I made my way north from my Moroccan adventures across southern Spain, I found myself walking down a deserted stretch of road that ran close by the Mediterranean Sea for a few miles, flirting at times with the waves that were half-heartedly lapping at the edge of a narrow bit of alluvial plain.

The air was heavy with moisture and it was extremely hot for late May and I had a long way to go before I could even hope to get a ride, so the sight of the little pomegranate orchard by the side of the road was tempting. There were just a half dozen or so trees next to a tiny weathered little cottage or hut, and a middle-aged woman sat in front of the hut washing some vegetables. I walked up to her, introduced myself, and asked if it were possible for me to buy a pomegranate from her. She rose smiling and, taking me by the hand, led me out into the orchard where she and I walked very slowly among the trees until she finally selected the pomegranate that she felt was just right for me, presenting it to me with her hands cupped carefully around the fruit, as through presenting something precious. She refused payment, still smiling, and once in a while I think of her and the moment when someone forgave me all of my sins.

*** * ***

I think that a lot of things caught up with me on a mountaintop above Malaga, Spain, as I made my way north. Vietnam. Frannie's pain. Too much had happened. Just when you think you've hit the end of your rope, the rope gets a little longer.

Anyway, I was standing there with my back to the highway, crying my little heart out when I heard car tires rolling off the pavement behind me and crunching onto the graveled shoulder. Caught in the act. A woman's voice with a Scandinavian accent called out to me. I wiped my face off as best I could with my sleeve and turned around.

At the wheel of the elderly Volkswagen van was a black man who turned out to be an American stationed with the US Air Force in Madrid, which is where they were headed. His wife was Swedish. My benefactors pretended as though they saw nothing out of the ordinary about a grown man standing by a road weeping on a mountaintop above Malaga. I caught a glimpse of myself in the rearview mirror and was mortified by what I saw. A shaggy grown man with bloodshot eyes, red-streaked cheeks, and snot dripping off my nose. Suave. I stayed with them in Madrid for a while, spending most of my time downtown, sitting in outdoor cafes and morosely contemplating my personal train wreck before heading north.

On the road to Santander, I let myself get caught on a mountain pass after dark. All I could do was keep climbing up the narrow, winding road with a sheer drop on one side and a cliff wall on the other. When the rare car came along, I sometimes had to press myself up against the cliff wall to avoid becoming roadkill. There was no question of trying to catch a ride. None of the vehicles showed any interest in investigating the strange character caught fleetingly in the glance of their headlights. Yeti in a slouch hat.

There were no lights in sight in this wilderness—no house lights, no streetlamps, no sign of habitation, no side roads or signs of exit. Just stone, pavement, and darkness—and the roar of water cascading invisibly in the chasm somewhere below the road. At this point, I would have settled for a spot wide enough to spread my sleeping bag out without the risk of becoming roadkill.

Finally, I saw some sort of dim light up the canyon. Ten minutes later, I came to a turnoff that dropped down to cross over the deep chasm on an ancient stone bridge. I could make out what seemed to be a small village on the other side of the bridge, with one window softly lit by what might have been a gas lamp or candle.

I turned off the highway to follow the road down into the village, thinking that even though it was much too late to seek lodging for the night, I at least should be able to find a piece of level ground big enough to roll out my sleeping bag. As I stepped out on to the bridge, I could make out the dark figure of someone walking towards me from the other side. It was an old man, and as we came face to face, he put up one hand as though to ward me off, making a sign of the cross with the other and saying something in Spanish to me in a voice that managed to convey both sternness and fear simultaneously. I had problems understanding what he was saying but I did understand the Spanish words for god and for the devil. I turned around and made my way back to the highway and resumed my ascent.

It seemed like a long time before I finally came to a kind of pullover or turnaround, just short of what appeared to be the summit of the pass. There was even a grassy spot wide enough for my sleeping bag, and I made a nest there, gratefully laying my weary body down. It was cold enough to frost the granite that rose all around me, and I climbed fully dressed into my sleeping bag, lit up a cigarette, and stared out into the darkness for a while. I finally drifted off to sleep to the sound of wolves howling in the distance. Wolves?

It was late when I arrived in Santander the next day, early enough to find a hotel room but too late to be particular. The hotel turned out to be expensive and not worth the price, but I was too tired to worry about it or do anything about it. As much as I had slept outside in my life, I seldom found myself feeling truly rested from the experience, so that a few days of sleeping out always left me a little tired. I hadn't eaten since breakfast but chose to go to bed with my hunger intact. I just wanted some rest. I'd deal with food and finding more reasonable lodging in the morning.

While I was having coffee at the first cafe I had come to in the morning, I got picked up by a sailor. Actually, what happened was that a sailor came into the cafe while I was having breakfast, sat down nearby and struck up a conversation with me, then followed me outside afterwards, trotting after me to introduce himself, speaking a lot better English than I spoke Spanish. Santander was his home port. He'd been ashore for three days, drinking all the time and, having reached the end of his money the evening before, was in desperate need of a morning bottle. He wanted to know if there was something he could do for me, perhaps as a guide, that might be worth a bottle of wine.

I liked the man. He was a hustler, but an honest, charming, and unapologetic one, a manipulator who had a way of making being hustled an enjoyable experience, worth at least a bottle of wine, perhaps even a good bottle. So, I told him that I planned on being in

Santander for a few weeks and needed a decent, reasonably priced room.

"So, we're making a deal? I find you a good place to stay, you buy me a bottle?"

"*Si.*"

"You pay in advance."

I laughed, "No, I pay you after I have a room, but I'll buy you a good bottle."

"Two bad bottles."

"We have a deal."

The thirsty rogue and his willing mark strolled arm in arm down the street.

He introduced me to an old man who showed me a four-bedroom apartment. He used one bedroom and rented out the others to single men, sharing the kitchen and living room with them.

The old man was a charmer, but I explained to him that I really needed a place to myself. He told me that his wife and he had lived in another apartment across town before she died, and it had stood vacant since he moved in with his other renters out of loneliness. I would be welcome to rent that apartment, which had two bedrooms and a lot of beautiful antiques.

I moved in and spent the afternoon on the beach, then took a shower and made a phone call. The couple who had picked me up outside of Malaga and who had been so kind to me in Madrid had given me as a goodbye present the name and a telephone number of a Spanish friend in Santander and had made me promise to call him.

They refused to elaborate but told me that I wouldn't regret talking to the man. He was whom I called now. I had wanted to establish myself before contacting him, so he wouldn't feel obligated to offer hospitality. However, when I introduced myself over the telephone, the man immediately and cheerfully suggested in very good English that we meet for coffee in a downtown cafe on the following afternoon, telling me that he would be wearing a dark suit and carrying an umbrella hooked over his forearm.

"I am the only person in Santander who will be carrying an umbrella on a day of sunshine, so you will have no problem."

There was no problem. In fact, I had arrived early and was still focusing on my first sip of coffee, not even looking at the door when I felt a tap on my shoulder. I glanced back to find a distinguished, middle-aged gentleman in an obviously expensive, conservatively cut suit standing behind me with a little smile on his face. Sure enough, he was the only person in the place who had an umbrella hooked over his forearm. Slightly built and immaculately groomed, the man made me feel a bit oversized. Still smiling, he glanced obviously around the crowded little cafe and said, "I am the only person in Santander who always carries an umbrella. You are the only person in Spain who looks like Buffalo Bill."

The Spanish gentleman ordered, and we stood at the counter for a while, chatting and sipping our coffee, talking mostly about our mutual friends in Madrid. After a half hour of comfortable conversation, my new friend suggested that we adjourn to another, more comfortable environment and have something to eat.

"There are two private clubs in town, and I belong to both of them. Which would interest you more, the tennis club or the yacht club?"

I had no idea what either one would be like or what the hell one did in a private club in Santander, Spain, but I had learned that in situations like this, the crucial decision was always whether to trust the other person's judgment. Either trust and follow their lead, or distrust and excuse yourself as soon as possible, but make up your mind. I opted for the yacht club simply because I had a lot more experience at being seasick than I had at playing tennis.

The club turned out to be a short walking distance away. It was built on pilings out on the bay and looked to be quite a place, even sporting a doorman who looked askance at my outfit. "I'm sorry, *señor*, but no one is allowed without a tie."

My host reached over and flicked the end of my red neck scarf with a fingertip. "I think that if we stretch our imaginations a bit, we can see this scarf as a tie."

The doorman obviously knew that he was being played, but he didn't seem to mind. He smiled at both of us, "*Si, señors,*" and opened the door to the club for us. The interior had a lot of old dark wood, yellowed photographs of yachts, and magnificent views of the sea from every table. My host headed directly for a corner table without waiting for anyone to seat us. A bottle of wine and food were ordered with a few words, and a conversation began that continued on and off for the next few weeks, becoming an essential part of my routine during my stay in Santander.

*** * ***

Most mornings, I got up early and wrote for a while before adjourning to a nearby cafe where I would sit for hours, doing my usual. At noon, I'd usually go for a long walk before hitting the beach for an hour or two. Many of my late afternoons were spent in conversations with my Spanish gentleman friend about the Spanish Civil War and its aftermath.

The *señor* had fought under Franco against the Republicans. One afternoon, he and I were sitting in his living room looking at a large coffee-table book that was filled with close-up photographs of corpses, victims of torture, and various forms of violent death that he told me had been at the hands of the Republicans. My host's spacious apartment was in a quiet upper-class part of the city, and only an occasional muffled yelp of traffic noise reached us from the street. I had never seen anything like the elegant, pale violet wallpaper of that living room, with its delicate raised patterns of what seemed to be some kind of velvet.

At the beginning of the civil war, the Republicans had held Santander, and they'd arrested my host and thrown him in a large stone outbuilding that still stood by an old lighthouse keeping vigil on a cliff overlooking the sea outside of town. He took me there one afternoon and showed me where they'd imprisoned him. "Every day, they'd take a few of the prisoners out and throw them off the cliff with their hands tied behind them. We never knew who was next. They would just come and get some of us, and often it seemed to be at random. They savored watching the fear on our faces as we waited to see who would die. The thing of it was that most of them were local people who knew us. Many of the prisoners and the executioners had known one another, in some cases had grown up together." He took me over to the cliff and showed me where they'd thrown his fellow prisoners off. "From inside our stone prison, we could hear them when they screamed."

He didn't tell me how he finally got out of there or what happened to his neighbors/captors when the town was taken by Franco's troops, and he was rescued. He didn't talk about what it was like to live in a town where an ex-captor or his son might bake your bread. Or maybe someone sees you on the street every day who knows *you* put a pistol to their father's head. I didn't ask him about these things, either.

I considered that there were probably thousands of people still alive in Spain who, at one time or another, had had the experience of being captor or captive, torturer or tortured. I tried to imagine seeing someone on the street who had tortured me, and whom I had perhaps tortured in my turn. There was a horrid kind of intimacy to all of it, an incest conducted with bullets and piercing steel along with penises and vaginas. A country of rapists coexisting with their victims.

"They would take prisoners out into the bay and tie chains around their legs before throwing them overboard," the *señor* told me. "For years, every once in a while, some diver would find himself in a little grove of skeletons, bony trees rooted to the earth with rusting chains, waving with the tides. One diver went insane after finding himself in such a forest."

The *señor* had fought as an infantryman until he'd been badly wounded in his legs and couldn't march long distances anymore. The Republicans had killed off many of the naval officers, so his superiors had made him some kind of naval officer for a little while, but he'd finally ended up in tanks.

Sitting in the *señor's* living room, I asked him what he would do if there were a counterrevolution tomorrow, if the Republicans rose against Franco. The slender, middle-aged *señor* in his carefully tailored suit leaped from his chair and strode across his living room to grab an imaginary rifle off the elegant violet wall, grinding words out between his teeth, "I would be in the street!"

\*\*\* \* \*\*\*

By the time I left Santander, about all I had to my name was a hundred dollars and a round-trip airline ticket. One of my landlord's tenants had been coming over weekly to collect the rent, and I told him that this would be my last week in the apartment, that I had to return to America. Three days later, I ran into my elderly landlord on the street. We were pleased to see one another, and the old man took me into his arms, insisting that I be his guest for lunch. We retreated to a cafe that was full of working men in dark blue coveralls, and they were all drinking wine and eating highly spiced, delicious little fish that were fried in front of us in huge frying pans with curved bottoms that resembled woks. It was a beautiful sunny afternoon, the old man was in uproarious good humor, and so were most of the other customers in the cafe, as was I.

I did some serious hitchhiking across northern Spain and up through eastern France back to Luxembourg to catch a flight back to the States, hitchhiking without heart. There was no place I wanted to go to, no one I wanted to be with, and nothing I wanted to do. All that I had was the knowledge that I needed to get back to the States before I was completely broke. That, and the need to talk to Frannie. I knew that I had burned my bridges, but I felt the need to apologize to her, to humble myself before her. She had at least that much coming. I had allowed my loneliness and confusion to drive me into a marriage that I was completely unsuited for, and I had made her and her family pay for my own confusion.

My obsession with extreme personal freedom was a mystery to me and, even though I fought for it like a drowning man instinctively fights for oxygen, the truth was that the lifestyle I had chosen required a discipline and wisdom on my part that I didn't possess, at least in the long run. It was beginning to dawn on me that for a man who had started out determined not to make anyone else pay for his freedom, I was running up quite a tab. The collateral damage in my wake was beginning to weigh on me.

After apologizing and saying goodbye to Frannie, I stepped out of the Port Authority telephone booth and, lighting up another cigarette, leaned against the wall next to my Kelty. Well, that was it. I decided that I would just stick it out there in the bus station for the night. There was a bus headed for LA at eight in the morning, and if nothing else occurred to me in the interim, I would just get on it and go as far as my money would take me. I couldn't afford the ticket, but even the thought of hitchhiking made me tired. West seemed like a good direction to me right then, but I was exhausted by motion and desperately wanted to be still for a while, at least for the night, before making my next move.

I picked the Kelty off the floor and went over to the bank of plastic chairs that stood in the lobby, placed the pack in one chair, and sat down next to it.

Wham! I abruptly sat up, almost jumping to my feet. A cop was standing in front of me, waggling his nightstick admonishingly at me. I realized that the guy has just struck me across the soles of my boots with the stick. "No sleeping here unless you can learn to sleep with your eyes open." After the cop had moved on, I looked around and, seeing other travelers sleeping who'd been ignored by the law, realized that all the sleeping travelers looked a lot more middle-class than I did. It was going to be a long night.

The seat on my left was occupied by my pack, but the seat on my right remained empty until around one o'clock in the morning, when a red-haired young woman quietly slipped into it. She had nothing with her, not even a purse, and looked like she had slept in her clothes but wasn't used to it. I guessed that she was also going to have to sleep with her eyes open.

It was too late in the night for the depot to be crowded and there were plenty of empty seats around, so my new neighbor obviously had made a choice not to sit alone. Yet she acted as though she were afraid of me, sitting huddled away from me in her chair and hugging herself, her head down and her eyes focused carefully on the floor at her feet. I said hello to her but got no response. At first, I just wrote it off as New York street attitude and went back to minding my own business, but I soon came to realize that there was something wrong with her. Her eyes were red-rimmed and watery, and her not terribly clean and underfed body trembled like the last leaf on a tree in an early snowstorm. Although I didn't know much about it, my guess was that she was in some sort of drug withdrawal, perhaps heroin.

It occurred to me to move away from her so that she could be more comfortable and so that I could get some sleep, but it also seemed to me that despite her body language, the woman had a need for at least the proximity of another human being, enough of a need to override her fear. I decided that it wouldn't hurt me to keep an eye on her through the night. Later on, I woke after briefly dozing off to find my hand fiercely clutched by my red-haired neighbor even as she carefully maintained a trembling distance from me, sitting with her eyes tightly closed, but not in sleep.

When dawn came, she seemed to be a little calmer, and I offered to buy her something to eat for breakfast.

"French fries. With a lot of ketchup." She was still not making any eye contact.

"You're sure that's all you want? I can pay for it."

No, she just wanted french fries and ketchup. I went upstairs where there was an in-house vendor and ordered a hot dog for myself and some french fries for the woman. What the hell. No sense getting too healthy. When the redhead tried to eat her food, the trembling in her hands and body made it difficult for her to manage the cardboard french-fry container, so gentleman Philip took off his sombrero and placed it upside down in her lap so she could use it as a crude breakfast tray. About three minutes later she managed to dump her entire container of french fries and ketchup into my hat.

We were both aghast at the sudden ugliness of my hat's interior. Even after I'd swabbed the worst of it out with some paper towels from the men's room, it still looked like some small animal had died a violent death in it. Trying to lighten the mood, I said, "Well, that wasn't too much of a plan, was it?" I could tell that the woman was devastated by the disaster she had made of my hat, but I didn't know how to reassure her. I was a little devastated myself. I tried again. "Well, the inside of that hat needed to develop a little character, anyway." She didn't laugh at that, either.

Feeling no need to be anywhere but needing to go *somewhere*, I left the waiting room to board the eight o'clock gray dog for Omaha with my bleeding hat firmly planted on my head. As I walked away, I glanced back for a sign of some sort from my red-haired companion of the evening, but she had no sign for me. She was just sitting there, huddled alone amid the ranks of orange plastic chairs, sleeping with her eyes open.

# CHAPTER 30

## *BROWNVILLE*

I woke as I had awakened every morning for the past two weeks, lying on a little canvas cot, my face covered with fine powdery dust. There was dust everywhere in the small attic room, even in my mouth. The only natural light was provided by two filthy little octagonal windows, one on each end of the room that I was making my nest in. Most of the dust was generated by the pottery downstairs, floating up constantly through the stairwell and the cracks in the crudely boarded floor, even when the potter wasn't working.

There was a little refrigerator I kept my peanut butter and milk in—which was pretty much what I had been living on ever since I had gotten into town—peanut butter, crackers, and milk. There was no running water, so my morning routine usually began with going outside naked, shaking the dust out of my clothes, then washing myself with the cold water from the freestanding spigot out in the middle of the yard. To avoid traumatizing any passersby, I made a point of performing my ablutions early, before the morning sun and morning traffic.

The little potter's cottage was on the east side of Brownville, Nebraska, and I could look out one of its dusty little attic windows and see across the Missouri River into the state of Missouri. Some of the dust in my room was provided by the unpaved street that ran by the cottage, a route which was seldom used by anyone, I was told, until they began building the nuclear plant downriver a year ago, and the little side street turned out to be the one and only access route. The little river town had approximately 170 permanent residents supporting a bar, a cafe, a general store, and a post office, but the construction of the nuclear plant had brought an unprecedented and extended boom to the village—mostly to the bar.

Brownville was one of the oldest towns in Nebraska, established when they built a ferry across the Missouri to accommodate the early pioneers and their wagons, but history had switched its attentions to Omaha and Lincoln long ago, leaving Brownville to become a quaint little backwater tourist attraction with a weekend-long fiddler's contest, some music camps, and a summer theater.

There was a large grain elevator on the riverfront, a meatpacking plant three miles across the river into the state of Missouri, and, of course, the nuclear plant. All of this combined to keep the village alive, if not thriving. The bar served as a social center for the entire community, including kids, dogs, and little old ladies during the day. After sundown, however, it was rumored that the devil made an occasional visit to the Brownville Tavern.

I had come into town late at night fresh from my overnighter at the Port Authority bus station, a long bus trip, and a hundred-mile hitchhike south from Omaha. My last ride was an old station wagon full of stolen television sets destined for delivery in Kansas City and driven by a devout born-again Christian who had insisted on saying a prayer for my soul before leaving me to my fate. So, we had knelt and prayed at an isolated intersection east of Brownville, our little ceremony illuminated by the headlights of his 1958 Buick station wagon, broken glass biting into my knee as a I received a scoundrel's blessings.

I had met Jim and his wife, Ann, while passing through Brownville a couple of years before, and had been an overnight guest at their home. Jim had been an effusively welcoming host and had made it clear to me that I would be a welcome guest any time. Well, sort of. It's clear to me now that he made that offer assuming that he would never see me again, and that when I took him up on that invitation, I was a confused and desperate man grasping at straws.

Anyway, Jim and Ann welcomed me now with some subtle reservations which I managed to ignore, and I ended up sleeping on their living room sofa for a couple of nights before moving into the attic over my host's pottery.

Jim was a potter and his pottery attic was a perfect temporary solution, providing me with shelter without intruding on anyone's privacy. For right now, the crackers and peanut butter tasted pretty good. I budgeted myself a daily beer and a pack of cigarettes as mental health necessities. For the price of that one beer, I felt comfortable spending an hour or so each evening at the bar, ensuring that I would have at least some social interaction every day. The rest of most days I spent writing, reading, and taking long walks to explore the town and the surrounding countryside.

The terrain rose abruptly on both sides of Brownville to form high bluffs overlooking the Missouri River, and the community cemetery was located on the highest of those bluffs. I went up there often and would sometimes sit for hours, watching out over miles of Missouri River Valley. We seem to give dead and eyeless bodies the best views. The only living people I ever saw in this graveyard were the white-haired old couple who were paid to dig the graves and keep the grounds spruced up.

There was a small shed that sheltered a battered old backhoe and their other tools—and the caretakers themselves when the weather turned sour. They kept a picnic table inside to take their breaks on. On a rainy day, they would often just open the garage doors and sit at the table and watch things get wet. The old couple befriended me, and the three of us would have an occasional little coffee klatsch there among the gravestones, looking out over the valley.

The meatpacking plant was three miles across the river into the state of Missouri, far from everything but a cheap labor pool of mostly small farmers or their wives in need of supplemental income. The work was harsh enough to keep a bit of a turnover going on, and I managed to get on. I was tired of being a little hungry all the time, and I didn't like being beholden to Jim Brown for the use of the pottery attic.

In a large, high-ceilinged room, there were three two-foot-wide conveyor belts carrying various cuts of beef down the middle of a long stainless-steel table. My job was to pull rib cage halves off the conveyor belt onto the stainless-steel table and strip the meat from between the ribs with my knife. There was a lot of time pressure. The place smelled of rancid fat so badly that just driving by on the highway with open car windows was an unpleasant experience. I'd never worked in a factory before, but I'd realize later that the meatpacking plant was one of the worst of the worst, even for a factory.

Many of the workers were women, and they were the most foul-mouthed crew I had ever worked with in my life. I realized that I was not among happy campers. These people acted more like hardened prison inmates than contented, God-blessed-by-being-born-American workers. The first time I walked out on the floor, I felt a little like I used to feel at times in Morocco before I began carrying a knife. Fresh meat.

In self-defense, I began wearing a pair of heavy, black-framed, army-issue sunglasses. Periodically, I would let out a wild scream and leap onto one of the beef halves which moved by behind me suspended from a sliding rail. Many of my fellow workers became convinced by these antics that I was either crazy or a drug addict or both, which was the effect I was looking for.

There was always the tang of old blood in the air and the place was kept cold as a well digger's ass, not much above freezing. The work was intense, but it was mostly in the hands, arms, and shoulders, so that my upper body was constantly sweating and stressed, while my lower body was relatively immobile and chilled through most of the day. Hemorrhoids were an occupational hazard in this place. By the end of the first week, my hands were so swollen that I couldn't get my ring off, and they remained that way until six months after I had quit the plant. I would be prone for decades afterwards to frequent and severe bouts of bronchitis.

The pay was just a notch or two above minimum wage, and it seemed that it had taken some pretty drastic efforts by the union just to get that. Stories were told of sabotage and armed guards at the plant during strikes, the tires of nonunion members and supervisors being slashed in the parking lot. I had a run-in myself with the union steward over his disrespectful attitude, but I managed to convince him of my homicidal tendencies, and I was left alone after that.

*** * ***

I settled in to stay for a while and save some money, at least until I came up with a better idea. Brownville's small size and isolated location promised to provide me with some much-needed stability and simplicity. I wasn't making much money at the plant, but Brownville was cheap. The work was a bit of an ordeal, but a man can get used to hell, and doing a little penance didn't seem like such a bad idea to me right then, anyway.

Shortly after going to work at the meatpacking plant, I moved out of the pottery attic and into the loft of the local art gallery, paying rent for a shared space with a young silversmith from Omaha who managed the gallery through the summer. The gallery was a converted carriage house with no running water, but there was an outdoor toilet with plumbing and access to showers in a neighboring building. I enjoyed having some company and being surrounded by art and light—and a diet that didn't include pottery dust.

In early fall, I was having a quiet beer in the tavern. A man named George Rogers was working behind the bar, while the regular barkeep shot some pool with an ironworker from the nuclear plant project. I usually did my drinking, such as it was, during the quieter hours—the afternoons or the early part of the week.

George Rogers interested me. He looked like a stereotypical used-car salesman, a small man with a slight paunch who liked to wear a white vinyl belt and matching shoes along with a bright-colored polo shirt and trousers. He owned a mega-sized car lot in Lincoln, but he seemed to have a soft spot in his heart for Brownville and kept a summer home there, an old clapboard pile high up on a bluff looking out over the Missouri. I figured that he was at least moderately wealthy, but he wore his money well and liked to take an occasional bartending shift at the tavern. Someone had told me that George had a son who had died in some strange accident a few years ago, and he had lost his wife in a car wreck soon after.

The regular barkeep, whose name was Red, was shooting pool with a man they called Big Tom. Besides George and myself, they were the only people in the tavern. George was using the slow time to do some cleaning behind the bar, and I was sipping my beer and staring out the front window at the weather. There was a little bit of rain coming down, just enough to make the pavement of Main Street shine in the streetlight that stood outside the tavern. There weren't many streetlights in Brownville. Just enough to keep pedestrians from walking into parked cars at night.

Suddenly, there was movement and raised voices behind me and I whirled on my barstool to behold Big Tom standing with his pool cue in one hand and Red's neck in the other, holding him up in the air so that he was barely touching the floor with his toes. Tom was shouting something that I couldn't make out, but he seemed to have the intention of pounding Red's head with that pool cue.

Now the thing was that Big Tom was really big. He stood around six foot five inches and must have weighed in at over 250 pounds. He was an ironworker, and very little of that weight was fat. I found out later from George that Big Tom was a Bataan Death March veteran.

I had just enough time to experience a twinge of resentment for being forced to interfere when paunchy little used-car salesman George Rogers went over the bar and somehow got between the two men, apparently completely oblivious to both his opponent's size and the pool cue in his hand. I had the sense that this wasn't just about saving Red, it was also about saving Big Tom from himself. George was practically levitating with fearless energy and moral force, and Big Tom didn't have a chance. He finally let the pool cue fall onto the floor, turned, and walked out the tavern door into the rain-softened night.

George Rogers stood in the middle of the tavern floor for a few seconds, taking a few deep breaths and staring at the closed door, before walking back behind the bar to put up three shot glasses and fill them to the brim with some prime bourbon. Red joined us at the bar and downed his bourbon with one gulp, looking a little green beneath the freckles.

"I think that man was just about to beat my head into punkin mush. Thanks, George."

George poured Red another shot, and the three of us stood there in silence for a bit. Finally, Red threw back the remainder of his bourbon, turned, and walked out the door. George locked the door behind Red, replenished the bourbon for both of us, and got a couple of ice-cold Budweisers out of the cooler. We sat there quietly in the otherwise empty bar for a while, smoking our cigarettes, sipping our drinks, and watching the rain dribble down onto the dark street outside, while George told me a tale of a young soldier dropped off on Japanese-occupied islands with assassin's tools, and living on fish and rice to avoid smelling like an American.

"I carried a forty-five mostly for myself, in case things went completely to hell. There were a couple of times when that forty-five got to looking pretty good to me."

He told me of coming back from the war, of sowing some wild oats before settling in to get his chunk of the American dream by getting married and selling more Fords and Lincolns than anyone else in Nebraska and having a son who turned out to be a golden boy—handsome, bright, a natural athlete and musician.

"The perfect wife and the perfect son. High cotton. If you didn't notice my bad dreams and the fact that Mommy and Daddy were drinking way too much."

George had arranged a construction job for his son the summer after high school graduation, and the boy was so excited about it he decided to skip graduation so he would be there when they broke ground.

"I'd wanted to be around and watch him start his first day, so I parked a fair distance away and watched as he stood out there in that empty lot in his brand-new work clothes, alone with his excitement and anxieties under the spring sun, leaning on a shovel and watching them try to fire up a cold-blooded backhoe.

"I was feeling pretty damn proud of him, but then I started thinking about where I'd been when I was his age, you know—getting ready to be a killer and all.

"Suddenly, instead of seeing my son, I was seeing myself, seeing everything that I'd been running from since the war. I realized that I'd been treating my wife and my sons as though they were perfect dolls in a perfect dollhouse of my creation, so I could tell myself that I was a normal person. So, there I was, sitting in my big new Lincoln spying on my son, and thinking dark thoughts about my old war souvenir forty-five in the glove compartment. Just then someone yelled, and I was running across that field towards the empty space that my son had just vacated.

"No one was ever able to tell us what killed him. He was perfectly healthy one moment and dead the next. He just stopped. You know how doctors talk when they're trying not to admit that they don't know what the hell they're talking about. My wife and I had been drinking instead of talking for years, but she really went off the deep end after our son died. A year later, she got herself killed in a drunken single-car accident. I'd tried to change things, tried to talk to her, but I'd waited a little too long."

On the following Saturday afternoon, I was back sitting on the same corner stool at the Brownville tavern and George Rogers was bartending again. Mostly old people, kids, and dogs hanging out. People still doing their drinking, but not as a serious sport. The bar had a lot of large windows and stood in the middle of an empty lot, so it lacked the shadowed murkiness of most bars. There was nothing in the place that wasn't needed to drink, smoke, listen to music, shoot pool, or all of the above.

So, I smoked my cigarettes and sipped my beer, watching the ebb and flow of a Brownville tavern Saturday afternoon while I eavesdropped on conversations, scratched a dog or a child behind the ears now and then, and occasionally entered into a bit of conversation with one of the regulars. I could see half the town's main street from my perch at the bar.

I happened to be looking out the front window of the bar when a car came to a screeching halt at the curb, and Red, the regular barkeep, jumped out and ran up the sidewalk and into the bar to demand that George call the police.

"Big Tom has gone nuts! He's holding Isabella hostage with a shotgun!"

Isabella was Big Tom's landlady and Red's girlfriend.

George wouldn't call the police. "I'll go talk to him. You take over the bar and don't let anyone near that phone for fifteen minutes. Promise." Red was pretty shaken up, but he also trusted George—especially after he had saved Red's bacon from Big Tom in the tavern that other night. Red finally agreed to the fifteen-minute wait. Without saying another word, George took off his apron, walked out from behind the bar, and headed out the door into the peaceful, sunlit Brownville Saturday afternoon.

I felt as though I were walking in deep mud as I followed him down the sidewalk to where his Lincoln was parked, not saying anything until we were in the vehicle and headed towards where Isabella's double-wide trailer was perched on top of a little rise on a side street. Apparently Red had been having coffee there with Isabella when Big Tom busted in the door with his shotgun, ready for business.

"George, you know these people and you know the ground, so you call the shots."

I had no idea what good I could do, but I couldn't stand the thought of George dealing with the situation alone, either. He told me to stay in the car while he went up to the trailer to try and talk to Tom.

"He doesn't know you, and if you walk up there with me, it might make him grumpy. You just stay put until either I signal you to come in or you hear a gunshot. If you hear a gunshot, you're on your own."

I don't know what I wanted to hear, but that wasn't it. We pulled into a long driveway at the end of which was a pastel green trailer with a lot of well-kept flowerbeds and pink flamingos. George parked back from the trailer a bit, and as he got out, I noticed that he was carrying a can of Budweiser casually in his left hand as he walked up the sidewalk.

"Hey, Tom. Where the hell are you?"

I sat there in the Lincoln's quiet, little, leather-upholstered world and watched George disappear into the trailer. After a while, its door opened again and a blond woman wearing pink shorts and a cream-colored blouse leaned out, beckoning for me to come in. It was Isabella. Well, this hadn't been included in George's short list of possible scenarios, but I didn't see anything for it except to march dutifully up the sidewalk. The things I get myself into.

When I came into the living room, Big Tom was pacing the floor holding a double-barreled shotgun with its muzzle wandering around here and there, like a bloodhound's muzzle seeking a scent. The big man kept going over to the front window and peeking out between closed curtains towards the driveway. He ignored me completely, which I took as a good sign, and he didn't seem to be directly threatening anyone in the trailer. George was sitting on the sofa with his legs crossed and the toe of one white patent leather shoe waggling elegantly in my direction. He grinned and waved a toast at me with his beer can. George had switched to Pabst.

We were having a party.

Big Tom finally acknowledged my presence.

"Get the man a beer, bitch."

It seemed to me to be a somewhat complex social situation, one which I felt incompetent to address, but I accepted my beer from Isabella and thanked her politely as she gamely attempted a hospitable hostess's smile through tear-smeared makeup. I sat in a chair where I could take an occasional peek out between the front window curtains.

George was nattering on somewhat maniacally about everything but Big Red's relationship with the shotgun and the police who were going to arrive at any moment. I was thinking that the local police were not exactly prepared to deal with the Big Tom situation. I was thinking that I wanted to see those cops coming before Big Tom did. I was halfway expecting them to come in the front door shooting. I also suspected that Tom might want them to do that very thing.

Finally, one of my furtive peeks between the window curtains caught an young uniformed cop coming up the driveway carrying a shotgun at port arms, his perfectly groomed David Niven mustache trembling slightly on his upper lip as though it might fall off its perch at any moment. I glanced back into the room to see George standing directly in front of Big Tom with his eyes locked onto those of the bigger man. He wasn't smiling or nattering on any longer, and his hands were extended in absolute expectation of receiving that shotgun. Tom had nothing to say. He just sighed and laid the weapon gently in George's hands.

Winter settled in and Brownville settled down. My routine out at the packing plant was neither stimulating nor glamorous. Five days a week I would walk into the malodorous factory in the dark before dawn, put in my hard and hemorrhoid-punishing eight hours at that giant clamorous refrigerator, then walk back out into the dark after sundown. The sun would look pretty good to me by Saturday morning, and I would find myself taking cloud-covered weekends personally. But my little traveling nut was prospering nicely, and I knew that unlike most of the other denizens of the meatpacking plant, my experience there would be relatively short-lived. I figured the swelling in my hands would eventually go away, along with the hemorrhoids.

One day, I was browsing through a recent *National Geographic* magazine and ran across an article describing a 350-mile backpacking trip that the author had recently made from Banff, Alberta, down through the Rockies into Oregon. The article even included a map showing the trails that the author followed. Why not? I began making plans, and while I was making plans for weeks wandering in the wilderness, I paid $500 of my hard-earned blood money for another blue Chevy, a souped-up 1964 Malibu station wagon.

The truth was that I was beginning to flail about a bit. There was a growing need in me to engage with society in some meaningful way, but I was not ready to face that need, and I was beginning to seek distractions, ways to avoid or delay confronting the need for change.

Another Christmas spent alone, this time in Brownville—but I didn't mind. On Christmas Day, I got into the Malibu and drove west until I found a tiny diner out in the middle of nowhere that was serving dinner for outliers like myself. There were almost twice as many customers as there were seats, but we managed. It was a good Christmas.

\*\*\* \* \*\*\*

Any Christmas spent anywhere was better than Christmas in Vietnam. People being killed all around while Bob Hope reigned over it all with his Santa Claus hat and his half-naked dancing girls, Ann-Margret performing fellatio on a microphone, then leading the teenage audience by their raging hard-ons into a tearful rendition of "Silent Night" while six movie cameras recorded it to present later as proof to the concerned American public that their teenaged boys were indeed enjoying themselves in the war zone. Sleep in heavenly peace.

\*\*\* \* \*\*\*

One day in early spring, I stepped out of the plant during lunch break to get some cigarettes out of my car. The stink of the place stayed with me all the way out to the parking lot, but as I was reaching to open the car door, the wind shifted and suddenly I got a shocking whiff of lilacs.

Lilacs? I stood there by my Chevy for a few moments, inhaling the traces of mystery lilac scent and watching the sky, letting the sun warm flesh almost permanently chilled by the hours, days, weeks, and months spent in that big, bloody refrigerator. I held my hands up in front of me, hands that seemed to be permanently swollen and aching now and wiggled my fingers.

I went back inside the plant, found my line foreman, and told him that I was done. He went into a bit of a tizzy. He couldn't believe that anyone would just walk out on a perfectly good cow-carving career. I shed my bloody coverall and went out into the parking lot to fire up the Chevy, anxious to get clear of the smell of dead cows.

That summer, I studied that *National Geographic* magazine and the map of that Rocky Mountain trail system until the magazine's pages began to tatter. I detasseled corn. I pruned apple trees and picked mushrooms. I bought myself a pair of running shoes and began trotting down the back roads around Brownville, learning where all the dirt roads were. I loved the feel of soft, powdered earth pillowing my footfalls, loved to have the first of the morning sun catch me loping along some fence line, breathing easily as the Missouri River began to throw light back up at the sky from the valley below.

However, the bloom *was* coming off the rose, or the lilacs, as it were. The harshness and isolation of the road had begun to overshadow the weightless moments and hours of pure freedom which were becoming fewer and further between. The price that I had forced my ex-wife to pay for my blundering confusion had left me feeling like a moral outlaw. I was turning into some sort of emotional and psychological Flying Dutchman with no harbor in sight, and I still wasn't admitting to myself how badly I needed one.

In early July, I left Brownville at the wheel of my souped-up blue Malibu, headed north for Banff National Park in Alberta.

# EPILOGUE

I'm not certain what I had in mind, but the fact is that I was an experienced outdoorsman of sorts abandoning my blue Chevy in a parking lot to launch myself into a 350-mile hike with inadequate equipment, very little food, and no plans for resupply. Some might describe my behavior as being self-destructive or even suicidal.

Well, the gods reached down and grabbed me by the nape of the neck, preventing me from throwing the dice I'd apparently loaded against my own survival. The proposed 350-mile trek turned out to exist only in the imagination of the *Geographic* article's author. I took my extreme frustration out on a somewhat saner forty-five-mile trek, setting a punishing and reckless pace all the way out and back to the blue Chevy, saving that car from interment in some Canadian junkyard. The gods take care of fools and drunks—and old blue Chevys.

*** * ***

I am not a drunk, but perhaps anyone who has visions is a fool—or crazy. Some will write me off as a great liar, and still others will see this book as a story of a troubled veteran taking his trauma out on the road, or as a story of someone seeking to escape a troubled childhood.

However, there is another possibility. Perhaps I am one of those people who, throughout history, felt an inexplicable compulsion to go out on some sort of solitary quest or pilgrimage into the unknown. Vision quests, hajj, the Holy Grail, Sitting Bull, Buddha, Jesus Christ, John the Baptist, Ulysses, and Otzi the Iceman come to mind. Plus, the many who didn't make it back, or did make it back and disappeared into obscurity—such as me, perhaps.

Perhaps there was a purpose to my odyssey that I didn't understand at the time, as humble as that purpose might have been. Perhaps the visions and experiences, even the confusion and despair, were all part of preparing me for that purpose. Perhaps the many people who helped me along the way were part of an ancient tradition of providing assistance and blessings to wandering monks, pilgrims, knights—and fools. Regardless, it is all a mystery to me.

*** * ***

In the fall of 1979, instead of committing suicide, I gutted up and enrolled in a master's program at the University of Montana, the shakiest grad student west of the Mississippi. Almost simultaneously I became aware of the lack of treatment available to Montana's Vietnam veterans suffering from war-related trauma.

The Flying Dutchman had found a harbor. My sudden awareness of the Vietnam veteran's predicament gave meaning to much of what had happened to me on the road and transformed me from a wanderer into a man with a mission, an advocate and activist, a public speaker writing essays and articles, interacting and coordinating with the Montana congressional delegation, and becoming a peer counselor for veterans. In 1982, I testified at a congressional hearing on the situation. In 1985, we were successful at bringing a vet center to Missoula, and a little later I went to work there, remaining there until 1993.

*** * ***

Since the train wreck I made of my marriage, I have lived alone. The ground keeps shifting beneath my feet, like sand being shifted by the tide. The visions come and go. What is knowledge today is a bad guess tomorrow. Failure turns out to be success. Disaster turns into a good story. There is something to be said for hitting the end of your rope occasionally, especially if you happen to survive. Comfort never taught me a damn thing, anyway.

Sixty-two years after they put Great-grandfather George down in the ground with a whisky bottle, I stood over his grave looking out over the hills towards the confluence of the Yellowstone and the Missouri Rivers where Sitting Bull surrendered. The black towers of the Snowden Bridge thrust up into my line of sight from where they had stood their hopeful vigil for coming up on a hundred years, yearning to raise their span for just one more riverboat.

# THE END

# ABOUT THE AUTHOR

Philip Burgess grew up on his family's ranch in Eastern Montana with his sleep haunted by the cries of wild geese and the wail of the last of the Great Northern steam engines across the Missouri River valley. Leaving behind an extended family of souls damaged by war, the Great Depression, mental illness, bad medical care, and reservation violence, Burgess went off to pursue higher education. He followed up four years of college with a less formal but somewhat more intense education as an army officer in Vietnam, where he managed to avoid being a hero. Afterwards, Burgess fulfilled a childhood dream by going out on the road and living a minimalist, drifter's life until he wound up in the mountains of Western Montana in 1980 where he has remained ever since, trying his best to earn his oats as a veteran's spokesman and therapist/poet and storyteller.

www.ingramcontent.com/pod-product-compliance
Lightning Source LLC
Chambersburg PA
CBHW021625120626
46545CB00002B/395